Beyond Medication

Beyond Medication focuses on the creation and evolution of the therapeutic relationship as the agent of change in the recovery from psychosis.

Organized from the clinician's point of view, this practical guidebook moves directly into the heart of the therapeutic process with a sequence of chapters that outline the progressive steps of engagement necessary to recovery. Both the editors and contributors challenge the established medical model by placing the therapeutic relationship at the center of the treatment process, thus supplanting medication as the single most important element in recovery.

Divided into three parts, topics of focus include:

- Strengthening the patient
- The mechanism of therapeutic change
- Sustaining the therapeutic approach.

This book will be essential reading for all mental health professionals working with psychosis including psychoanalysts, psychiatrists, psychologists and social workers.

David Garfield is Professor, Associate Chair and Director of Residency Training in the Department of Psychiatry and Behavioral Sciences at Rosalind Franklin University of Medicine and Science, Chicago Medical School. He is also faculty at the Institute for Psychoanalysis, Chicago.

Daniel Mackler is a psychotherapist in private practice and a filmmaker, New York City.

The International Society for the Psychological Treatments of the Schizophrenias and Other Psychoses Book Series

Series editor: Brian Martindale

The ISPS (International Society for the Psychological Treatments of the Schizophrenias and Other Psychoses) has a history stretching back some 50 years during which it has witnessed the relentless pursuit of biological explanations for psychosis. The tide is now turning again. There is a welcome international resurgence of interest in a range of psychological factors in psychosis that have considerable explanatory power and also distinct therapeutic possibilities. Governments, professional groups, users and carers are increasingly expecting interventions that involve talking and listening as well as skilled practitioners in the main psychotherapeutic modalities as important components of the care of the seriously mentally ill.

The ISPS is a global society. It is composed of an increasing number of groups of professionals organized at national, regional and more local levels around the world. The society has started a range of activities intended to support professionals, users and carers. Such persons recognize the potential humanitarian and therapeutic potential of skilled psychological understanding and therapy in the field of psychosis. Our members cover a wide spectrum of interests from psychodynamic, systemic, cognitive and arts therapies to the need-adaptive approaches and to therapeutic institutions. We are most interested in establishing meaningful dialogue with those practitioners and researchers who are more familiar with biological-based approaches. Our activities include regular international and national conferences, newsletters and email discussion groups in many countries across the world.

One of these activities is to facilitate the publication of quality books that cover the wide terrain that interests ISPS members and a large number of other mental health professionals and policymakers and implementers. We are delighted that Routledge Mental Health has seen the importance and potential of such an endeavour and have agreed to publish an ISPS series of books.

We anticipate that some of the books will be controversial and will challenge certain aspects of current practice in some countries. Other books will promote ideas and authors well known in some countries but not familiar to others. Our overall aim is to encourage the dissemination of existing knowledge and ideas, promote healthy debate and encourage more research in a most important field whose secrets almost certainly do not all reside in the neurosciences.

For more information about the ISPS, email isps@isps.org or visit our website www.isps.org.

Other titles in the series

Beyond Medication

Therapeutic engagement and the recovery from psychosis

Edited by David Garfield and Daniel Mackler

Routledge
Taylor & Francis Group

LONDON AND NEW YORK

First published 2009
by Routledge
27 Church Road, Hove, East Sussex BN3 2FA

Simultaneously published in the USA and Canada
by Routledge
270 Madison Avenue, New York, NY10016

Routledge is an imprint of the Taylor & Francis Group, an Informa business

Typeset in Times by Garfield Morgan, Swansea, West Glamorgan
Printed and bound in Great Britain by T J International Ltd, Padstow,
Cornwall
Paperback cover design by Hybert Design

This publication has been produced with paper manufactured to strict
environmental standards and with pulp derived from sustainable forests.

British Library Cataloguing in Publication Data
A catalogue record for this book is available from the British Library

Library of Congress Cataloging in Publication Data
Beyond medication : therapeutic engagement and the recovery from
psychosis / edited by David Garfield and Daniel Mackler.
       p. ; cm.
   Includes bibliographical references.
   ISBN 978-0-415-46386-7 (hbk) – ISBN 978-0-415-46387-4 (pbk.)
   1. Psychoses—Treatment. 2. Psychotherapist and patient. 3. Therapeutic
alliance. I. Garfield, David A. S. II. Mackler, Daniel, 1972–
   [DNLM: 1. Psychotic Disorders—therapy. 2. Professional–Patient Relations.
3. Psychotherapeutic Processes. 4. Psychotherapy—methods. WM 200
B5735 2009]
   RC512.B49 2009
   616.89—dc22
                                                              2008021537

ISBN: 978-0-415-46386-7 (hbk)
ISBN: 978-0-415-46387-4 (pbk)

Contents

Contributors

Daniel Dorman
Private Practice Psychiatrist, Beverly Hills, California; Assistant Clinical Professor of Psychiatry, UCLA School of Medicine, Los Angeles.

Elizabeth Faulconer
Inpatient Attending Psychiatrist, Evanston Hospital, Evanston, Illinois; Assistant Professor, Department of Psychiatry and Behavioral Sciences, Northwestern University and Evanston Northwestern Healthcare.

Robert Foltz
Private Practice Psychotherapist, Park Ridge, Illinois; Assistant Executive Director, Camelot Residential Treatment Center, Des Plaines, Illinois.

Patricia L. Gibbs
Private Practice Psychoanalyst, Dearborn, Michigan; Lecturer, Michigan Psychoanalytic Institute.

Joanne Greenberg
Professor of Fiction Writing and Anthropology, Colorado School of Mines.

Bertram Karon
Professor of Psychology, Michigan State University.

Julie Kipp
Private Practice Psychotherapist, New York City; Administrative and Clinical Supervisor, Bronx REAL Continuing Day Treatment Program; Adjunct Professor of Social Work, New York University.

Brian Koehler
Private Practice Psychotherapist, New York City; Adjunct Professor of Psychology, New York University and Long Island University.

Catherine Penney
Registered Nurse, Morongo Valley, California.

Garry Prouty
Professor of Psychology and Mental Health, Prairie State College, Illinois
and the Chicago Counseling and Psychotherapy Center.

Warren Schwartz
Clinical Psychologist, Coordinator of Adult Services, Riverbend Com-
munity Mental Health/Twin Rivers Counseling Associates, Franklin, NH;
Adjunct Professor, New Hampshire Technical Institute, Concord, New
Hampshire; Newsletter Co-Editor for ISPS-US.

Ann-Louise Silver
President of ISPS-US; Adjunct Professor of Psychiatry, Uniformed Services
University of the Health Sciences.

Ira Steinman
Private Practice Psychiatrist, San Francisco, California.

Frank Summers
Private Practice Clinical Psychologist and Psychoanalyst, Chicago, Illinois;
Training and Supervising Analyst, Chicago Institute for Psychoanalysis;
Associate Clinical Professor, Department of Psychiatry and the Behavioral
Sciences, Northwestern University Medical School.

Foreword

Bertram Karon and Ann-Louise Silver

It is all too common today to read statements like "by now, everyone agrees that medication is the first line treatment of psychosis." This statement grows, not from scientific knowledge, but from the advertisements of the pharmaceutical industry. A clinician may decide that medication is necessary to bring psychotic panic under control, but the currently available medications are not curative, and they come with significant side effects, especially when administered chronically or in complex regimens. The mental health field is overrelying on these agents, while simultaneously undervaluing the power of psychotherapy to quell psychotic terror and to bring understanding and insight to bear.

Everyone suffering from psychosis deserves to have someone with whom to team up, someone who has the confidence and commitment to stay with the sufferer for as long as that sufferer needs this help. All field workers and hospital psychiatric technicians should know that their teamwork with their clients can profoundly change the course of that person's life. This book contains chapters written by clinicians who, because of the evidence presented to them by their daily work and daily lives, have come to specialize in working with the severely ill. This volume also contains two chapters written by people who recovered from schizophrenia, detailing what worked for them in favor of their recovery, and what did not.

One feature comes across clearly in these chapters: that each of us works differently, bringing our own unique personalities to the engagement with the uniqueness of each patient. Each of us uses the clinical literature to support us, finding our favorite writers who speak to us through their publications. Our patients have their voices, and we have ours.

We hope this book will guide readers into some remarkably evocative and inspirational understandings. There is no "right way" to treat psychosis; both therapist and client bring their creativity and strengths to the task, and search for common ground, be it shared experiences, shared knowledge of a particular part of the country, or shared pleasure in an activity – maybe touch football, maybe needlepoint, maybe history or astronomy. Or perhaps the commonality, as noted by Davoine and Gaudillière (2004), will be a shared history of trauma.

We hope to support the reader in searching for a more creative, less standardized, more hopeful way of being present with those struggling with psychotic disorders. These are disorders of profound loneliness, and clinical friendship mitigates this isolation. In this vein, we recommend that the reader follows the present text by reading another book in this series: *Models of Madness* (Read, Mosher, and Bentall, 2004). In the current climate of efficiency and overcommitment to biological factors in mental illness, these writings offer a way into a humanly subjective approach to treating insanity. Clinicians need more confidence in their own unique subjectivities, our most powerful instruments for healing.

The meaning in madness

When observed through the concepts of psychodynamic theories, the "meaningless" utterances and acts of patients diagnosed with schizophrenia often have obvious meanings. As one works with the sufferer to unravel the meaning, this effort in itself gives the patient evidence of our sincere interest and hopefulness. Usually, communication becomes clearer. We know we are succeeding when others start questioning the accuracy of the original diagnosis. How could this be "real schizophrenia" if the person is communicating so much more clearly? As we pursue meaning, even with patients considered "incurable schizophrenics" by other professionals, a very good therapeutic outcome often occurs, as the chapters in this book demonstrate. (Also see Silver, 1989, and Karon, 2003.)

In contrast is the oft-repeated view, held by the majority of mental health professionals today – professionals who have never listened carefully to a patient with schizophrenia – that meaning and life history are irrelevant, since schizophrenia is a biological disease (even though the biological hypotheses may be inconsistent with each other: e.g., Torrey et al., 1995). Nowhere is the apparent contradiction between psychodynamic, humanistic, and cognitive therapy, on the one hand, and biological psychiatry, on the other, so dramatic as in the treatment of schizophrenia. We reject Kraepelin's pronouncements of pessimism – that schizophrenia is a deteriorating brain disease – conveyed to this day in DSM-IV (Frances, 1994: 282–283), especially in light of the realization that Kraepelin's original cohort of deteriorating "schizophrenic" patients probably included many with the then not-yet-delineated viral influenza *encephalitis lethargica* (Boyle, 2002; Whitaker, 2002: 165–166).

False attacks on the psychotherapy of psychosis

The most extreme rejection of psychotherapy for patients diagnosed with schizophrenia was the PORT report (the Schizophrenia Patient Outcome

Research Team report, funded by the National Institute of Mental Health), which concluded that psychoanalytic therapy should never be used, nor should any form of family therapy that implied a relationship between symptoms and events in the family (Lehman et al., 1998). Most of its recommendations concerned how to use medications or electroconvulsive therapy. As Ver Eecke (2003) has pointed out, the recommendations against psychotherapy were based, according to this group themselves, on their weakest level of evidence, "expert opinion" rather than empirical data. Ann-Louise Silver and Tor Larsen (2003) edited a special issue of the *Journal of the American Academy of Psychoanalysis and Dynamic Psychiatry* replying to the PORT report, in which the authors were all ISPS members (International Society for the Psychological Treatments of the Schizophrenias and Other Psychoses). In addition to Ver Eecke's careful review of the logic and data of the PORT report were articles summarizing the empirical and clinical evidence for the effectiveness of psychotherapy for schizophrenia, all of which were left out of the PORT group's considerations.

Interestingly enough, at the meetings of the ISPS-US (the United States chapter of ISPS) and at the international meetings of the ISPS, it is striking that psychoanalytic therapists of seemingly different theoretical schools (including ego analysis, interpersonal, object relations, self psychology, relational, and Lacanian) understand each other and each other's work, because they understand the problems with which each therapist is trying to cope. There is also a mutual understanding between the psychoanalysts and the serious non-psychoanalytic therapists like the humanistic psychologist Garry Prouty (2003) and the cognitive therapists (e.g., Larsen, Bechdolf, and Birchwood, 2003) who work with people suffering from schizophrenia.

We encourage our patients to let us in on their life stories. It is noteworthy that all therapists of any school modify their technique on the basis of their experiences with patients in general and of their experience with each individual patient. Consequently, all therapists tend to understand each other. Psychodynamic approaches, in particular, sometimes take on the form of a serious, at times epic, quest in which clinician and patient join forces to quell terror and to create a place of security in which the patient's and therapist's talents can flourish and new relationships can develop.

Beyond medication

There are legitimate differences of professional opinion as to whether medication is always necessary, never necessary, or sometimes useful; whether medication is a lifelong treatment or whether it is useful at the beginning or during crises but should be withdrawn as the patient can tolerate; whether it is helpful in the short run but hurtful in the long run; whether it is always helpful, sometimes helpful, or never helpful.

Our own clinical experience as well as our reading of the literature indicates that if the patient, the therapist, and the setting (hospital, family, etc.) can tolerate it, psychotherapy seems most effective with a minimal reliance on medication. But this is a complicated issue, worthy of extended discussion. All settings are not alike, nor are all psychotherapies, nor all psychotherapists, nor all medications. But sharing real clinical experience is invaluable, especially when one's colleagues do not practice exactly the way we do, and hence can observe things we might not have a chance to observe.

This is not a rejection of neurology and biochemistry, but a rejection of simplistic models, which do not come close to describing the complexity of the human nervous system and consequently do not seem to be therapeutically effective. The journalist Robert Whitaker (2002) has documented the fact in the published research literature that medications for psychosis are not as helpful as is commonly believed. For example, the World Health Organization studies found consistently that the 5-year outcomes for patients diagnosed with schizophrenia in countries where nearly all of them are medicated are far worse than in poor countries where, because they cannot afford the medications, a much smaller percentage of patients with schizophrenia are medicated. Moreover, there has been a constant and massive increase in the percentage of chronically disabled patients with mental illness in the United States, from 3.8 per 1000 in 1955 to 20 per 1000 in 2003 (Whitaker, 2005), paralleling the increase in the use of medication and the decrease in the use of psychotherapy for serious mental illness. Clearly, the overreliance on medications has proven very deleterious.

The brain and behavior are not that simple

Current biological psychiatry does not attempt to take into account what modern biology knows about the complexity of the nervous system. The complexity of a central nervous system of billions of cells, each of which has ten thousand direct connections to other cells, and which are constantly changing their connections on the basis of each conscious experience, has been described by modern biology, but mechanistic models that can comprehend such complexity do not exist. In the words of Erich Kandel (personal communication with B. Karon, 1998), who deservedly won the Nobel Prize for his work on the biology of memory, "There is nothing we are learning which is inconsistent with anything in psychoanalysis. We are simply learning some of the mechanisms by which these things happen." Alan Shore and Brian Koehler are among those who are attempting to integrate complex modern biological knowledge with accurate psychological models. We believe that it is in the experiences of the complex interaction between human beings, especially in psychotherapy, that this complex neurobiological organ can complexly and subtly change itself more effectively than can any direct crude physical or chemical intervention.

The effectiveness of psychotherapy: empirical studies

Not only does clinical experience with individual patients considered incurable by other professionals attest to the power of psychotherapy (e.g., Karon, 2003; Robbins, 1993), so too do studies like those of Benedetti and Furlan (1987), who reported from Italy and Switzerland a series of 50 severe cases of patients with schizophrenia treated with intensive psychoanalytic therapy (2–5 sessions per week) for 3–10 years by supervisees, with very good results in 80% of the cases. Schindler (1980) in Austria reported that in a 10-year follow-up that studied such criteria as working, taking care of children, and relating to a spouse, bifocal family therapy was more effective than medication. Revere et al. (1983) found that psychotherapy led to discharge and employment, as well as improved psychological functioning, in 15-year inpatients at St. Elizabeths Hospital, but not in medicated controls. It was noteworthy that the patients who did best in the outside world were often rated by the ward staff as less well-adjusted to the ward just before discharge than their medicated controls. These unmedicated patients showed more initiative and less unquestioning "robotic" compliance, traits useful in real life but not usually valued by hospital staff. Deikman and Whitaker (1979) instituted a regimen of purely psychological treatment (without medication) on one experimental ward of a psychiatric hospital. Their ward program decreased rehospitalization. There were no suicides, suicide attempts, or elopements during the 11 months in which the ward was fully operative. A comparison ward, more fully staffed and using expert psychopharmacology, had three suicides in the same period, and sent its more disturbed patients to a long-term state hospital.

The Michigan State Psychotherapy Research Project (Karon and VandenBos, 1981) randomly assigned patients with schizophrenia to one of three groups: (a) an average of 70 sessions of psychoanalytic psychotherapy; (b) medication used effectively; or (c) a combination of the two. Blind evaluation showed that psychotherapy alone, or with initial medication that was withdrawn as soon as the patients could tolerate being without it, led to earlier discharge from the hospital, kept the patients out of the hospital, and improved their thought disorders more than medication alone. Patients treated with psychotherapy lived a more human life in a variety of ways. Psychotherapy with maintenance medication was better than medication alone, but not as good in the long run as psychotherapy alone or with initial medication that was withdrawn. Psychotherapy with maintenance medication resulted in less improvement in the thought disorder compared to psychoanalytic therapy alone, and reduction in the thought disorder was the best predictor of not being re-hospitalized.

Gottdiener (2006) summarized all the published controlled studies by means of a statistical meta-analysis. Supportive therapy, cognitive therapy, and psychoanalytic therapy are more helpful than medication alone, but psychoanalytic therapy and cognitive therapy are much more helpful than supportive therapy. While psychoanalytic therapy with or without medication was more helpful than medication alone, there were no published controlled studies of cognitive therapy without medication.

Alanen (1991, 1997) in Finland demonstrated what a real community mental health system providing psychotherapy can do. The first session is always a family session to which all members of the family are invited. It begins with the invitation: "Six months ago your son, daughter, husband wife, father, mother was not psychotic, now they are. Something must have happened. Can you help us try to figure out what might have happened?" They have developed sensitive theories of which family interventions are most likely to be helpful to the designated patient as well as to the other members of the family. The three- or four-person treatment team decides which option or combination of options – individual therapy, family therapy, medication, hospitalization – is most likely to be helpful to this individual and family at this point in time. Since this system has been in effect, the amount of medication used has decreased, as well as the necessity for hospitalization. The data show that it is cheaper than the previous system of American-style community treatment emphasizing medication without meaningful psychotherapy. More importantly, the patients are restored to a more human and productive life.

Principles of treatment: therapeutic engagement

Patients respond to insight and to internalizing a tolerant, kind, confused, and stubborn therapist, one who is there to help, can tolerate negative affect as well as not understanding, and who does not quit. We match our stubbornness against their stubborn symptoms. We need confidence in our unique subjectivities, as they are our most powerful healing instruments. A rich array of theory and technique has evolved, providing security for clinicians. Most effective therapists, however, are more concerned with helpfulness than with theoretical consistency. Clinician and patient join forces to quell terror and create a secure place for creativity. Shared understanding of psychotic experience inspires hope. A strengthening mutual trust provides the glue that repairs the shattered ego. Our patients diagnosed with schizophrenia form inherently analyzable transference reactions.

This relational transition from I-It to I-Thou (Buber, 1958) marks the essence of spirituality. Psychotherapy of psychosis, by necessity, addresses the patient's spirit: striving to bring order out of chaos, helping patients recover confidence in their humanness, seeking something of a "resurrection," returning the patient to emotional life from a position of psychic deadness.

As noted by Fromm-Reichmann (1950), some unifying principles emerge:

1   Primary process in dreams, psychosis, and creativity all have meta-phoric significance. Insight converts raw anxiety into sublimated cohesive work.
2   A psychotic person's emotional responses to the analyst and the analyst's countertransference each provide clues to understanding and thus containing anxieties.
3   Life events, both traumas and sources of security, contribute to each person's unique attempts to adapt to an always unknowable future.
4   Developing respect for each patient's stubbornly fixed defenses is therapeutic.

Summary

Few clinicians of psychosis work exclusively with psychotic patients. All see mental health and illness on a continuum. All human beings could become psychotic, all have entered its territory (Winnicott, 1974), and those suffering psychosis can recover. As Sullivan (1953, 1962) pointed out, we all are more simply uniquely human than otherwise. As humans, we can say how we think and feel; we know the inevitability of our death. We all strive to make our lives meaningful. Working with psychotic patients is frequently exhausting, sometimes scary, sometimes irritating, but it can also be exciting and deeply satisfying.

Fromm-Reichmann (1989: 481) spoke for all of us who work with difficult patients when she said: "If you want to know something for my epitaph, you could say I had a lot of fun, but a different sort of fun from other people. It was a special kind of fun."

References

Alanen, Y. (1991, August). *Psychotherapy of Schizophrenia in Community Psychiatry*. Paper presented at the Xth International Symposium for the Psychotherapy of Schizophrenia, Stockholm, Sweden.

Alanen, Y. (1997). *Schizophrenia: Its Origins and Need Adapted Treatment*. London: Karnac Books.

Benedetti, G. and Furlan, P. (1987). Individual psychoanalytic psychotherapy of schizophrenia. In G. Benedetti (Ed.), *Psychotherapy of Schizophrenia* (pp. 198–212). New York: New York University Press.

Boyle, M. (2002). *Schizophrenia: A Scientific Delusion?* (2nd ed.). London: Routledge.

Buber, M. (1958). *I and Thou*. New York: Charles Scribner's Sons.

Davoine, F. and Gaudillière, J.-M. (2004). *History Beyond Trauma*. New York: Other Press.

Deikman, A. and Whitaker, L. (1979). Humanizing a psychiatric ward: Changing from drugs to psychotherapy. *Psychotherapy: Theory, Research, and Practice*, 16: 204–214.

Frances, A. (1994). *DSM-IV*. Washington, DC: American Psychiatric Association.

Fromm-Reichmann, F. (1950). *Principles of Intensive Psychotherapy*. Chicago: University of Chicago Press.

Fromm-Reichmann, F. (1989). Reminiscences of Europe. In A.-L. Silver (Ed.), *Psychoanalysis and Psychosis* (pp. 469–481). Madison, CT: International Universities Press.

Gottdiener, W. (2006). Individual psychodynamic psychotherapy of schizophrenia: Empirical evidence for the practicing clinician. *Psychoanalytic Psychology*, 23: 583–590.

Karon, B. (2003). The tragedy of schizophrenia without psychotherapy. *Journal of the American Academy of Psychoanalysis and Dynamic Psychiatry*, 31: 89–118.

Karon, B. and VandenBos, G. (1981). *Psychotherapy of Schizophrenia: The Treatment of Choice*. Northvale, NJ: Jason Aronson.

Larsen, T., Bechdolf, A., and Birchwood, M. (2003). The concept of schizophrenia and phase-specific treatment: Cognitive behavioral treatment in pre-psychosis and in non-responders. *Journal of the American Academy of Psychoanalysis and Dynamic Psychiatry*, 31: 209–228.

Lehman, A., Steinwachs, D., and the Survey co-investigators of the PORT project (1998). Translating research into practice: The schizophrenia patient outcomes research team (PORT) treatment recommendations. *Schizophrenia Bulletin*, 24: 1–10.

Prouty, G. (2003). Pre-therapy: A newer development of schizophrenia. *Journal of the American Academy of Psychoanalysis and Dynamic Psychiatry*, 31: 59–74.

Read, J., Mosher, L., and Bentall, R. (2004) *Models of Madness: Psychological, Social and Biological Approaches to Schizophrenia*. London: Brunner-Routledge.

Revere, V., Rodeffer, C., Dawson, S., and Bigelow, L. (1983). Modifying psychotherapeutic techniques to meet the needs of chronic schizophrenics. *Hospital and Community Psychiatry*, 34: 361–362.

Robbins, M. (1993). *Experiences of Schizophrenia*. New York: Guilford Press.

Schindler, R. (1980). Die Veranderung psychotischer Landzeiteverlaufe nach Psychotherapie [The change of long term progress of psychotics after psychotherapy]. *Psychiatrica Clinica*, 13: 206–216.

Silver, A.-L. (1989). *Psychoanalysis and Psychosis*. Madison, CT: International Universities Press.

Silver, A.-L. and Larsen, T. (2003). The schizophrenic person and the benefit of the psychotherapies: Seeking a PORT in the storm. *Journal of the American Academy of Psychoanalysis and Dynamic Psychiatry*, 31 (Special Issue).

Sullivan, H. (1953). *The Interpersonal Theory of Psychiatry*. New York: W.W. Norton.

Sullivan, H. (1962). *Schizophrenia as a Human Process*. New York: W.W. Norton.

Torrey, E., Bowler, A., Taylor, E., and Gottesman, I. (1995). *Schizophrenia and Manic-Depressive Disorder: The Biological Roots of Mental Illness as Revealed by the Landmark Study of Identical Twins*. New York: Basic Books.

Ver Eecke, W. (2003). The role of psychoanalytic theory and practice in schizophrenia. *Journal of the American Academy of Psychoanalysis and Dynamic Psychiatry*, 31: 11–30.

Whitaker, R. (2002). *Mad in America: Bad Science, Bad Medicine, and the Enduring Mistreatment of the Mentally Ill*. Cambridge, MA: Perseus Press.

Whitaker, R. (2005). Anatomy of an epidemic: Psychiatric drugs and the astonishing rise of mental illness in America. *Ethical Human Psychology and Psychiatry*, 7: 23–35.
Winnicott, D. (1974). Fear of breakdown. *International Review of Psycho-Analysis*, 1: 103–107.

Acknowledgements

Working with severely disturbed patients in meaningful therapy has been the lifeblood of my career and I am deeply indebted to my patients who have shared their hearts and souls with me. I am grateful to Daniel Mackler, whose great energy, acumen, and deep collaborative spirit made this endeavor possible. The ISPS-US authors/contributors to this volume are all, to a person, outstanding human beings and I am fortunate to have had their sustaining company in my professional life for over twenty-five years. Dr. Nutan Vaidya, my chair and friend at the Department of Psychiatry at RFUMS/The Chicago Medical School, has been a consistent advocate for my academic writing, as has the late Dr. Marian Tolpin from the Chicago Institute for Psychoanalysis, to whom I owe much inspiration. Finally, I am extraordinarily fortunate to have a wife and colleague, Dr. Bonnie Garfield, who counseled me during the production of this book and, as well, my daughter and son, Jenny and Jake, who challenge me to stay with my passion in life.

David Garfield, M.D.

First and foremost I am deeply indebted to David Garfield, who welcomed me into this project with trust and respect. I couldn't have asked for a better collaborator – and guide. I also offer my deep gratitude to Ann-Louise Silver, who brought me out from the wilderness of private practice and into ISPS-US – and now into publication. She saw my value not just as a clinician but as a writer as well. Finally, I have three personal thanks: first, to Joanne Greenberg, my hero on many levels; second, to Fred Timm, a friend and therapist who gives the best feedback I know; and third, to all my patients, whose courage inspires me daily.

Daniel Mackler, LCSW

Part 1

Engaging the patient

Chapter 1

Strengthening the patient

David Garfield and Daniel Dorman

Introduction – into psychosis: the case of K.

There are many roads into psychosis and there are many key ingredients to the road out. When the emotional pain of living becomes unbearable and internal and external support begins to lose its ability to hold things together, a profound new and different reality sets in. In the midst of this "falling apart," at the center of this "going crazy," the patient has, in a way, lost his or her mind. Yet, what does that really mean? What is it that is lost?

K. had struggled since she moved to her new wealthy suburb at the age of 11. As the oldest of four girls and one youngest boy, K. had set the pace. She excelled in soccer, was considered creative and verbally advanced by her teachers, and enjoyed the respect of both her parents. Yet, in the new school, she was a "duck out of water." There were many talented children there. Her family was at the low end of the income bracket in this town. She had left her close friends, and found it difficult to make new friends. Girls in her grade made excuses as to why they could not sleep over. K.'s mother also felt out of place. She drove a Mercedes but felt that others would see that they did not live in a big house and would think that she drove it for "show." When cut off by nasty drivers in town, K.'s mother would think that she was being targeted because she drove a Mercedes – that people were jealous of her.

K. felt her old self-confidence slipping away. To compensate, she made up elaborate fantasy stories in her own mind about Dalia, a mythical 30-year-old artist who was talented and known for her creativity. Dalia also possessed secret physical powers that allowed her to fend off and deter would-be assailants. Dalia was not only a painter but also a writer and K., in real life, would emulate Dalia's style as she imagined it in her fantasies. After 2 years in the new junior high school, K. had no good friends. Luckily, she had her little sisters to play with, but she began to worry about her body as she was going through puberty. When she was younger, K. had always felt good about her body. She was a good athlete. At the new junior high, K. had not tried out for the soccer team. Her father, a hardworking, "never home" attorney, pushed her to play sports in school. She tried lacrosse but was quite self-conscious. Her body image oscillated dramatically. Was she too fat? Was she too tall? K. could not get a fix on her own body during this time. She would have spurts of being quite good at lacrosse and at other times her self-confidence would give way to intense self-consciousness and awkwardness. She took refuge in her fantasy world with Dalia.

K. found herself "dissociating" at times during class. She had no seizures or medical problems, but she would lose track of time and would feel like she was "not in her own body." She tried to adjust her eating to make her body "come out right." She would command and direct her little sisters so she could feel like she had something to offer. As she entered high school, K. kept away from boys. She went to church frequently, which gave her some sense of belonging. Yet, she continued to have disturbing "dissociative" experiences at school and sometimes at home. There was no history of abuse. She felt like she was not doing well with her life; she knew there was something "wrong" with her but did not know what it was. She found herself becoming more and more anxious.

Louis Sass (1992) described how normal emotionality is replaced by a certain kind of anxiety as psychosis sets in. He divided the process into four stages. First, a period of "unreality" sets in where things just do not seem the same. Here is where we find our patient K. The second stage is what Sass calls "mere being." In this state, nothing has any more emotional value than anything else and "significance" evaporates. A devastating car accident may carry the same weight as dropping a turkey sandwich on the ground. The third stage is called "fragmentation" and involves the inability to compare one thing with another. The cow and the calf are not seen as mother and offspring – these kinds of relationships are not noticed anymore. It is just two different sizes of cow. A tire is not seen as part of a car but rather as two separate unrelated items. Finally, in a desperate search for meaning, the fourth stage of "apophany" appears. Apophany is the Greek word for "to become apparent." Now, everything has meaning. Each little noise, each little word, each glance, each opening of a door all become terribly meaningful, but the patient cannot figure out how. The patient is forced to remain on guard at all times to try to make sense of it.

The developing self

Defining one's self, one's unique identity, is a central part of human psychological development. That developing self is challenged throughout our lives, but more at some ages and under some circumstances. For example, if K. had a stronger sense of her self, she might not have felt like a "duck out of water" at the new school. A move would be a challenge to any child, since he or she depends on the consistency of the external world, but

K. did not have enough confidence in herself to accommodate the change. The demands of the external world increase as we grow older, which is why K. experienced increasing problems. Her self, her "I," was not able to keep up with the increasing demands. Her lack of confidence led her to construct Dalia, a fantasy self who had strength and power. K.'s dependence upon a fantasy identity, vicariously living through Dalia's secret powers, added to her increasing sense of unreality. But the cost of constructing an identity is that further growth is impeded. Actual growth is the accumulation of actual experience. K. was freezing herself in place. She experienced a gradual erosion of her "I," adding to her sense of unreality. As her "I" eroded, she no longer had a reference point for her emotionality, thus she gradually slipped into a life without meaning. The awareness of a diminutive "I" accounts for much of the pervasive anxiety referenced by Sass. As she retreated into a solipsistic state, K. lost the ability to confirm or validate her sense of self. Thus she experienced herself in fragments. She then desperately searched for meaning, for what was real and what was not real, which resulted in paying attention to every little sensation and every little detail of her life. She desperately sought solutions, such as declaring with certainty that her changing body was the problem, or that she needed to join a group to secure an identity. But these efforts did not fix her gradual self-dissolution. K.'s overwhelming anxiety caused her to try to shut down her mind, resulting in periods of dissociation. Some people shut themselves down to such an extent that they become catatonic.

To the outside observer K. is psychotic. But her experiences are not just "delusions," or misrepresentations of reality. Life *was* becoming unreal. K.'s anxiety was, in fact, overwhelming. Her experience of herself in fragments can be understood, since she no longer experienced herself in a cohesive way. Even her efforts to shut herself down make sense, since she did not know what else to do. The psychotic person is not so strange or so different from anyone else. His struggles, even his solutions to his difficulties, are entirely human. He can be understood.

The road out of psychosis demands addressing the problem at the core: K.'s diminutive "I," her lack of self, must be strengthened. A therapist who tries to understand the psychotic person will find that he or she always has a remnant of self. It may be buried, but it is there. It is possible to help affirm his or her remaining self, and to help him build a stronger self. The remnant of self is not a static thing, but rather it has a nascent vitality. Although this remnant is a result of a significant developmental arrest (Stolorow and Lachmann, 1980), it is constantly seeking to re-engage. Marian Tolpin (2002), the Chicago self-psychology psychoanalyst, labeled this alive remnant the "forward edge of development," and notes that it is the therapist's job to attend to its manifestations and to provide the kind of responsive environment that can facilitate its developmental trajectory. Let us turn to the example of Ms. C. for an initial understanding of how this happens.

Engaging the sequelae of psychosis: the case of Ms. C. – looks can be deceiving

Ms. C. had been in a halfway house for about 15 years. She had been married to a terribly abusive alcoholic man to whom she had devoted herself. She had been an active little girl, the only child of a beautiful mother who was a housewife and a father who was a wealthy attorney and an abusive, alcoholic husband. Ms. C. reported that as a little girl she was constantly told, by her father, how she was pretty like her mother. Her mother was described as sweet but quiet and unengaged. Later, Ms. C. would relate that she was sure her father had been consistently unfaithful to her mother and that caused her mother to be depressed. She grew up in a big house in the Hamptons on Long Island.

Ms. C. had done well in school and had become something of an environmentalist before it was fashionable. She was an avid birdwatcher and took over her mother's gardening when her mother was too depressed to keep it up. She had many boyfriend suitors and she dated in high school. She wanted to go away to college but her mother wanted her nearby, so Ms. C. went to junior college. She was "swept off her feet" by a charismatic young man who was in law school and who wanted to go into politics. At the age of 22, she married and quickly had two children in the span of 3 years. Her husband was elected to the state senate and she entertained regularly. She was the "belle of the ball" and delighted in her role as the "woman behind the man." Ms. C. ignored reports that her husband was "a bit like Jack Kennedy with the women." She, in fact, adored Jackie Kennedy, so she was initially pleased by the comparison. But her husband's infidelity became more difficult to ignore. On top of that, he became very demanding of how she should dress and what she should serve to guests, and he would come home very late, drunk, and smelling of another woman's perfume. When she confronted him about this, he would deny it, become furious, and hit her.

Ms. C. felt that she could not tell her mother about the situation. Her own father died and Ms. C. noted "I didn't cry at the funeral." Ms. C. became depressed. She felt that her mother needed Ms. C.'s "belle of the ball" lifestyle as something that kept her mother from being depressed. Ms. C. became anxious. She began to believe that she was ugly and disgusting. She voiced the delusion that her face had changed and she was deformed. One night when her husband did not come home, she could not sleep the whole night. He did not call or return in the morning either. She called his office and he had come in but was in a meeting. Ms. C. went into the kitchen, found a plastic bottle of liquid bleach, poured it over her head and face, and lit herself on fire. Her mother was to come over for lunch and found Ms. C. whimpering in a corner of the kitchen.

Ms. C. was completely disfigured from the self-inflicted immolation. She refused plastic surgery. After her wounds had healed, she was transferred to a psychiatric inpatient unit. Her husband insisted that she stay there for 6 months. She came home and she knew that he would not be able to tolerate her. She had a difficult time explaining what had happened to her two little girls. She became withdrawn. Ms. C. had covered her hands with the bleach as well, so they were completely disfigured, as were her neck and upper chest. Many of her caregivers at the hospital found it hard to look at her. Ms. C. understood this. She retreated into a world of her own. Every time she attempted to return home in the first 2 years, she found it impossible to return to "my old life. I was now as ugly and disgusting on the outside as I felt on the inside." She entered a halfway house associated with the hospital.

Her husband sought a divorce and remarried quickly. He took custody of their children although she wrote to them and called them several times a week. They would visit her in the halfway house on holidays. Ms. C. settled into a life "amidst outcasts." She routinely participated in all the group sessions, made insightful comments to the other patients and to staff, and she volunteered in the hospital gift shop. Her social interactions, however, were difficult because staff were sometimes disturbed by her grotesque appearance, and since she did not want to cause them distress she would leave the group. Sometimes, patients would sense that she was hiding behind her wounds and they would address this, which would be difficult for her and would cause her to leave the group.

After 15 years in the halfway house and many staff therapists, one of us (D.G.) was assigned as her therapist. Warnings had been issued by the staff as to what the initial reaction might be. What was memorable was exactly how startling it was to find that Ms. C. had beautiful, brilliant blue eyes.

Ms. C. was worn down by her years on trifluoperazine (Stelazine) and her routine in the hospital and halfway house. She had never heard voices, never had persistent delusions, and yet had been labeled with schizoaffective disorder for several years. The new therapist focused on her blue eyes and over a period of weeks of twice-a-week therapy became more comfortable with her disfigurement. Ms. C. was somewhat startled that the therapist was not repulsed by her appearance. She did not know quite what to make out of the suggestion to meet twice a week but she was happy for the conversation. She related the entirety of her story and her terrible remorse about her life without her daughters.

The patient was confused by other aspects of the therapist. He did not push medication and, in fact, suggested that maybe she did not need it. It took several months to taper her dose down and she was fine. Although he had in mind that her act of self-immolation was not only a peak experience of masochism and "turning against the self," he also was aware of the amount of rage and self-hatred that accompanied it. Both realized that this was not going to be the "status quo" infrequent medication management/ no change therapy that had taken place over the last 15 years.

Over the first year, Ms. C. reported having more feelings. She missed her daughters, she was annoyed with the hospital, and she pitied and was very angry with her mother. The therapist's modest office at the State Hospital became a kind of refuge for her to talk. It was in the second year that something small but remarkable occurred.

One day Ms. C. came in and made a comment about how the pathos ivy plant in the office needed more water. Although it was a brief, off-the-cuff observation, she had never made a comment, critique, or observation like this before. The therapist latched onto it and said that he thought that one was supposed to soak them and then let them dry out a lot. She then went into a small treatise on plant watering. She also touched upon a Boston fern as well. This was about more than her becoming a teacher in that moment. Here she was expressing something important to her that she was now fully sharing. It was no longer just her blue eyes that were impressive, it was the breadth of her knowledge of and passion for plants.

How the little "I" becomes a bigger "I": engaging affects

A person's internal perception of what feels organic or real is his authentic self. Ms. C. developed a false self as a person who did not cry. Her more natural, or real, self was to be depressed. A person's "I" is his separate-from-others or individual identity, which arises from his authentic self.

Ms. C.'s "I," her individual identity, seems to have been ignored in childhood. She developed a false identity as "pretty and unengaged," like her mother. Ms. C.'s experience of herself in her marriage as her husband's "belle of the ball" was what her husband wanted, but was not a reflection of her true identity, who she was as a real person. But Ms. C.'s efforts to please her parents and her husband probably represented some authentic part of her being.

Paradoxically, Ms. C.'s self-immolation was an act that came from her authentic self, or what was left of it. That act expressed her rage and her despair that she was an "outcast," not a valued member of the human family. She also may have experienced a sense that her act would punish her husband. And it could have represented her authentic feeling that she should live as she felt herself to be: disgusting. People commonly come to the conclusion that if their true self is not acknowledged or accepted, they must be disgusting or worthless.

The power of therapy is that "I" development can be encouraged, even in those whose "I" development has come to a standstill, or where the individual's "I" only exists in fragments. Part of the therapeutic task is to listen for and respond to these fragments. For example, burying one's "I" is an act of self-defense, therefore an act of the authentic self. The therapist, by placing himself in a position to learn *who* his patient is, will hear his patient's truth. Ms. C. must have recognized that her therapist's interest in her was authentic, or she would not have responded in a genuine way by suggesting how he might better care for his plants.

Much of therapy involves the experience of the moment. This moment-by-moment process involves mutual acknowledgement and addition. The therapist acknowledges or recognizes his patient's "I." His patient senses the truth of this recognition. For example, Ms. C. likely recognized that her therapist highly regarded her eyes, thus he was not put off by her disfigurement. She also recognized her therapist's desire to know her, to know who she really was under her skin. She responded by revealing her passion for plants. By knowing her, Ms. C.'s therapist changed. He added an increment to his own "I." His patient's "I" too had changed, added to, by knowing her therapist. His responses became part of her. Each acknowledgement adds to the other's "I." Each exposes an enlarging "I" to the other, bit by bit.

Ms. C. began to feel more because a "space," created by her therapy, existed within which she could be authentic. This "space" is not a physical place, rather a metaphor for an experience, a mental operation wherein an individual might find an internal representation of his individual self, his "I" (Jaynes, 1990). Ms. C.'s increased feelings likely will include her previously split-off pain, which is why patients often appear "worse" to the outsider as therapy progresses. Ms. C.'s pain, however, is her authentic response to her condition. Her once diminutive "I" has begun to expand. Strength or confidence can be defined as trusting one's perceptual apparatus. As Ms. C. begins to trust her self-perceptions, she will likely be encouraged to continue her expansion.

The central role of emotional development in strengthening the self

What does it mean when a chronic psychiatric patient becomes more affectively alive? Like the sap that flows through a tree, affect circulates. The usual pathways that have been blocked or unused for long periods of time now begin to open up. There is a small change, and sometimes a big change, that occurs within the patient. The patient becomes engaged – engaged by someone and engaged with something. An old unused capacity is revived. A repertoire is expanded. The old psychoanalytic language for this was that the therapist had provided an auxiliary ego to the patient. Yet, under closer inspection, the mechanisms that underlie this "coming to affective life" take on greater clarity.

The therapeutic alliance, which has been the stalwart of psychotherapy success, sets the stage for an engagement that activates certain processes within the patient. When the patient's personal interests are touched upon, the passions or feelings connected to those interests also become activated.

Now what? When the therapist or analyst recognizes, participates in, or attunes to these interests, an interesting phenomenon occurs. Through the blue eyes or through the leaves of the plant, two minds come into contact with one another. In the back and forth, turn-taking process of verbal and non-verbal communication, categorical and dimensional aspects of emotional life are set in motion. The categorical aspects, such as happy or sad states, may arise. Also, dimensional aspects emerge as well.

Vitality affects

Vitality affects are distinguished from categorical affects (Stern, 1985, 2004). The categorical affects represent discrete behavioral states and have been studied by a number of researchers (Ekman, 1982; Emde 1990; Izard, 1991; Tomkins, 1962). Joy, fear, sadness/distress, anger, disgust, shame, and interest/surprise have varying intensities and hedonic tone but are individual feeling states with corresponding somatic expressions. Ekman has been in the forefront of detailing the facial expression and recognition of the categorical affects. Vitality affects, as introduced by Stern (1985), are somewhat different. These are subjective experiences that are characterized by their kinetic dynamic motion. Tomkins (1962), another emotion researcher, also placed great emphasis on the kinetic components of affect.

Vitality affects parallel the vital bodily processes such as breathing, swallowing, vomiting, defecating, muscles moving, and the body turning, starting, stopping, or even falling asleep. We can describe them in various ways. They are fading, exploding, collapsing, slowing down, drawing out, or drifting feelings. These qualities of experience, as opposed to the categorical affects, are always present. Yet they can combine with the categorical affects, in that we can have an eruption of anger or we can have an eruption of fear as the toddler strays too near to the street. The vitality affects are induced by internal and external events. Stern (2004) notes:

> Vitality affects are intrinsic to all experiences in all modalities, domains, and types of situations. They occur both in the presence and absence of Darwinian categorical affects. For example, a rush of anger or joy, a sudden flooding of light, an accelerating sequence of thoughts, a wave of feeling evoked by music, a surge of pain, and a shot of narcotics can all feel like "rushes." They share a similar distribution of excitation/ activation over time, a similar feeling-flow pattern – in other words a similar vitality affect.
>
> (p. 64)

Thus, vitality affects have three dimensions – duration, frequency, and intensity. They have what Stern (1985, 2004) calls an "activation contour." The three dimensions combine to form this contour shape of a vitality affect. The psychoanalytic clinician expresses vitality affects all the time from the "uh huh" to the "mmmm" to the myriad of other sounds, noises, simple utterances, and "body language" that characterize the ebb and flow of communication in any given session.

Affect and vitality affect attunement is a self-object function

The central role of affective change and modification is becoming recognized as the mechanism of therapeutic change in psychoanalysis (Clyman, 1991; Lane and Garfield, 2005; Spezzano, 1993). Heinz Kohut (1971), the grand-father of self psychology, noted that just as people do not notice that oxygen is essential to their life when they are functioning normally, human beings do not notice that important self-object functions are essential for psycho-logical function. He pointed to two sources of this psychological oxygen. He called the first "mirroring" experiences, and labeled the second as "ideal-izing" experiences. Later, he added a third category of "likeness" or "twin-ship" experiences. These were vital avenues through which the nascent self or "I" would grow and become more intact and coherent. Through the lens of self psychology, psychopathology represented the breakdown products of the self. Key self-object functions were lacking and in extreme cases psychosis could be the result.

The old adage that affect and cognition are two sides of the same coin may be giving way to a new adage: that affect and self-esteem are two sides of the same coin. Socarides and Stolorow (1987) have been among the first to note the critical role of affects in self-object function. Garfield (2001) has pointed out how cross-modal attunement through the use of vitality affects can serve as a "mirroring" self-object experience that expands a faltering self in psychosis. So much of psychosis involves the patient not having access to sustaining and enhancing aspects of their inner world. "When I feel you feeling me, then I connect with a part of myself which has been off limits to me. I connect to myself through you." In these natural inter-subjective ways, the self becomes stronger.

Countertransference issues

The developmental process does not eliminate the primitive self. Rather, subsequent development layers over the earlier, more primitive versions of the self. The psychotic person's state of developmental arrest often appeals to the therapist's buried primitive self, thus countertransference issues arise. Ms. C.'s therapist, for example, might have reacted to his own experience of being small and helpless, a remnant of his early "I," as resonating with Ms. C.'s disfigurement, or by identifying with her many years of feeling that she was an outcast. Had he reacted in this way, he might have displayed "too much" empathy, which would have been picked up by Ms. C. as not having to do with her, as would his attempt to be "too helpful."

Harold Searles (1965) writes about many countertransference issues that arise when one treats psychotic patients. For example, he cautions:

> . . . he [the therapist] will not need to shield himself, through the maintenance of an urgently and actively 'helpful' or 'rescuing' attitude, from feeling at a deep level, the impact of the fragmented and dedifferentiated world, with its attendant feelings, in which the patient exists.
>
> (p. 530)

The therapist must also be cautious about placing too much emphasis on the *content* of his patient's delusions, as opposed to considering the feeling implications (Searles, 1965). Ms. C.'s feeling that she was an outcast is just as important, perhaps more so, as how and why (the content) she became an outcast.

The therapist should be cognizant of developing hubris as a result of his importance to his patient's growth and development. The therapist may be tempted to regard himself as too important to his patient, as if he is in the position of a parent. Despite his patient's lack of development, the patient should not be related to as a child. A large part of the treatment resides in the respect that a therapist has for his patient. Such respect confirms a patient's self-respect, that is, the patient's experience, however constricted, that he is an autonomous person. Respect also means that the therapist possesses the strength to allow his patient to find his own way. Ms. C.'s therapist, for example, allowed her the room to discover her authentic self.

The therapist would do well, too, not to hurry the treatment. The process of "I" development occurs in increments of experience and cannot be truncated. Often, perhaps usually, the therapist may become despairing over his patient's lack of progress, or what appears to him as worsening of his patient's condition. Additionally, working with psychotic patients may cause the therapist to despair because he may feel a lack of acknowledgement. The therapist should not visit his despair upon his patient by trying to force change. Patience really means respect for his patient's internal processes.

Bipolar psychosis: the case of Ellen V.

Ellen was a 40-year-old married woman who had worked as an occupational therapist for some 20 years. She grew up on the North Side of Chicago, the second daughter to a well-to-do cardiologist. Her mother was a "stay at home" mom. Ellen had suffered a mild depressive episode during college and had several hypomanic episodes during the early years of her marriage. After the birth of her second child, at the age of 30, Ellen went through a rough postpartum depression and had to stop breastfeeding. She was started on fluoxetine (Prozac) but later developed a manic psychosis where she became "lost" in the world of Oliver Stone's *JFK* conspiracy movie. She corresponded extensively with those who believed that the late president's death was part of a right-wing plot, and she idealized Oliver Stone and fantasized about being his lover.

Ellen's husband, Bob, was a mild-mannered fellow who suffered from low self-esteem and chronic frustration at not being promoted from his middle management position at an insurance company, despite being quite competent. He had not finished college and felt that this deficit prevented him from real advancement, yet he was scared of going back to school and potentially "not doing well." He was a committed, although not very present, father and husband. He supported his wife as she went from psychiatrist to therapist, despite her not really making much change.

Even when Ellen was stable in terms of her mood, she harbored fantasies about Oliver Stone. When she became depressed, she thought she was a "piece of shit" and did not deserve to live. She readily accepted her diagnosis of bipolar affective disorder with psychotic features and she took just about whatever medication was prescribed. Yet, after a few weeks, she would opt out of most of it due to side effects. She would later profess that she liked her fantasies about Oliver Stone and that the lithium or valproate (Depakote) would take those away. When she was depressed, she would also be angry. She was more apt to continue taking her fluoxetine (Prozac) despite the fact that it prevented her from having an orgasm.

One of the most distinguishing characteristics of Ellen's upbringing was her relationship with her older brother. Four years her senior, Allan monopolized the entire family scene. He was bright, although no brighter than Ellen, but insisted that the entire family cater to his whims, worries, and concerns. Both parents favored Allan over Ellen and her role was to tend to whatever her brother needed. This arrangement would have been satisfactory to her if Allan had been appreciative but, in fact, he would not only depreciate her efforts but would also be sadistic to his little sister. He would grunt at her when she helped him to tidy up his room, telling her she was "almost worthless," and when she protested he would spit at her. He would hit her hard on the back of the head when she forgot to get everything he asked for when she ran errands to the bookstore for his school supplies. If she complained to her parents, Allan would deny it and turn even more violent and cruel towards her. She learned not to complain.

Ellen started her psychotherapy after she had suffered a severe dystonic reaction from haloperidol (Haldol). She had been discharged from an inpatient hospitalization where she been manic and also, subsequently, severely depressed and suicidal. During this latter period she had become delusional, believing that she had cancer and was "rotting in her insides." She was discharged on risperidone (Risperdal) and valproate (Depakote) with a small amount of haloperidol at night. She went home to her husband who did not know how to help her, and she saw a psychiatrist for medication management. When the psychiatrist increased the evening haloperidol dose and she had the dystonic reaction and he did not want to hear about Oliver Stone, she fired him and decided to start with someone new who would also do therapy.

For the first 6 months, Ellen tested her new psychiatrist/analyst. She was morose and unhappy and told him nothing was helping. He tapered her off the haloperidol, and later the risperidone. She did not want to be on the valproate because it made her "fat." She refused to go on lithium or carbamazepine (Tegretol) for the same reason. She wanted to be on an antidepressant. She wanted to be on bupropion (Wellbutrin). She finally agreed to be on lorazepam (Ativan) as well, which seemed to control her hypomania such that she did not become manic. She refused the standard psychopharmacological approach to bipolar disorder. The new doctor went along with her wishes as long as things were safe from a medical perspective. He could justify the combination pharmacologically and therapeutically even if it was far from optimal. More importantly, he wanted to know why she was so unhappy. In a spurt of upset one day, she confessed that she had no one to talk to about Oliver Stone, JFK, or anything. She "knew" that the new guy did not want to hear it either. Despite his protest, she stormed out of the office. She was his last patient of the day and as he was walking to his car Ellen was nearby. She yelled, "I might as well walk with you as I am parked near you."

She then went on to snort, "You think I'm worthless and you think you are so smart, but nothing you do helps me." She spat in front of him. He simply said, "You are very angry – there is the spitting," and got into his car. Her whole demeanor changed from then on. They discussed her brother. He understood that her transference to him had been around the brother and her unhappy life as a child in his presence. He asked about JFK. She began to feel that he was really interested in her. She felt that she got nothing from her husband other than his pity. There was no understanding there. It was like life with her parents.

Ellen went on to reveal deep and extensive masochistic fantasies about being raped by Oliver Stone. First, the lover would have to spank her and this would sexually arouse her. Then she would have him hit her on the back of the head and she would fall down and then she would spit at him and then he would force himself on her and she would have multiple orgasms at the same time that he did. She could sexually satisfy her husband but she noted that "he gets freaked out when I ask him to spank me. He won't do that." She revealed that she had had masochistic fantasies as a latency age girl as well. She realized in therapy that she would not be ridiculed for her inner life. They discussed how isolated she had become. In fact, Ellen had no friends. She worked, somewhat slavishly, for her children and her household. She had great difficulties setting appropriate limits with her two children. Over a 6-year, twice-weekly period of time, all of this was discussed. Ellen became more aware of how her emotional state brought her either into a "flight" into fantasy that isolated her or into a descent into "worthlessness" that made her not want to live. She established a fairly stable positive "father" transference to the analyst wherein she could rebuild her occupational therapy career, as she and the analyst had the health care profession in common. This was an idealizing transference that helped her to establish a middle ground between the psychosis of mania and the "rotting" delusions of melancholic depression. She eventually self-titrated her lorazepam and bupropion, while always notifying the therapist, and she had no psychiatric relapses. At the same time, the Oliver Stone fantasies abated as she realized that she wanted a powerful man like her father to take definitive interest in her and that she felt this same attachment need, now fulfilled from her therapist. She wondered if she could wean herself off him.

As her sadomasochistic defenses were discussed and set aside for more adaptive measures (she joined a movie club and volunteered to help the high school students make documentaries), she felt less isolated. She was able to set some reasonable limits with her children. She was talking about cutting down on sessions or maybe taking a break. It was around that time that her husband got a big promotion in another state and Ellen ended up moving. She called frequently over the next 2 years and continued her life in a fairly stable way.

The struggle to maintain a self

Manic-depressive illness is a person's attempt to maintain self and/or "I" consistency. One can imagine, as children often do, that one is superman or powerful in a myriad of ways. The depressive component is that the authentic self – the person's sadness – "leaks" through anyway, provoking flight into the imaginary self. A vicious cycle ensues.

Ellen's sense of her individual self, her "I," was that she was a "piece of shit." Her identity was similar to that of Ms. C. in that they both felt worthless. Without a reasonably strong "I" it is difficult to feel that we can change or direct our own affairs. Thus Ellen and Ms. C. felt helpless and at the mercy of others.

Ellen's anger and depression were expressions of her individual identity. Her "delusion" that her insides were rotting was also an expression of her authentic self – she knew that something was terribly wrong. To combat her very negative experience of herself, Ellen imagined that she had power over powerful people, like JFK and Oliver Stone. Power really means that she tried to convince herself that her "I" was not small and weak. But her fantasies of power did not represent an authentically strong "I."

By relating to his patient's authentic self, that is, by acknowledging her depression, her anger, and her attempts to maintain self-consistency by imagining herself to be powerful, her therapist acknowledged Ellen's authentic self. It is a paradox that despite developing a life around a poorly developed "I," there is nevertheless an "I," a part of a person that recognizes, even searches for, acknowledgement. As Ellen developed a stronger "I" in her therapy by incrementally acknowledging the validity of her self-experience, she no longer needed fantasies of strength. She was, then, no longer as sad or angry and thus had less need to stabilize or regulate swings from depression to mania as she developed self-regulatory capacity.

Conclusion

Whether it is schizophrenia, psychotic depression, or manic-depressive psychosis, patients struggling with the breaking apart of their inner universe need real assistance in putting themselves back together again. The self needs to be strengthened. Psychotic patients come to clinical attention in a variety of different ways and there are many tools that clinicians pull out to help them in this effort. The self cannot be strengthened by medication management. This effort requires a collaborative working together between patient and therapist to enliven and cultivate buried parts of the person such that a new cohesion can emerge and gain force. In being a catalyst for emotional change, clinicians must attend to the experience and meaning of their psychotic patients' inner and outer communications. Contact must be made with the affective power of the patient's true self and both parties must find a way to make good use of this power in the purpose of strengthening the patient.

The therapeutic alliance, working with the inner and outer environment of the patient, common obstacles to treatment, sustaining recovery, and the experience of cure from the inside out are but a few of the topics that this book hopes to address. When James Joyce consulted the great Swiss analyst, Carl Jung, about his "schizophrenic" daughter, Lucia, Joyce was heartbroken and befuddled. He wanted to know why it was that Lucia was called psychotic and he was called a literary genius when his stream of consciousness was so similar at times to her neologisms. Jung replied, "You both go into the same river, but you dive and she falls." Our aim in this book, in our work with patients, is to get them strong enough so that they can swim once again.

References

Clyman, R. (1991). The procedural organization of emotions: A contribution from cognitive science to the psychoanalytic theory of therapeutic action. *Journal of the American Psychoanalytic Association*, 39: 349–382.

Ekman, P. (1982). *Emotion in the Human Face*. New York: Cambridge University Press.

Emde, R. N. (1990). Mobilizing fundamental modes of development: Empathic availability and therapeutic action. *Journal of the American Psychoanalytic Association*, 38: 881–913.

Garfield, D. (2001). The use of vitality affects in the coalescence of self in psychosis. *Progress in Self Psychology*, 17: 113–128.

Izard, C. E. (1991). *The Psychology of Emotions (Emotions, Personality, and Psychotherapy)*. New York: Springer.

Jaynes, J. (1990). *The Origin of Consciousness in the Breakdown of the Bicameral Mind*, Boston: Houghton Mifflin.

Kohut, H. (1971). *The Analysis of the Self*. New York: International Universities Press.

Lane, R. and Garfield, D. (2005). Becoming aware of feelings: Integration of cognitive-developmental, neuroscientific, and psychoanalytic perspectives. *Neuro-Psychoanalysis*, 7: 1–26.

Sass, L. (1992). *Madness and Modernism*. New York: Basic Books.

Searles, H. F. (1965). Phases of patient–therapist interaction in the psychotherapy of schizophrenia. In *Collected Papers on Schizophrenia and Related Subjects* (pp. 521–559). New York: International Universities Press.

Socarides, D. and Stolorow, R. (1987). Affects and selfobjects. In R. Stolorow, B. Brandchaft, and G. Atwood (Eds.), *Psychoanalytic Treatment: An Intersubjective Approach* (pp. 105–119). Hillsdale, NJ: Analytic Press.

Spezzano, C. (1993). *Affect in Psychoanalysis: A Clinical Synthesis*. Hillsdale, NJ: Analytic Press.

Stern, D. (1985). *The Interpersonal World of the Infant*. New York: Basic Books.

Stern, D. (2004). *The Present Moment in Psychotherapy and Everyday Life*. New York: W.W. Norton.

Stolorow, R. and Lachmann, F. (1980). *Psychoanalysis of Developmental Arrests*. New York: International Universities Press.

Tolpin, M. (2002). Doing psychoanalysis of normal development: The forward edge transference. *Progress in Self Psychology*, 18: 167–190.

Tomkins, S. (1962). *Affect, Imagery and Consciousness*. New York: Springer.

Chapter 2

The initial engagement in the psychotherapy of psychosis, with and without an asylum

Elizabeth Faulconer and Ann-Louise Silver

Editors' Introduction: So often in the therapeutic work with severely disturbed patients conventional "rules of engagement" simply will not work. Whether it is a caricature of the "silent analyst" or the convention of the outpatient office with the leather couch, therapists who work with patients struggling with psychosis soon find that flexibility in approach is the operative word of the day.

Drs. Elizabeth Faulconer and Ann-Louise Silver, both of whom worked at the psychoanalytic inpatient hospital Chestnut Lodge, share this essential requirement for flexibility with us in their beautiful description of work with three very different psychotic patients in three very different settings. Dr. Faulconer's work with Maria in a supportive asylum and with Isabel in a standard general hospital inpatient unit both highlight how initial relationship engagements can be fostered by the former and complicated by the latter.

Dr. Silver's work with David demonstrates creative flexibility at its maximum. Here, the therapist realized that engaging the family and the patient where they live was the only way to jumpstart an effective treatment. Psychodynamic individual therapy and family therapy were provided at the same time in order to create a milieu where David, despite serious resistance, could eventually be engaged in meaningful work.

Introduction

When the patient struggles with psychosis, the start of a therapeutic relationship varies with the treatment setting. The patient has an entirely different experience arriving at an institution where the therapist is an integral part of a therapeutic community, versus when the therapist is part of hospital staff having little knowledge of each other, or when patient and therapist are meeting for the first time in the therapist's office or the patient's home. Similarly, the past experiences of both parties are vital: is this the patient's fifteenth therapist? Has this therapist been working for 1 year or 15 years? This chapter explores the differences in these treatment settings, and notes how they affect the emerging treatment of psychosis. Development of rapport, the therapeutic alliance, and transference and countertransference phenomena are all shaped by first engagements. Both patient and therapist bring a host of expectations, wishes, fears, and biases to their initial contact based on past experiences, on what they have heard about one another, and on their feelings of comfort in the environment of their meeting. Each comes with a treatment philosophy and a perceived notion of how the relationship "should" evolve, and each is guarding against past pitfalls.

Sometimes patient and therapist have heard something about the other before the first meeting – and sometimes not. This prelude mixes cultural and environmental forces. Has the patient researched and chosen the therapist? Have family members done this work, thus bringing their biases to bear? Is the choice left to chance, through a telephone call to emergency services or a visit to the emergency room? And what has the patient been told? What prejudices have formed through reading, watching television, going to the movies? (Are you a "Freudian" or a "Jungian"?) Likewise, what attitudes does the therapist bring to the relationship? Is the therapist affected by economic anxiety, by concerns about his or her place in the treatment community, by a recent assault, or perhaps by high praise over a treatment success? Many feelings are at play long before the initial encounter. Some kind of image is already forming in both parties' minds before the first "hello." And if the patient is being admitted to a hospital by his or her outpatient clinician, the patient most likely is struggling with feelings of defeat and abandonment, which will color the meeting with the new clinician.

Setting 1: Maria in an asylum

Maria, aged 36, came to Chestnut Lodge from another inpatient psychiatric hospital. Chestnut Lodge was a private psychiatric hospital that rose to prominence in the 1940s and 1950s under the therapeutic guidance of Frieda Fromm-Reichmann, who was one of the world's pre-eminent clinicians for psychosis. Chestnut Lodge provided patients with a range of staff members devoted to their treatment, and all patients met with their analysts for at least 4 hours each week and lived on a unit managed by an administrative psychiatrist they saw daily. Additionally all treatment providers were encouraged to obtain their own analytically oriented therapy. Frieda Fromm-Reichmann and Chestnut Lodge were both immortalized by Joanne Greenberg in her classic novel depicting her own recovery from schizophrenia, *I Never Promised You a Rose Garden*, and are addressed further by Greenberg in Chapter 11 of this volume.

Maria had a remarkable movement disorder, apparently resulting from neuroleptics, also known as antipsychotics; she had won a lawsuit against her previous prescribing psychiatrist. Consultants said, "If this is tardive dyskinesia, it is unlike any I have seen before." She had an unsteady gait and her arms flailed about. She preferred crawling to walking, and tended to fall out of chairs. She had hypertrophy of her muscles from apparent dystonia, and was presently taking clozapine, the drug of choice for psychotic patients with tardive syndromes, as it was the antipsychotic least likely to exacerbate this disorder. She was admitted to the hospital unit that specialized in treatment-resistant psychotic disorders.

Due to Maria's movement disorder, she may have expected her therapist, Dr. Faulconer, to greet her as a "freak" or "victim" – or as a patient with "special needs." One wonders if she had any hope or insistence of falling into one or more of these roles. In the first therapeutic encounter, however, which took place on the hospital unit, neither therapist nor patient fulfilled any of these potential expectations. Maria said that she was a poet. She shared copies of work she had written 10 years earlier, poems on existential themes. She discussed her year as a young adult traveling in France, where she worked in vineyards and enjoyed meeting the very friendly French people. She had a lovely French accent. Dr. Faulconer told Maria that she, too, had worked in France, in the American Hospital of Paris, and spoke French well, though not as well as Maria. The two spoke French in session and Maria corrected Faulconer's imperfect accent, giving Maria the regular opportunity to help her therapist improve and thus solidifying her feeling of autonomy and control.[1] This shared familiarity allowed for the possibility of the formation of an instant, if tenuous, bond that would be much less likely to be formed in a treatment setting with less structured support for both patient and therapist.[2]

To an extent, Dr. Faulconer's degree of self-disclosure worked. They addressed each other informally as "*tu*," as the young people up into their twenties in France do among themselves but not with older people outside the family. At first Dr. Faulconer had addressed Maria as "*vous*," but then Maria suggested "*tu*" because of their supposed youth. The use of "*tu*" supported the emerging therapeutic alliance. Maria saw them as two young adults who had their "whole lives" ahead of them – a hopeful portent for treatment, and certainly a positive portent for a future therapeutic alliance.[3]

Having a secure community supporting a new dyad allows the therapist greater flexibility and spontaneity in forging a bond with a new patient who is psychotic. Her inevitable mistakes can be mitigated by others in the team. The patient's doubts can be softened (or hardened) by members of the treatment team and by other patients, who have their own history of interactions and observations of that therapist. Concurrently, the therapist knows whom she likes and trusts, and whom she does not. That is, there cannot be a real group situation without the full range of competitions and animosities; but in a psychodynamic community one hopes that these tensions are being addressed. The therapist's relatively greater security in this setting provides a calm with which the new patient may identify. The therapist introduces the patient to a potentially healing home, hopefully to be outgrown and abandoned once the course of work and therapeutic change has been firmly established.

Despite her disturbances, Maria believed not only that she was not ill, but that she was married to a psychiatrist practicing and pursuing research in an institution near Chestnut Lodge. She reported that this local psychiatrist, whose actual name, address, and phone number she knew, had testified against her psychiatrist in the lawsuit that had won her money. She stated that she had agreed to come to Chestnut Lodge not for its high treatment reputation but because of its proximity to him. Maria focused obsessively on seeing this man – and on calling him and his actual wife – because Maria insisted she was married to him.[4] Dr. Faulconer talked about the reasons she must not call his home. Maria, however, insisted that she had to call the wife because the wife was a usurper, and several times did call the wife, even threatening her. As a result, Chestnut Lodge's Clinical Administrative Psychiatrist put Maria on telephone restrictions – preventing her from making such calls. Had Dr. Faulconer been the one to limit or police Maria in this way, it is doubtful the therapy could have progressed as well as it did – if at all. More than likely Maria would have retaliated by refusing to talk in therapy. This is exactly the kind of situation that led Chestnut Lodge to institute a "therapist–administrator split" in the 1940s. This split, one not followed by many other treatment facilities, served well for those with schizophrenia or with borderline conditions.

However, splitting these staff roles can create tension between staff members, which, if unresolved, can negatively affect patient treatment. Psychoanalyst Alfred Stanton and sociologist Morris Schwartz, in their classic book, *The Mental Hospital*, documented the strong correlation between disagreements between members of the treatment team and regression in the patient. Resolution of the intrastaff tension led to significant reintegration in the patient about whom they disagreed (Morse and Noble, 1942; Stanton and Schwartz, 1954).

Meanwhile, Chestnut Lodge's hospital milieu setting allowed Dr. Faulconer to conduct treatment in other unconventional ways that enhanced Maria's initial engagement. For instance, Maria was a born-again Christian, loved the Bible, and wanted it read to her, something that Dr. Faulconer, given the supportiveness and safety of the treatment environment – an increasingly rare phenomenon today – was able to do. During sessions, Maria discussed in detail what the Bible meant to her. Meanwhile, Maria could not sit in a chair because of her flailing movements, and instead sat on the floor and rolled around. Dr. Faulconer joined her on the floor and read the Bible passages that Maria chose. Maria also enjoyed playing with words, yet could not write them down because of her movement disorder. Dr. Faulconer volunteered to take dictation, which Maria enjoyed immensely – both for the control and autonomy it provided her.

It is important to note how the initial engagement was colored by the setting of the treatment. The setting enhanced the possibility that all was in the service of securing a solid therapeutic alliance. These efforts became the starting point for intensive psychotherapy, in which patient and therapist met 4 days per week for 50-minute sessions. Dr. Faulconer met Maria where she was, rather than demanding that Maria conform to the dictates of a less supportive setting – the standard of today's treatment setting for psychosis – that stressed social conformity and efficient behavioral changes.

The tradition in Chestnut Lodge was to meet the patient where he or she was. With psychotic patients, who had often been regressed for years, it was an important step to model the usual activities. Faulconer and Maria often talked about Maria's confusion concerning issues of daily life and, if the patient inquired about them, about physiological processes and sensations. One common topic involved Maria's questions about bathing and its relation to offensive body odor. Ogden (1989: 31), in a vivid clinical summary, demonstrates how:

> The autistic-contiguous position is a primitive psychological organiza-tion operative from birth that generates the most elemental forms of human experience. It is a sensory-dominated mode in which the most inchoate sense of self is built upon the rhythm of sensation, particularly the sensations at the skin surface.

While acknowledging the primitive levels of experience, therapists at Chestnut Lodge sometimes escorted patients into the nearby town to shop or to have tea – something beyond the range of possibility for many treatment providers in other settings. Therapists often found that meeting with patients outside the mental health environment allowed them to reveal their potential for socially appropriate conduct, which they kept hidden at the hospital (Silver, 1997). Just as each staff member develops a unique transference–countertransference relationship with a given patient, each seeing different aspects of the patient's personality, based on each person's past experiences and interrelationships, different settings will bring out different aspects of the patient as well. Our current reliance on office-based treatment limits the range of experiences open to patient and therapist. Shared activities in different settings give an ever-fuller awareness of the patient's range of expression.

Setting 2: Isabel: from emergency room to general hospital unit

Isabel, age 55, was admitted involuntarily to the inpatient unit of a general hospital via the local emergency room. She came to the emergency room because of intense emotional conflicts with her mother and stepfather, with whom she had been living. Although the emergency room may have a certain degree of validity, especially with some psychotic patients who are imminently suicidal or homicidal, for many it only heightens the hopelessness, alienation, and loneliness that are at the core of their psychotic disturbances (Fromm-Reichmann, 1959).

In Isabel's case, the emergency room staff determined that she was psychotic and felt that an inpatient unit was the best setting for her, and transferred her there. Isabel was tiny, slightly taller than 5 feet, and weighed 89 pounds. She had many obsessional issues around food. She arrived disheveled, but wore attractive rings on her fingers. Although psychologically disabled, she had lived independently for 30 years. Before she became disabled, she had been a technical writer and editor for several organizations, and until very recently had enjoyed spending time and taking classes in the city's natural history museums.

Recently, however, her apartment had been destroyed by a flood, which forced her to move in with her mother and stepfather, who both quickly realized how difficult it was for her to function. Isabel denied hallucinations but during conversations with others she talked in asides to herself or to someone who was not present. She had difficulty organizing her thoughts, and often behaved unusually. She removed her false teeth during meals and conversations, which was considered socially inappropriate, if not downright bizarre. She was very afraid of gaining weight, and took 2 hours to eat even part of a meal. She had thought-blocking and poverty of content of speech.

Once in the hospital (which was a more standard or conventional psychiatric hospital than Chestnut Lodge, in that antipsychotic medications were the standard basis of treatment and the setting had less of a milieu environment) Isabel refused medications but accepted psychotherapy. Isabel, however, was not responding to the milieu therapy the hospital provided – various groups and individual psychotherapy with Dr. Faulconer. In spite of the awareness that our current medications are not curative, Dr. Faulconer found Isabel too disorganized for talk therapy and decided that she needed to take her to court to enforce the taking of medications. There is strong economic pressure to avoid taking patients to court. Dr. Faulconer decided to do so despite the pressure because she had seen the benefits of clozapine for withdrawn patients.

Dr. Silver worked at Chestnut Lodge from 1975 until its closure in 2001 and watched the hospital transition (in the 1980s) from an institution that worked with patients to recover without medication to a more conventional institution that increasingly relied on antipsychotic medication. Although Dr. Silver observed that many psychotic patients at Chestnut Lodge became more actively and directly communicative once on medications, she also noted that their relationships with their treatment providers became more shallow and less intense, and that this often resulted in less long-term and less significant overall change and overall recovery.

In the case of Isabel, the two went to court, and the judge determined in favor of forcing Isabel to take medication – against Isabel's wishes. Once Isabel started taking the court-ordered medications – haloperidol to begin with – she began to talk more. Dr. Faulconer was aware that the initial court-ordering of medications left them with a shaky foundation of trust, which can be damaging for initial engagement with a patient, but she hoped that the relationship would improve. In time it did. Once on medication, Isabel started eating more, and her ability to articulate her thoughts improved. In therapy she focused on her various interests, such as aquarium fish, and several of her rigid beliefs. She spoke regularly about her teeth, about which she had several peculiar ideas. She felt sugar was good, even essential, for the well-being of teeth. Most of her teeth had been removed because of decay through neglect. She had had implants placed to hold a bridge for her upper teeth. The implants were surrounded by infected tissue and had to be removed.

The contrast in initial therapeutic approaches to the cases of two significant emotionally disturbed patients, Maria and Isabel, reflects differences in the treatment philosophies of different psychiatric settings, and demonstrates differences in approach by the same therapist.

Regarding her medication, Isabel did not find haloperidol comfortable and agreed to take clozapine instead. Gradually she talked more, she ate less slowly, and she led the unit meeting. Yet she reported fidgetiness, akathisia, which she attributed to the medicine. Medication to counter akathisia was adjusted to eliminate the side effect. Therapist and patient also studied other issues that could be involved in her feelings of fidgetiness, including loss of independence – both by being in the hospital and having lost her home. She was angry a lot of the time. She did not wish to go to the group home where her family wanted her to go and to which her inpatient team agreed she should go. She felt she was being controlled. She was.

After 2 months, Isabel was ready to leave the inpatient unit, and she was discharged from the hospital. For the first few months, a staff member from the group home to which she was transferred brought her to her weekly appointments with Dr. Faulconer. Much of their discussions focused on issues of people eating other people's food in the group home. This issue preoccupied her. Gradually, however, her focus shifted toward her other interests and about the activities she wanted to do. Dr. Faulconer and Isabel discovered they were both subscribers to *Natural History* magazine, and they spoke about this common interest, which provided some degree of rapport. Isabel's language had become impressively articulate and fluent. At times she discussed language from an editor's point of view. Meanwhile, she complained that the medicines were still making her fidgety; medicines to decrease akathisia were adjusted further. She said that she felt more comfortable being around others who were also taking medicine; with them, she felt less peculiar. They went together to lectures at natural history museums in the community; Dr. Faulconer could comment with shared evidence that Isabel was not behaving peculiarly. They went on to discuss other sources of anxiety and how anxiety about increasing activities might be involved, not just the medicine. Faulconer decreased the medicine gradually; medicines remained at the minimum therapeutic blood levels.

Isabel's independence increased as well. She began to take the subway to Faulconer's office alone. Isabel talked more about relationships with other people in the group home. A group of people went together for medical appointments, and she enjoyed these trips.

Meanwhile, Isabel progressed beautifully; she looked good, felt good, and socialized increasingly comfortably. Dr. Faulconer's roles in the first and second cases differed, and she has needed much internal flexibility and adaptability in these very different environments. Both patients responded to clozapine and both needed intensive psychotherapy in addition.

Setting 3: David: an outpatient psychotherapy of psychosis – in the patient's home

David, age 28, had been housebound almost continually for nearly a decade when he was referred to Dr. Silver. His mother had used the internet to research local clinicians and had found Dr. Silver's involvement in the ISPS-US along with a group she had founded, the Columbia Academy of Psychodynamics. She had read papers by Dr. Silver and liked her orientation. She was amazed, on calling her, to find her willing to meet with her son at their home, not far from Dr. Silver's home-office.

David's anguish manifested as muscle pains and spasms that left him nearly paralyzed, sometimes in odd postures, for such long intervals that he developed bruising in his feet and lower legs. Physical therapists warned him that if this continued he could develop gangrene requiring amputation. Medical evaluation revealed no autoimmune disorder or other medically treatable explanation for his pain. Psychosis can manifest in extraordinary anxiety without clear delusions and hallucinations – as in the case of catatonic schizophrenia. It can be so profound that the sufferer is literally immobilized, caught in intense ambivalence about whether to move forward into adult life and sexuality or to retreat into a life dependent on his or her parents meeting his basic needs.

David reported that his anxiety was so great that thinking itself brought on waves of pain. Having matriculated in a prestigious college at age 18, he left midway through and had been unable to complete college requirements locally. He was very lonely, but since the break-up of his one unconsummated romantic relationship had left him devastated he was terrified of another love relationship.

David lived about 10 minutes from Dr. Silver's home-office, and since he had difficulty moving or traveling at all she offered to meet with him at his home. This grew from her experience decades earlier when she had made a home visit to a patient and her husband in a rural community far from her home or from the range of her life experiences. The picture of that patient's life became infinitely clearer when meeting with her in the home she and her husband had created (Silver, 2005). Also, she was accustomed to beginning work with new Chestnut Lodge patients by meeting them on their units, and she sought out experiences that would link her with that lost asylum. As professionals, our relative inflexibility, verging on agoraphobia, costs us much, because we as a profession have set a standard of meeting with patients almost exclusively in our offices, or perhaps in hospital rooms at institutions where we have hospital privileges. And although it costs clinicians much, it costs our patients far more, because it is they who suffer more if they cannot adjust to a psychiatric one-size-fits-all paradigm.

Greeted by the patient's mother, Dr. Silver and David were introduced and then sat together on his front porch, the house located in a quiet well-established wooded development. There seemed to be an instant rapport. He had attended the same college as one of Dr. Silver's own children, but not concurrently, and from his descriptions she guessed his dorm immediately.

Midway through this first hour, his mother asked if she could say something, and spoke about the situation of his birth, and about the complex family traumas surrounding it. She seemed to be saying nearly explicitly that she had inadvertently sown the seeds for her son's emotional disorder. He sternly informed her that this was his hour not hers, and could she please do something else. He also said he thought he had heard this story before, though he was not altogether sure. He had been on antipsychotic medications for 5 years and said he was "a zombie" the entire time. Therefore, he now refused to take medication.

"Regression" does not mean a return to the way one thought at an earlier age; it means using patterns characteristic in a general way of earlier, less sophisticated ways of processing information. Abstract thinking depends upon an ability to form generalizations: to reflect on the specific instance and place it in a larger context. The more anxious one feels, the less one is able to call on the cognitive strengths one has developed, and the more one falls back on reflexive responses such as "fight or flight" or "good or bad."

Metaphor is less available, and concrete evidence is more important than abstraction. The regressed patient lacks a dependable sense of selfhood, and will borrow, or "incorporate," the therapist's self as a mental crutch – if the therapist literally "goes the distance" to be with the patient, having a strong enough sense of self that she is not afraid of losing herself in the patient's space. Thus concrete thinking can proceed into the abstract, and this is the spark of hope for recovery.

Perhaps the therapist will go the distance in the therapy, enduring the inevitable phases of negative transference. There is concrete meaning for the therapist as well, literally seeing "where the patient lives." "I see" easily translates to "I understand." Doctors of whatever stripe have hidden behind professional elitism in saying that "home visits are the jobs of the social workers," implying that the doctors are too busy with important issues of the mind, and should relegate such tasks to the doers so that they can think in their offices. Antiquated gender roles immediately come to mind, along with enlightenment-era chauvinism. Coming to the patient's own territory conveys a message of "I am your humble servant – how may I be of use?"

Like the social worker on a home visit, Dr. Silver noticed many home maintenance tasks left undone, even as an important family event drew closer, and she saw how her patient's difficulties were magnifications of those of his parents. The notion that the patient is a failed family therapist was illustrated in the family's environment.

Meanwhile, Dr. Silver continued to work with David at his family's home, and with his parents as well, in sessions also in their home. This all fostered a strong initial engagement, and it seemed that the treatment would proceed well until an incident occurred that nearly ruptured the treatment – and created an extreme backlash of "negative transference" towards Dr. Silver. The incident involved David eavesdropping on a family session that he was supposed to be attending but had not come to, and he overheard his parents complain that he was too demanding, either requiring them to make trips to the specialty restaurant nearby, thus disrupting their workday, or calling out for snacks in the middle of the night. Dr. Silver was first helping them to feel more comfortable in saying "no," and then providing them with less taxing substitutes.

Afterward David confronted Dr. Silver, and fired her. He said it was not helpful that she came to his home: it fostered dependency and isolation, thus keeping him sick. He stated that he knew a psychiatrist whose office he could get to. As Dr. Silver was leaving, she told him, "I don't fire so easily. You have two stubborn pains: one is your illness, and the other is your therapist." They both laughed; after all, a strong bond had been formed between the two, and his negative reaction was likely coming less from the weakness in their relationship than from his feelings of betrayal for what he had overheard.

Nevertheless, he agreed to have another session with Dr. Silver, although he elected to hold it over the telephone, putting a safe distance between the two of them. This eliminated the danger he may have felt of his shattering the therapeutic relationship by physically attacking Dr. Silver (something that had never happened in previous treatments nor towards his parents). Again, this resonated with Chestnut Lodge work, where patient and therapist would hold sessions on the unit rather than in the doctor's office, in case the nursing staff needed to step in for protection. The two reviewed the previous session, with acknowledgements on both sides that things could have been handled better.

At present, Dr. Silver's work with David is still ongoing – and in flux. It is to the benefit of their work together that she has the flexibility to meet him in any number of settings. She will probably find a family therapist for the family as a whole, and try "simply" to be his therapist. She is encouraging him to drive to her office at any time and take a look at the house, the office entrance, and the back patio where they could have sessions if he would prefer, since he does, with increasing frequency, venture out in his car. The two are striving towards his improved autonomy and mobility, something that would benefit all involved.

Dr. Silver comments: It is a great hardship to go through life starved of affect. This reflects the profound difference that the milieu environment can make. If a treatment provider cannot say, "We have time" – time to let the therapeutic relationship unfold and evolve organically, without medication, without behavioral pressure to conform – and if a treatment provider is forced to produce results efficiently, then the treatment provider must take an attitude that something "must" be done. Imposition of such "standards of the community" – standards of treatment care in which medication is considered the only way – have pitted "psychiatric survivors" against psychiatrists. Psychiatrists seek court support to enforce outpatient medication, while groups of patients find this an unconstitutional restriction of freedom, a cruel and unusual punishment handed down to those who have committed no crime. The two best resources for background are the website of PsychRights (www.psychrights.org), constructed by psychiatric survivor and activist-lawyer James Gottstein, of Anchorage, Alaska, and Robert Whitaker's (2002) *Mad in America*.

Conclusion

While our literature contains many excellent and now-classic descriptions of the initial contact between patient and therapist, almost all are based on work done within secure institutions (Fromm-Reichmann, 1950; Greenberg, 1964; Searles, 1965; Silver, 2005; Sullivan, 1954). A beautiful exception is Vittorio Gonella's description of his innovative work with a chronically institutionalized man, work done in parallel with his disser-tation on the contributions of Harold Searles (Gonella, 2005). Somehow, we need to bring back healing communities, for our patients and for ourselves. They do not need to be large places. Only a century ago, it was the rule rather than the exception that "alienists" (as psychiatrists were then known) oversaw small sanatoria, where they employed very few people as additional staff. Now, for many clinicians in private practice settings who work with patients with psychosis, it is their job, and often an impossible job, to provide their own one-on-one mini-sanatoria. This is the result of a mental health climate where all too often medications are considered the sole treatment for psychosis and where psychotherapeutic work with psychosis is thought to be outmoded or even dangerous. How lonely this is for the clinician attempting to reach the soul of the patient – and how frustrating for the patient who is desperate to be reached, yet reaching out and finding no hand to grip for emotional support.

Yet loneliness is not just in the patients and the clinicians. As a nation we must realign our values, pouring less money into wars and more into helping the most vulnerable members of our communities. We need a net-work of safe and supervised homes, perhaps modeled on Loren Mosher's pioneering Soteria House, where staff that are not "highly trained" are supported by these theorizing professionals as they get to know the resi-dents, supporting their social efforts and coming to understand them (Mosher, Hendrix, and Fort, 2004). Our current medications are not curative; they sometimes blunt the patient's emotions. As stated earlier, it is a great hardship to go through life starved of affect, being told that medications are key to stabilization and yet not having someone dedicated to really getting to know one and staying with one for as long as is needed. We need initial interviews conducted by people who are supported by their employers first to really get to know their patients, and second to stay with them for as long as it takes the person to become confident in his or her autonomy and social network.

Notes

1 Another Lodge therapist, Ilan Treves MD, now living in Tel Aviv, Israel, made dramatic progress with a previously unreachable autistic, paranoid, and combative man, since Treves began working with this man soon after he, Dr. Treves, arrived also from Paris. He did not understand American slang and did not know his way around the hospital campus. An immediate bond formed since this patient could help him improve his English, and could guide him around the hospital. The patient was the expert, Treves his grateful student, with whom he could identify, thus being able to learn from him and incorporate Treves' empathic sociability, temporarily putting aside his bitter resentments.
2 Dr. Silver had a similar bonding with a very psychotic patient at Chestnut Lodge; both claimed the same hometown, about 350 miles from the Lodge. They knew

each other's neighborhoods, movie theaters, candy stores, and schools. This geographic alliance gave both of them comfort at a difficult time, as both were new to Chestnut Lodge (Silver, 2001). See also Gutheil and Havens (1979).

3 Maria's temporal regression to an age before matrimony resonated with the temporal regression of another Mary, Eugene O'Neill's depiction of his mother's regression as she relapsed yet again into morphine addiction, as depicted in his autobiographical play, *Long Day's Journey Into Night*. This play was strongly influenced by American psychoanalysts (Silver, 2001).

4 Her attack on the psychiatrist whose testimony led to her acquiring the money needed for her treatment hints at her unconscious guilt regarding this victory, and her underlying need to sabotage her treatment. Was her religious conversion also accompanied by unconscious guilt? And was this delusional "husband" standing in for her father? Had her parents' marriage dissolved, and did she feel at some level responsible, needing punishment?

References

Fromm-Reichmann, F. (1950). The initial interview. In *Principles of Intensive Psychotherapy* (pp. 45–68). Chicago: University of Chicago Press.

Fromm-Reichmann, F. (1959). Loneliness. *Psychiatry*, 22: 1–15.

Gonella, V. (2005). The contribution of Harold F. Searles to an emerging therapeutic relationship with a chronic schizophrenic man. *Journal of the American Academy of Psychoanalysis*, 33: 705–728.

Greenberg, J. (1964). *I Never Promised You a Rose Garden*. New York: Holt, Rinehart and Winston.

Gutheil, T. and Havens, L. (1979). The therapeutic alliance: Contemporary meanings and confusions. *International Review of Psycho-Analysis*, 6: 467–481.

Morse, R. and Noble, D. (1942). Joint endeavors of the administrative physician and psychotherapist. *Psychiatric Quarterly*, 16: 578–585.

Mosher, L., Hendrix, V., and Fort, D. (2004). *Soteria: Through Madness to Deliverance*. Philadelphia: Xlibris Corp.

Ogden, T. (1989). The autistic-contiguous position. In *The Primitive Edge of Experience* (pp. 47–82). New York: Jason Aronson

Searles, H. (1965). Phases of patient–therapist interaction in the psychotherapy of chronic schizophrenia. In *Collected Papers on Schizophrenia and Related Subjects* (pp. 521–559). New York: International Universities Press.

Silver, A.-L. (1997). Chestnut Lodge, then and now: Work with a patient with schizophrenia and obsessive-compulsive disorder. *Contemporary Psychoanalysis*, 33: 227–249.

Silver, A.-L. (2001). American psychoanalysts who influenced Eugene O'Neill's *Long Day's Journey into Night. Journal of the American Academy of Psychoanalysis*, 29: 305–318.

Silver, A.-L. (2005). In the footsteps of Arieti and Fromm-Reichmann: Psychodynamic treatments of psychosis in the current era. *Journal of the American Academy of Psychoanalysis*, 33: 689–704.

Stanton, A. and Schwartz, M. (1954). *The Mental Hospital.* New York: Basic Books.

Sullivan, H. S. (1954). *The Psychiatric Interview.* New York: W.W. Norton.

Whitaker, R. (2002). *Mad in America: Bad Science, Bad Medicine, and the Enduring Mistreatment of the Mentally Ill.* Cambridge, MA: Perseus Press.

Chapter 3

Making contact with the chronically regressed patient

Garry Prouty

Editors' Introduction: Garry Prouty, the originator of the Pre-Therapy Method, clearly lays out the tools to make contact with an extremely regressed or psychotic patient. His point of view is a "client-centered/experiential" one that has its roots in existential psychiatry. Prouty extends Rogers' and Gendlin's work to deeply regressed and disorganized patients and posits the ever-present existence of a nuclear "pre-expressive self" inside the patient that is in need of contact. The effect of that contact is to bring the patient, through the use of a variety of contact techniques, to a less regressed, more integrated, more functional state of being.

The three pillars of Prouty's work on contact are: (1) the contact reflections (the work the therapist does); (2) the contact functions (client psychological process); (3) contact behaviors (measurement). Note also the importance of a non-directive approach to Prouty's method and how it flies in the face of current psychiatric orthodoxy, which emphasizes "giving structure to the regressed and psychotic patient."

Prouty divides psychological progression out of psychosis into three areas. First, the patient needs to become aware of people, places, things, and events (Reality Contact), and Prouty provides a range of methods by which to help the patient accomplish this task. Next, the patient becomes aware of moods, feelings, and emotions (Affective Contact). Prouty demarcates how the therapist can facilitate this process as well. Finally, the patient develops or re-engages their capacity to symbolize (Communicative Contact). Prouty looks for these manifestations as guides to the progression of the treatment.

Introduction

Psychiatry has long supported a market-driven and reductionistic ideology of neuroleptic treatments for psychosis (Mosher, 2004; Whitaker, 2002). In recent years, however, we have witnessed the emergence of alternative views. First, we have the hypotheses that certain neuroleptic medications lack efficacy, safety, and efficiency (Jackson, 2005; Whitaker, 2004). Others express concern about their dangerous side effects (Breggin, 1991, 1997). We also have the research findings of Karon and VandenBos (1981), who report that patients receiving psychoanalysis show greater gains than patients receiving drug treatment only. Next we have the clinical case histories of successful treatments without neuroleptics (Dorman, 2003; Prouty, 2004). Last, we have findings that link child abuse, trauma, and schizophrenia (Read et al., 2004). These elements point toward the possibility of a reduced role for the use of medications and an increased role for psychotherapy. It is within this context that the Pre-Therapy Method is presented.

Pre-Therapy

Pre-Therapy involves making contact with highly regressed, difficult to reach patients, such as those with chronic schizophrenia or psychotic mental retardation. These patients are often out of touch with their own senses of self and are rarely considered available for psychotherapy. Although Pre-Therapy might be considered a method for setting the stage for later forms of psychotherapeutic treatment, what it accomplishes is itself a form of treatment.

Pre-Therapy had evolved primarily, but not exclusively, from the theory and practice of Carl Rogers' client-centered psychotherapy (Prouty, 1994). Although client-centered therapy has an informal reputation of being relevant mostly to high-level, functional patients, it actually has been one of the more productive modalities used by humanistic researchers in the psychotherapy of schizophrenia (Hinterkopf and Brunswick, 1981; Pugh, 1949; Rogers et al., 1967; Teusch, 1981; Truax, 1970; Vanderveen, 1967).

Rogers (1957) defines three "core attitudes" of the therapist that best facilitate the growth of the client: unconditional positive regard, empathy, and congruence. Rogers (1957) defines unconditional positive regard as "a warm acceptance of each aspect of the client's experience" (p. 98), empathy as "sensing the client's private world as if it were your own" (p. 99), and congruence as the allowance for the therapist, within the therapeutic relationship, to be "freely and deeply himself, with his actual experience being presented by his awareness of himself" (p. 97).

Rogers et al. (1967) noted that those patients diagnosed with schizophrenia exposed to the highest level of these core attitudes showed the greatest level of emotional processing, and also that clients exposed to the highest level of empathy showed the most improvement on the MMPI (Minnesota Multiphasic Personality Inventory) and TAT (Thematic Apperception Test) instruments. It is for this reason that these three core attitudes form the foundation of Pre-Therapy.

Additionally, the non-directive attitude (Raskin, 1947), a powerful element in Rogerian therapy, is integral to Pre-Therapy, and forms its basic respectful nature. The non-directive attitude is defined as a "surrendered" following by the therapist of the client's own intent, directionality, and process. This is especially vital in working with highly regressed patients, as this chapter's upcoming vignettes attest to.

Pre-Therapy also bases itself on the concept of the Pre-Expressive Self (Prouty, 2000). The Pre-Expressive Self is formulated on the idea that there exists an underlying self, albeit a pre-expressive one, even in patients who are extremely regressed and demonstrate little or no sense of self at all. Garfield and Dorman, in Chapter 1, also noted the vital role of engaging a "fragment" of the authentic self or "pre-expressive self" that is central to the recovery from psychosis.

Speaking from personal experience, my first encounter with the Pre-Expressive Self came to me in my childhood. As a young boy I lived with my younger brother who was dually diagnosed with severe mental retardation and psychosis. He lived in an autistic-regressed state. One day I invited a friend of mine to come fishing at our home on the river, and my brother, who only interacted in a minimal way, was along with us – as silent and non-interactive company. While my friend and I were talking I said, "I wonder if my brother understands what we say." Although my brother had never given any indication that he could understand our conversation, much less reply to it, he stated, to my complete surprise, "You know I do, Garry." He then lapsed back into his autistic-regressed state.

For years I was haunted by this experience, as it gave me the feeling that "someone was in there." It was not until decades later, after the publication of my first book, that I realized the connection between the descriptions of Dr. Luc Roelens, a Belgian psychiatrist concerned with non-medical explanations of psychosis, and my "haunting experience" with my brother. In the forward of my text (Prouty, 1994), Roelens describes cases of sudden and unexpected contact. In one, a woman who had remained hospitalized for many years with chronic and severe catatonic symptomology was informed that her husband had fallen off the roof and badly hurt himself. Her response was to say she needed to go home immediately and take care of things. For some time afterward she, who for years had expressed little or nothing of a self or any form of interaction, experienced no relapse into catatonia, so she went home to follow through taking care of her home. At 4- and 10-year follow-ups there was no evidence of pathology except for some degree of withdrawal from social interaction.

Another of Roelens' reported cases concerns a male patient who had been in a dementia-like state. While being fed intravenously and drinking cola, he coughed and spat all over the nurse. Suddenly the patient spoke: "Excuse me, I did not intend to do that." He then relapsed into silence. These case histories and the experience of my brother suggest the presence of a Pre-Expressive Self underlying autism, regression, psychoses, retardation, and senility. For some clinicians, making contact with a Pre-Expressive

Self is quite similar to the psychoanalytic notion of a therapeutic regression leading to contact with a developmentally arrested or "fixated" part of the patient.

Pre-Therapy aims to assist the therapist in making contact, and in optimizing this contact, with this Pre-Expressive Self and enhancing it for the betterment of the patient.

Techniques of Pre-Therapy

Contact reflections

Contact reflections form the basic arsenal of tools for the therapist who attempts to engage a severely regressed, disconnected client in Pre-Therapy. Contact reflections are ultra-concrete reflections by the therapist of the client's immediate behavior or surroundings. There are five contact reflections (each defined in depth below, and then illustrated later in case vignettes): (a) situational reflections (abbreviated to SR), (b) facial reflections (abbreviated to FR), (c) word-for-word reflections (WWR), (d) body reflections (BR), and (e) reiterative reflections (RR). They allow the therapist to establish contact with the client at the client's level of expression – that is, to meet the client where he is. They are extraordinarily concrete so as to "fit" the concrete cognitive style of the regressed patients with schizophrenia (Arieti, 1955; Freidman, 1961; Goldstein, 1939; Goldstein and Scheerer, 1941; Gurswitch, 1966; Mazumdar and Mazumdar, 1983). In light of the reality that all too often non-concrete attempts to relate to highly regressed patients with schizophrenia fail, the following five concrete contact reflections allow the therapist not only to empathize with the client, but also to demonstrate this empathy to the client – and thus relate to one who is so often considered not capable of being related to:

1   *Situational reflections (SR).* The therapist performs a situational reflection by reflecting back to the client some concrete element of the situation experienced by both therapist and client. For example, if there were a child pushing a toy train on the floor of the room of the therapist and client, the therapist might say, "The child is pushing the train." Another example, if it were happening in the room, could be "David is petting the cat." The function of these reflections is to restore, develop, or facilitate reality contact for the client.

2   *Facial reflections (FR).* The therapist performs a facial reflection by reflecting back to the client some concrete element of the client's facial expression. The human face, a marvelously "expressive organ," contains not yet formed, pre-expressive affect. Facial reflections facilitate the experiencing or expression of affect and develop the client's ability to make affective contact. For example, if the therapist noted a sad

look on the face of the client, the therapist could say, "You look sad" or, more concretely (assuming it were true), "There are tears in your eyes." Another example befitting a different situation could be the therapist saying, "You look angry," or, more concretely, "Your jaw muscles are tight."

3   *Word-for-word reflections (WWR)*. The therapist performs a word-for-word reflection by reflecting back to the client the client's exact words. Many geriatric clients, as well as clients diagnosed with schizophrenia or mental retardation, present verbal symptoms of incoherence. For example, many clients with schizophrenia present echolalia, neologisms, or word salad interspersed with social language. Such a flow of communication by a client with schizophrenia could be as follows: "[unintelligible word], stamp, [unintelligible word], hat, [unintelligible word], dog." Even though this makes no conventional sense, a therapist engaging in Pre-Therapy with a client would reflect the social language just as it occurs, word for word – in this case: "stamp, hat, dog." This word-for-word reflection offers the client the experience of being received as a human communicator – and this constitutes a healing factor in itself, especially when we consider how rare being related to is for a regressed client.

4   *Body reflections (BR)*. The therapist performs a body reflection by reflecting back to the client the client's bodily expression. There are two types of bodily reflections. In the first, the therapist verbally expresses the body expression of the client, such as by saying, "Your arm is in the air" or "You are standing on one foot." In the second type of body reflection the therapist literally reflects back to the client the client's bodily expression – the therapist holding his own arm in the air or standing on one foot.

5   *Reiterative reflections (RR)*. The therapist performs a reiterative reflection by repeating any of the previous four types of contact reflections that produced a response from the client. Reiterative reflections are not specific techniques and instead embody the principle of making "re-contact." To use an example of a short-term reiterative reflection, there was a patient who remained silent and only touched her forehead, and the therapist repeatedly performed the same action with her own body and also expressed this verbally. Here the patient eventually said "Grandma." Word-for-word reflections by the therapist eventually moved the client into expressing some real feelings about her grandmother's death. An example of long-term reiteration occurred when an extremely regressed client pointed at her stomach in various therapy sessions. The therapist performed a reiterative reflection in a long-term mode by saying at the start of a new session (in which the client was not pointing to her stomach), "Last week you said 'baby' and pointed to your belly." Gradually, the process unfolded into the client telling a

true story about a real pregnancy she had had and the trauma she suffered by having an abortion.

These five types of contact reflections, when combined and applied over a period of time, will result in an increase in the client's contact with the world, self, and others. In more technical terms, when therapists employ contact reflections with severely regressed clients, their clients display more reality, affective, and communicative behavior. But in more detailed terms, one might ask what has actually occurred. These contact reflections expose the client to a web of contacts that facilitate his efforts to be connected with others. Second, these contact reflections meet the client at his level, which is something that few other conventional therapies do – or have the theoretical background to do – with severely regressed clients. Third, if this facet of Pre-Therapy is successful then the client's increased reality, affective, and communicative functions enable him to be more accessible to "classical" client-centered therapy or other approaches – hence the meaning of the prefix "Pre" in Pre-Therapy.

The following case vignette, from Prouty (2003), illustrates this process. The client was one of 13 children. His parents were farmers of Polish nationality. His mother had been hospitalized several times for schizophrenic problems. Family observation revealed at least one sibling who, although not hospitalized, displayed psychotic symptoms. The family brought the client to the United States for evaluation. A preliminary observation confirmed that the client was potentially responsive to Pre-Therapy.

Psychiatric documents described the client in these ways: "mute," "autistic," "catatonic," "making no eye contact," "exhibiting trance-like behavior," "stuporous," "confused," "not establishing rapport," "delusional," "paranoid," and "experiencing severe thought blocking." He had been diagnosed with various pathologies: as manic-depressive; hysterical reaction; disorganized schizophrenic; paranoid schizophrenic; catatonic schizophrenic; profound schizophrenic; and schizophrenic, affective type. He had received six electroshock treatments, as well as numerous chemical interventions including diazepam (Valium), imipramine (Tofranil), chlorpromazine (Thorazine), clomipramine (Anafranil), phenothiazine, haloperidol (Haldol), and trifluoperazine (Stelazine).

The client returned to his home for several months while the therapist and family made plans to transition the client into residential care. My associate therapist arrived at the client's home and found that the client, kept at home for several months, had deteriorated into psychosis. His parents had not rehospitalized him. He was in a severe catatonic state, having withdrawn to the lower portion of the three-story home. He no longer ate meals with the family and instead crept out at night to use the family refrigerator. He had lost considerable weight, and his feet were blue from being cramped and stiffened due to lack of movement and circulation.

What followed was an unusual 12-hour process that illustrates the therapist's application of contact reflections, which resulted in the successful resolution of the catatonic state and the development of communicative contact – all without medication or electroconvulsive therapy (ECT). (ECT, along with benzodiazepines, is widely recognized in psychiatry as being a very effective biological treatment for catatonia.)

When the therapist arrived the patient was sitting on a long couch, his body very rigid and his arms outstretched – perfectly straight and at the level of his shoulders. His eyes stared straight ahead, his face was mask-like, and his hands and feet were blue-gray from lack of movement. The therapist sat on the opposite side of the couch, making no eye contact with the patient. The therapist made contact reflections with the patient at intervals of about 5–10 minutes. Throughout most of the following vignette the reader should note the therapist's non-directive attitude and non-directive verbalizations.

Segment One

(begun at approximately 2:00 p.m. and lasting about an hour and a half)

Therapist [performing SR]:   I can hear the children playing.
Client: [No response, no movement.]
(The therapist waited 5–10 minutes before making the following, and between making all subsequent contact reflections.)
Therapist [performing SR]:   It is very cool down here.
Client: [No response, no movement.]
Therapist [performing SR]:   I can hear people talking in the kitchen.
Client: [No response, no movement.]
Therapist [performing SR]:   I'm sitting with you in the lower level of your house.
Client: [No response, no movement.]
Therapist [performing SR]:   I can hear the dog barking.
Client: [No response, no movement.]
Therapist [performing BR]:   Your body is very rigid.
Client: [No response, no movement.]
Therapist [performing BR]:   You are sitting very still.
Client: [No response, no movement.]
Therapist [performing BR]:   You are looking straight ahead.

Client: [No response, no movement.]

Therapist [performing BR]: You are sitting on the couch in a very upright position.

Client: [No response, no movement.]

Therapist [performing BR]: Your body isn't moving. Your arms are in the air.

Throughout this segment the client exhibited no response and made no movement. The therapist then brought over a chair and sat in it directly in front of the patient, mirroring his body position exactly (including out-stretched arms) – a literal body reflection.

Segment Two

(begun at approximately 3:30 p.m.)

Therapist [performing verbal BR]: Your body is very rigid. You are sitting on the couch and not moving.

(The therapist remained in this position for approximately 15–20 minutes. No response from client.)

Therapist: I can no longer hold my arms out-stretched. My arms are tired.

Client: [No response, no movement.]

Therapist [performing verbal BR]: Your body is very stiff.

Client: [No response, no movement.]

Therapist [performing BR]: Your arms are outstretched.

Client: [No response, no movement.]

Therapist [performing BR]: Your body isn't moving.

The client then put his hands on his head, as if to hold his head, and spoke in a barely audible whisper.

Client: My head hurts me when my father speaks.

Therapist [performing WWR]: My head hurts me when my father speaks.

Therapist [performing literal BR]: [Therapist placed her hands on her head in the same way as the patient did.]

Therapist [performing RR/WWR]: My head hurts when my father speaks.

The client then continued to hold his head in his hands for 2–3 hours.

Segment Three

(begun at approximately 8:00 p.m.)

Therapist [performing SR]: It's evening. We are in the lower level of your home.

Client: [No response, no movement.]
Therapist [performing verbal BR]: Your body is very rigid.
Client: [No response, no movement.]
Therapist [performing BR]: Your hands are holding your head.
Client: [No response, no movement.]
Therapist [performing RR/WWR]: My head hurts when my father speaks.

Client: [Immediately dropped his hands to his knees and looked directly into the therapist's eyes.]
Therapist [performing BR]: You've taken your hands from your head and placed them on your knees. You are looking right into my eyes.

Client: [Sat motionless for hours, and then at one point dropped his head to his knees.]
Therapist [performing RR/BR]: You dropped your hands from your head to your knees.

Client: [No response, no movement.]
Therapist [performing SR]: You are looking straight into my eyes.

Client: [Immediately, he speaks in a barely audible whisper.] Priests are devils.
Therapist [performing WWR]: Priests are devils.
[It later unfolded in the therapy that the patient was the victim of a sexual overture from the family priest.]
Therapist [performing BR]: Your hands are on your knees.
Client: [No response, no movement.]
Therapist [performing verbal SR]: You are looking right into my eyes.
Client: [No response, no movement.]

Therapist [performing BR]:	Your body is very rigid.
Client [speaking in a barely audible whisper]:	My brothers can't forgive me.
Therapist [performing WWR]:	My brothers can't forgive me.

The client then sat motionless for approximately 1 hour. Note the non-directive, non-questioning attitude of the therapist.

Segment Four

(begun at approximately 1:45 a.m.)

Therapist [performing SR]:	It is very quiet.
Client: [No response, no movement.]	
Therapist [performing SR]:	You are in the lower level of the house.
Client: [No response, no movement.]	
Therapist [performing SR]:	It is evening.
Client: [No response, no movement.]	
Therapist [performing BR]:	Your body is very rigid.

The client then immediately, in slow motion, put his hand over his heart, and then spoke.

Client:	My heart is wooden.
Therapist [performing BR then WWR]:	[In slow motion, puts her hand over her heart and talks:] My heart is wooden.
Client: [Feet start to move.]	
Therapist [performing a verbal BR]:	Your feet are starting to move.
Client: [More eye movement.]	

The therapist then took the patient's hand and lifted him to stand. Although I do not have the information to know why the therapist took this directive action, I suspect she felt some "life surge" in the patient and responded empathically and intuitively.

They began to walk. The patient then walked with the therapist around the family farm and in a normal conversational mode spoke about the different animals. He brought the therapist to newborn puppies and lifted one to hold. The client had good eye contact.

The client continued to maintain communicative contact over the next 4 days and was able to transfer planes and negotiate with customs officers on the way from Poland to the United States. He was able to sign himself into the residential treatment facility, where he underwent classical person-centered/experiential psychotherapy.

This vignette illustrates the workings of Pre-Therapy, which enabled the restoration of the client's psychological contact, thereby facilitating a more interactive level of treatment. Very clearly, this client's reality and communicative contact improved sufficiently for him to enter psychotherapy.

Another case example, previously described (Prouty, 1994), illustrates the value of applying contact reflections when resolving a psychotic episode in a woman diagnosed with disorganized schizophrenia. The therapist was a mental health paraprofessional taking a group of clients on a community visit.

As quoted in Prouty (1994):

> The client was one of seven on an outing from a halfway house. She was seated in the rear seat of the van. As I looked in the rearview mirror, I observed the patient crouched down into the seat with one arm outstretched over her head. The client's face was filled with terror and her voice began to escalate in screams. I pulled the van off the road and asked the volunteer to take the other patients out of the van. I sat next to the client, sharing the seat. The client's eyes were closed and she was wincing with fear.
>
> (pp. 55–57)

Client [in a rising voice]:	It's pulling me in!
Therapist [performing WWR]:	It's pulling me in.

The client continued to slip further down into the seat, with her left arm outstretched. Her eyes remained closed.

Therapist [performing BR]:	Your body is slipping down into the seat. Your arm is in the air.
Client: [No response.]	
Therapist [performing SR]:	We are in the van. You are sitting next to me.
Client: [Screaming.]	
Therapist [performing SR]:	You are screaming, Carol.
Client:	It is pulling me in.
Therapist [performing WWR]:	It's pulling you in.
Client: [No response.]	

Therapist [performing SR]:	Carol, we are in the van. You are sitting next to me.

The client had a terrified look on her face as she screamed.

Therapist [performing FR/SR]:	Something is frightening you. You are screaming.
Client [still screaming]:	It's sucking me in.
Therapist [performing WWR]:	It's sucking you in.
Therapist [performing SR/BR]:	We are in the van, Carol. You are sitting next to me. Your arm is in the air.
Client [beginning to sob very hard – arms dropped to lap]:	It was the vacuum cleaner.
Therapist [performing WWR]:	It was the vacuum cleaner.
Client [making direct eye contact with therapist]:	She did it with the vacuum cleaner.
Client [continuing in a normal tone of voice]:	I thought it was gone. She used to turn on the vacuum cleaner when I was bad and put the hose right on my arm. I thought it sucked it in.

The client then exhibited less terror. It should be noted that this patient would daily kiss her arm up to her elbow and stroke it continually.

Therapist [performing SR]:	Your arm is still here. It didn't get into the vacuum cleaner.

The client then smiled and let herself be held by the therapist.

Later that afternoon, a regular psychotherapy session was held and the client began to delve into her feelings about punishment she received as a child.

It should be noted that medications, which would often be a standard treatment in many modern mental health facilities in such situations, were not needed to resolve this crisis.

Psychological awareness and contact (contact functions)

The purpose of Pre-Therapy is to make contact with the highly regressed patient. Though regressed, they have the ability to connect to themselves, to others, and to the world through their own psychological processes. It is our work as therapists to engage patients where they are at and enable and enhance the workings of their psychological processes.

Pre-Therapy divides the psychological processes of the patient into three categories: making contact with reality, that is, having awareness of people, places, things, and events; having an awareness of affects, that is, having an awareness of moods, feelings, and emotions; and being able to communicate, that is, to symbolize to others the reality of the world and of the self.

The enhancement and manifestation of these three processes are illustrated in the following case example. Prouty (1994: 42–43) presents the following vignette involving a student therapist and a very chronically psychotic woman.

Client: Come with me.

Therapist [performing WWR/BR]:   Come with me.

[Therapist's commentary: The patient led me to the corner of the day room. We stood there silently for what seemed to be a very long time. Since I couldn't communicate with her, I watched her body movements and closely reflected these.]

Client: [putting her hand on the wall]:   Cold.

[Therapist's commentary: She had been holding my hand all along, but when I reflected her, she would tighten her grip. She began to mumble word fragments. I was careful to reflect only the words I could understand. What she said was beginning to make sense.]

Client: I don't know what this means anymore. [She touches the wall: making contact with reality.] The walls don't mean anything anymore.

Therapist [performing WWR/BR]:   [Touching the wall:] You don't know what this is anymore. The walls and chair don't mean anything to you anymore.

The client began to cry, signifying her awareness of affects. After a while she began to talk again, and this time she spoke clearly, demonstrating communication.

Client: I don't like it here. I am so tired – so tired.

Therapist [performing WWR]:   [Therapist's commentary: As I gently touched her arm, this time it was I who tightened my grip on her hand. I reflected her words back to her:] You are so tired, so tired.

The patient smiled and told the therapist to sit in a chair directly in front of her and began to braid the therapist's hair, which is a relational form of communication.

Research into the effectiveness of Pre-Therapy (contact behaviors)

Many behaviors emerge in clients undergoing Pre-Therapy. These behaviors, resulting from expressions of the client's psychological processes, provide the material for operationalized scientific measurement. For instance, a patient's ability to make reality contact, that is, to demonstrate his or her contact with the world, can be operationalized as the client's verbalization of people, places, things, and events. A patient's ability to make affective contact, that is, express his contact with or awareness of the self, can be operationalized as the bodily or facial expression of affect. Affective contact may also be operationalized through the use of "feeling words" such as "sad" or "angry" or "lonely." A patient's ability to communicate is operationalized through his or her use of social words or sentences.

Hinterkopf, Prouty, and Brunswick (1979) utilized the Pre-Therapy Method with patients and found significant increases in reality and communicative contact for patients with chronic schizophrenia when compared with a control group receiving recreational therapy. The patients had an average hospitalization of 20 years, providing researchers a chance to explore the genuinely chronic portion of the schizophrenic continuum that lacked previous client-centered research.

A single case study (Prouty, 1990) measured the effects of the Pre-Therapy Method on a client diagnosed with schizophrenia/autism and mental retardation who had a Stanford Binet IQ of 17. The report noted large increases in reality, affective, and communicative contact. A clinical evaluation was provided by a psychologist who was unaware of the research purpose. He reported that the client demonstrated reduced aggressiveness as well as an improved ability to tolerate frustration. He also reported that the client showed greater internalized self-control mechanisms as well as greater emotional and behavioral stability. This report provided the first client-centered exploration of psychosis at the lower end of the intellectual continuum.

In another single case report of Pre-Therapy, Prouty (1994) studied the interrater reliability of psychological contact through the use of the Pre-Therapy Scale. The client was a young woman who was hospitalized with schizophrenia and mental retardation. Two sets of observations were taken of the client – one set for a single day and one for a 3-month period. The single-day observations consisted of 24 pairs of rater scorings drawn from the beginning, middle, and end of the session (1–20, 40–60, and 80–100 percentiles). A correlation coefficient of 0.9847 was obtained with a p value of .0001. The pairwise *t-test* produced a value of 2.3738 with a p value of .0526. These results indicate no difference between scoring at the .01 or .05 level of significance. The 3-month observations consisted of nine pairs of mean scores from independent raters that yielded a correlation coefficient of 0.9966 with a p value of .0001, presenting strong evidence against the null hypothesis. The pairwise *t-test* resulted in a value of 0.0964 with a p value of .3528. These results indicate no difference between scorings.

In yet another pilot study, DeVre (1992) further confirmed interrater reliability and developed evidence of reliability for the Pre-Therapy Scale. There were three clients. The first two had chronic schizophrenia and normal intelligence and the third was mentally disabled. The first client's measure of agreement was $k = .39$. The same raters, with a second client, obtained $k = .76$. Again, with the same raters and a third client the raters obtained $k = .87$. The reliability measure was obtained by using independent psychiatric nurses trained in the Pre-Therapy Scale. The first effort produced a low measure of $k = .39$. With improved English to Flemish translation, the nurses produced $k = .7$ at a .0005 level of significance.

Dinacci (1997) produced a video study of clients receiving Pre-Therapy. This pilot study involved a single therapist, two experimental clients receiving Pre-Therapy, and two control clients, all diagnosed with both schizophrenia and mental retardation, each hospitalized for 30 years. The experiment produced strong clinical and quantitative evidence for marked increases in verbally communicative behaviors in the near-mute clients, using the Evaluation Criterion for the Pre-Therapy Interview (ECPI) scale, which measures verbal coherence and severe levels of disorganization. Reporting a beta coefficient of .77, Dinacci found a corresponding confidence of 97.5% that the differences will fall between 16,195 and 28,257 communicative units. Controlling for first-session differences, Pre-Therapy patients averaged communicative scores that were 22.226 units higher than the control group. The difference was significant at $p > .02$. This statistical interpretation revealed that the client communication scores fell within the range predicted by a much larger sample and was not the result of extraneous variables. Qualitatively the video shows clients who are more lively and expressive.

Conclusion

Pre-Therapy offers clinicians a new set of theory and tools for making contact and ultimately fostering connection and conversation with difficult-to-reach clients. It offers a method for helping free those whose selves live trapped and isolated within a pre-expressive or pre-communicative state. Through Pre-Therapy a vital part of the patient transforms into consensually validated symbolic communication by first engaging the patient at the most basic place of experience. Pre-Therapy affords therapists a client-centered and ultimately respectful means to forge essential contact with those who are so often written off, or simply medicated, by the current mental health field.

This essential contact – neither invasive nor arcane, but rather gentle, patient, and trusting – offers a profound reminder to mental health workers that some of the most withdrawn and seemingly unavailable people actually have quite a capacity for interaction if only we can listen to their messages, reflect their humanity, and take their lead. This offers an entire paradigm for psychotherapy with the most disturbed patients, and perhaps many who are not so disturbed: If we only are able to tap into the latent inner capacity for growth and follow these inroads, they will guide us in the direction that they most need to go.

References

Arieti, S. (1955). *An Interpretation of Schizophrenia*. New York: Robert Brunner.

Breggin, P. (1991). Schizophrenic overwhelm and neuroleptic drugs. In *Toxic Psychiatry* (pp. 21–117). New York: St. Martins Press.

Breggin, P. (1997). *Brain Damaging Treatments in Psychiatry, Drugs, Electroshock and the Role of the FDA*. Norwell: Springer.

DeVre, R. (1992). *Prouty's Pre-Therapie*. Master's Thesis, Department of Psychology, University of Ghent, Belgium.

Dinacci, A. (1997). Ricera sperimentale sul trattamento psicologico de pazenti schizopfrenici con la Pre-Terapia. *Psicologia della Persona*, 2: 3–8.

Dorman, D. (2003). *Dante's Cure: A Journey out of Madness*. New York: Other Press.

Freidman, G. (1961). Conceptual thinking in schizophrenic children. *Genetic Psychology Monographs*, 63: 149–196.

Goldstein, K. (1939). The significance of special tests for the diagnosis and prognosis in schizophrenia. *American Journal of Psychiatry*, 96: 575–588.

Goldstein, K. and Scheerer, M. (1941). Abstract and concrete behavior: An experimental study with special tests. *Psychological Monographs*, 53: 51.

Gurswitch, A. (1966). Gelb-Goldstein's concept of "concrete" and "categorical" attitude and the phenomenology of ideation. In J. Wild (Ed.), *Studies in Phenomenology and Psychology* (pp. 359–384). Evanston, IL: Northwestern University Press.

Hinterkopf, E. and Brunswick, L. (1981). Teaching therapeutic mental patients to use client-centered and experiential skills with each other. *Psychotherapy: Theory, Research and Practice*, 18: 394–403.

Hinterkopf, E., Prouty, G., and Brunswick, L. (1979). A pilot study of Pre-Therapy method applied to chronic schizophrenics. *Psychosocial Rehabilitation Journal*, 3: 11–19.

Jackson, G. (2005). *Rethinking Psychiatric Drugs: A Guide for Informed Consent*. Bloomington, IN: Authorhouse.

Karon, B. and VandenBos, G. (1981). *Psychotherapy of Schizophrenia: The Treatment of Choice.* New York: Jason Aronson.

Mazumdar, D. and Mazumdar, T. (1983). Abstract and concrete behavior of organic, schizophrenic and normal subjects on the Goldstein-Scheer Cube Test. *Indian Journal of Clinical Psychology,* 10: 5–10.

Mosher, L. (2004). Drug companies and schizophrenia: Unbridled capitalism meets madness. In J. Read, L. Mosher, and R. Bentall (Eds.), *Models of Madness* (pp. 115–130). New York: Brunner-Routledge.

Prouty, G. (1990). Pre-Therapy: A theoretical evolution in the person-centered/ experiential psychotherapy of schizophrenia and retardation. In G. Lietaer, J. Rombauts, and R. Van Balen (Eds.), *Client-Centered and Experiential Psychotherapy in the Nineties* (pp. 645–658). Leuven, Belgium: Leuven University Press.

Prouty, G. (1994). *Theoretical Evolutions in Person-Centered/Experiential Therapy: Applications to Schizophrenic and Retarded Psychoses.* Westport, CT: Praeger (Greenwood Press).

Prouty, G. (2000). Pre-Therapy and the Pre-Expressive Self. In T. Merry (Ed.), *The BAPC Reader* (pp. 68–76). Ross-on Wye: PCCS Books.

Prouty, G. (2002). Humanistic psychotherapy for people with schizophrenia. In D. Cain and J. Seeman (Eds.), *Humanistic Psychotherapies: Handbook of Research and Practice* (pp. 579–601). Washington, DC: American Psychological Association.

Prouty, G. (2003). Pre-therapy: A newer development in the psychotherapy of schizophrenia. *Journal of the American Academy of Psychoanalysis and Dynamic Psychiatry,* 31: 59–73.

Prouty, G. (2004). De Hallucinatieals het onbewuste zelf (The hallucination as the unconscious self). *Tidjdschrift Clientgerichte Psychotherapie,* 42: 85–98.

Pugh, R.W. (1949). *An Investigation of Some Psychological Processes Accompanying Concurrent Electric Convulsive Therapy and Non-Directive Psychotherapy with Paranoid Schizophrenia.* Dissertation. Chicago: University of Chicago.

Raskin, N. (1947). *The Non-Directive Attitude,* unpublished manuscript.

Read, J., Goodman, I., Morrison, A., Ross, C., and Alderhold, V. (2004) Childhood loss and stress. In J. Read, L. Mosher, and R. Bentall (Eds.), *Models of Madness* (pp. 223–252). New York: Routledge.

Roelens, L. (1994). Foreword. In G. Prouty (Ed.), *Theoretical Evolutions in Person-Centered/Experiential Therapy: Applications to Schizophrenic and Retarded Psychoses* (pp. xi–xx). Westport, CT: Praeger (Greenwood Press).

Rogers, C. (1957). The necessary and sufficient conditions of therapeutic personality change. *Journal of Consulting Psychology,* 21: 95–103.

Rogers, C., Gendlin, E., Kiesler, D., and Truax, C. (1967). The findings in brief. In C. Rogers (Ed.), *The Therapeutic Relationship and its Impact: A Study of Psychotherapy with Schizophrenics* (pp. 73–93). Madison: University of Wisconsin Press.

Teusch, L. (1981). Positive effects and limitations of client-centered therapy with schizophrenic clients. In J. Lietaer, R. Rombauts, L. Teusch, U. Beyerle, H. Lange, K. Schenk, and G. Stadmuller (Eds.), The client-centered approach to schizophrenic patients: First empirical results. *European Conference on Psychotherapy Research,* II: 141–147.

Vanderveen, F. (1967). Basic elements in the process of psychotherapy: A research study. *Journal of Consulting Psychology*, 29: 19–26.

Whitaker, R. (2002). *Mad in America: Bad Science, Bad Medicine, and the Enduring Mistreatment of the Mentally Ill*. Cambridge, MA: Perseus Press.

Whitaker, R. (2004). The case against antipsychotic drugs: A 50-year record of doing more harm than good. *Medical Hypotheses*, 62: 5–13.

Chapter 4

The role of the therapeutic alliance in the treatment of seriously disturbed individuals

Warren Schwartz and Frank Summers

Editors' Introduction: Schwartz and Summers lay out the next requisite phase in the psychotherapy of psychosis – the establishment of a therapeutic alliance. This is not just a relationship, but a relationship with a structure, a purpose, and an explicit or implicit contract or agreement. Like in a marriage, the partners in this life project become a "couple." They establish a way of living and working together in the time they share together. And the effects of their common purpose vis-à-vis the patient's symptoms and life trajectory will, if their alliance is effective, persist even during the times when they are not together.

Building on Faulconer and Silver's views on the importance of the setting in initial engagements, Schwartz and Summers detail why reliability, predictability, and dependability are so important to the success of the therapeutic alliance. In an inner world of chaos in hallucination and delusional fantasy, a securing rhythm becomes a secure port in the storm.

Finally, the therapeutic alliance is not just a structure but a way of working together, a set of "rules of engagement." These include being non-judgmental and non-impinging, navigating between "providing for" and "understanding with," and paying attention to affect and action. This chapter provides a portable toolbox for the techniques that Garry Prouty enumerated in the previous chapter – and provides a roadmap for constructing that toolbox.

Introduction

Psychotherapy with seriously disturbed patients is a challenging endeavor. These individuals are commonly terrified, can think and behave in frightening, uncustomary, and downright bizarre ways, and require persistent and intensive attention. Many practitioners are not inclined to invest in and engage with patients presenting with such conditions and needs. Here is the impetus for sparse, disengaged, "symptom management" types of treatments. The lack of an engaged relational presence characterizing these common treatment approaches precludes the potential for healing. The patient holds on to his symptoms under such interpersonal conditions because he does not have the emotional security to open himself up and grow into other ways of managing his world.

A psychotherapeutic process that fosters desired clinical outcomes necessitates a sufficient *alliance* between patient and practitioner – a relationship characterized by steady and emotionally intimate work. The emergence and maintenance of such an alliance functions as a bridge to therapeutic action. But the alliance is also a *result* of a clinical process. Our mission here is to delineate the elements of the therapeutic alliance, understand how it is established, and identify how it supports further therapeutic action in work with seriously disturbed individuals.

First, it will be helpful to define the therapeutic alliance more specifically and to understand its relationship to other aspects of the treatment relationship. This clarification will prepare us to see how the alliance is established and maintained and how it paves the way for therapeutic change.

Defining the therapeutic alliance

The therapeutic alliance involves an agreement between patient and therapist that they will be working toward the patient's symptom abatement and greater life satisfaction. It involves the acceptance that both parties will be working toward helping the patient better understand himself and that this self-understanding will lead to positive change. The alliance is a mature, positive attachment that sits behind the transference and the chaotic experience of symptoms. When it is established and maintained, it is always there in the background, even in difficult times.

There are times when a treatment goes on and on and both parties seem satisfied, yet no therapeutic alliance has been established. Such is the case when patient and therapist understand the patient's psychological disturbance as purely biologically driven, as there may be no agreement in such a case that the patient's disturbance can be mitigated or solved by a human process. In these cases, an alliance has been established, but not a therapeutic one. Such a relationship usually involves a mutual avoidance of subjective contact, which does not foster the patient's growth and integration. An arrangement such as this involves a work agreement, but the agreement is not characterized by a mutual investment in the understanding and growth of the patient.

When an alliance is established, transference inevitably occurs, and there is an acceptance, by both patient and therapist, that the patient is bringing something to the relationship – that his history and worldview lead him to think and behave in certain ways. This mutual acceptance represents the opening of a third set of eyes that can reliably gaze on the treatment situation and be referred to by both parties to inform the nature of the patient's condition.

We can further elucidate the nature of the alliance by comparing it in more detail with other elements of the treatment relationship. What we would like to do, with the help of Meissner's (1996) thorough and scholarly work on the subject, is quickly "pan-out" a definition of the therapeutic alliance by making these comparisons. Once we can separate out the alliance from other aspects of the clinical relationship, we will be prepared to examine the factors that allow for its establishment and, later, how it serves as a base for therapeutic action.

The therapeutic alliance can be distinguished from transference in that the alliance is a more rational, stable, mature aspect of the relationship while the transference is typically of a less mature and more chaotic quality (Meissner, 1996). Again, the alliance is characterized by an agreement (explicit or implicit) between patient and practitioner that they will be working toward the patient's betterment by helping him understand and transform his symptomatic life. Transference, on the other hand, can be seen as the patient's enactment of his early determined relational patterns in the treatment. It is the alliance that facilitates the clarification and understanding of these dysfunctional patterns.

While there may be elements of positive transference in the therapeutic alliance, these are usually more mature and foster growth rather than regression and resistance. Freud (1912) referred to this as the unobjectionable component of the positive transference. While the alliance involves an attachment to the therapist and this attachment contains elements of positive transference, these elements foster, rather than inhibit, the working agreement.

A brief word is in order about the real relationship and how it compares with the therapeutic alliance and the transference. In terms of its uniqueness from these other aspects of the relationship, the real relationship involves the actual qualities as perceived and responded to by the other rather than filtered through the lens of transference and countertransference, and is distinguished from the therapeutic alliance because it does not involve any work agreement as the therapeutic alliance does.

While a therapist might have a personality that lends itself toward good psychotherapeutic work, it is how his personality is mobilized in session that determines the patient's trust in him and fosters his growth. A therapist with a warm, empathic personality could very well be perceived as persecutory by the patient, particularly by a paranoid patient, and particularly if the therapist does not manage his actions in a way that is sensitive to the patient's psychodynamics. Furthermore, while a therapist may possess certain potentially therapeutic qualities, if these qualities are only mobilized in work characterized by non-therapeutic interventions (e.g., medication-only treatment), the reality of his personality has little or no therapeutic effect and the alliance is thus a non-therapeutic or counter-therapeutic one. Again, it is how this "real relationship" is mobilized that determines a therapeutic effect and potential. We do not see empathy, kindness, or a capacity for engagement as elements of the therapeutic alliance when these qualities are utilized to get the patient to comply with anything other than the psychotherapeutic task of personal development and integration.

To summarize, the therapeutic alliance is a relatively mature attachment containing an agreement that the therapeutic dyad will be working toward the patient's betterment. Additionally, the alliance is what allows the therapeutic action to occur. The real relationship is also mature and often positive but does not contain a work agreement. The transference is usually not mature and can work against the goals of the alliance, whether positive or negative. With these definitions, let us move to the factors and processes that allow for the establishment and maintenance of the therapeutic alliance.

The frame: theater of engagement

According to Winnicott (1965), the mother performs two sets of functions for the infant. The *environmental mother* provides the conditions necessary for the child's growth and development. For example, she keeps the room temperature, noise, and stimulation at manageable levels. The *object mother* is the mother whom the child loves and hates, who is the object of the child's affective states. The child works out her affects and relationships with the object mother, but the establishment of these relational patterns is possible only if the environmental mother provides the conditions under which the child can experience a variety of affects toward her. Analogously, the frame is the aspect of the alliance that provides the conditions within which the transference can be resolved, and the therapist must provide these conditions. Transference resolution takes place with the therapist as the target of the patient's affects and desires. The ability of the therapeutic couple to make use of the transference is dependent on the frame provided by the therapist in her role as environmental mother.

As with the frame's function with the patient, the frame provides the therapist with some stability and predictability and thus contains some of the anxiety that otherwise would potentially overwhelm the process. Reverie, the associative flow of countertransference, becomes difficult to access when the therapist's mind is broken up by unmanaged chaos. The therapist has much difficulty formulating and communicating her experience of the patient under unanchored circumstances.

Aspects of a therapeutic frame include: a consistent, comfortable, and quiet physical space; regular, predictable meetings bound by a relatively consistent time-frame; and a physically and emotionally safe environment. When these elements are in place, the alliance is more likely to unfold.

Time and space considerations

It is important to provide the patient, who may be disoriented, with a relatively temporally and physically consistent setting that facilitates introspection and allows for comfortable contact with the therapist.

It is usually best if the therapist faces the patient rather than "using the couch" in the more traditional psychoanalytic fashion. Fromm-Reichmann (1950) and Sullivan (1970) noted that giving the patient the opportunity to observe the therapist relieves her of anxiety that would otherwise interfere with treatment. A therapist who interactively responds to the patient provides her with visual and audible markers of reality. Such intersubjective conditions, facilitated by the frame, create a new, anchoring reality that helps secure the alliance and begins the strengthening process described by Garfield and Dorman in Chapter 1.

The room should be quiet enough so that the therapist and patient are not distracted. While many clinicians work in institutions with limited choices of space, finding one that is comfortable and quiet is important, and a therapist should do whatever she can to find one. Additionally, a room with a lock on the door can ensure privacy and minimize intrusions from other patients and staff. It is appropriate for a therapist to assert to the team or administration that such a space is important for patients' treatments.

A regular time cycle is an important component of the frame. In the beginning of therapy it is helpful to determine, as well as possible, how often and frequently the therapist will be meeting with the patient. Patients vary in their tolerance of session length.

Working with more seriously disturbed patients on the frequency of at least twice a week fosters a strong therapeutic alliance. Just as it is important for a mother to be predictably responsive to her baby's needs, the therapist must be as available as possible to the patient.

While predictability of sessions in terms of length and when they are held is important, it is also important that one is flexible enough to accommodate the patient's needs by extending, shortening, adding, or skipping sessions.

Safety – an important function of the frame

Without safety, the therapeutic alliance cannot be established, as the anxiety for either or both parties is too overwhelming for any work to get done (Karon and VandenBos, 1981; McWilliams, 2004). The most pervasive affect for the patient with schizophrenia is terror, specifically annihilation anxiety (Atwood, Orange, and Stolorow, 2002; Becker, 1973; Karon and VandenBos, 1981; Searles, 1961). For this reason, Karon and VandenBos recommend explicitly dealing with this terror at the outset of treatment with these patients. With severely regressed patients, they say something like "I am not going to kill you and I am not going to let anyone kill you." It might be important to add "I am not afraid that you are going to kill me." This can be enormously helpful in reducing their fear and solidifying the therapeutic alliance. Such statements are only helpful if the therapist really believes them. Of course, if the therapist has a real basis to be afraid of the patient he might tell him this and should take precautions to protect himself from being harmed.

The provision of safety is an essential element of the frame and what Modell (1991) means by the iconic/containing function of the analyst. When the therapist is able to provide a safe environment, the patient feels "held" by the therapeutic situation. McWilliams (2004) suggests that the therapist should assess the patient's fear of her by directly asking him about it and by observing his body language. It is sometimes a good idea to invite the patient to sit closer to the door. Of course, the therapist might want to sit closer to the door if the patient does really frighten her.

An important part of the frame is the management of suicidal and other potential or actual self-directed dangerous behavior. Safety is a necessity and should be the highest priority with the dangerous patient. Only after safety has been established should a therapist investigate, along with the patient, the meanings of the act or potential act.

Emotional safety is promoted by the therapist, who carefully observes the patient and provides him with consistently well-timed, empathic, non-intrusive feedback. This respectful stance with the patient usually differs from how others have responded to him (including other professionals) and is often a welcome and freeing surprise (Karon and VandenBos, 1981).

In sum, the frame facilitates the establishment and maintenance of the therapeutic alliance because it provides both patient and therapist with a predictable and safe space that binds anxiety, enabling the work agreement to unfold.

Further solidification and maintenance of the therapeutic alliance

We will now investigate the types of conditions that facilitate the emergence of the therapeutic alliance and the types of conditions that foreclose on it.

Being non-judgmental and non-impinging

The alliance is an engagement based on the trust that the patient develops in the therapist. This trust is fostered by the therapist's willingness to adapt to the patient's needs rather than impose an agenda on her. Such a practice is in contradistinction to purely psycho-educational approaches, which typically involve a transmission of something from the outside in.

All psychotic patients are suspicious or downright paranoid of others. Their delusions almost always consist of the sense that they are being influenced or maligned by a malevolent other or others. It is thus critical that we allow the patient as much control over the treatment as possible, while still respecting basic aspects of the frame that permit the work. We strive to listen wholeheartedly to what the patient is communicating, however disturbing or apparently nonsensical, as he can only feel that we take him seriously if we make an effort to take him in as he is.

Once the patient can trust that the therapist is there for the patient (rather than to satisfy the therapist's own needs) the alliance is strengthened. The patient's experience of the therapist's willingness to accommodate him tells him that his experience matters, and makes possible the patient's use of his experience. If, however, the patient senses that the therapist has an agenda to impose, as frequently happens in the case of psycho-education-only or medication-only treatments, the patient might join him in a relationship of convenience, but will not form a therapeutic alliance that would facilitate the task of self-understanding.

The tension between "providing for" and "understanding with"

While we want to provide the patient with certain experiences that solidify and maintain the alliance, there are times when "providing for" as opposed to "understanding with" the patient might steer the dyad the wrong way.

Children need assistance from parenting figures to relieve distress and solve problems. If the parent either offers no such aid or always resolves the child's tension for her, the child gains no belief in her ability to alleviate negative states and enhance well-being. Likewise, as therapists, if we provide too little the patient may not be able to *tolerate* facing her pain; if we provide too much, she might not be *motivated* to face her pain. A sufficient psychotherapeutic alliance encourages the patient's ability to tolerate negative states while providing containment and soothing when these states threaten to disrupt the patient's psychic equilibrium. This strategy mirrors the attitude that Demos (1988) finds in parents who are successful in helping the child manage affects. By employing this balance and not swaying too far in one direction or the other, we abide by the vision inherent to the alliance that the patient will eventually develop the capacity to tolerate, regulate, and understand her experience.

We want to be kind and generally accommodating to the patient to build the safe, trusting alliance that makes therapy possible. This might mean offering the patient a cup of coffee or glass of water – which is only fair to do, especially if we are sipping from our own cup (Karon and VandenBos, 1981). As Karon and VandenBos (1981) note, we need to provide the severely disturbed patient with a certain amount of protection and gratification, at least in the beginning of treatment. Here we accept some of the patient's omnipotence in the service of building the relationship that makes therapeutic action possible, including the resolution of the patient's omnipotent expectations.

It is important for a therapist to sometimes take an educative role. For example, the therapist might provide the patient with information about housing, transportation, or benefits. Many seriously disturbed patients come from families that were either neglectful or unable to provide them with the informational and material resources necessary to navigate life (Karon and VandenBos, 1981). If the patient is being seen in a clinic, the educative role is usually assumed by the case manager, but even in these situations it is often necessary for the therapist to provide some information to him. This does not usually detract from the alliance unless a patient becomes overly dependent on the therapist at the expense of developing his own autonomy.

A key component of the patient's trust in the therapist and the establishment of the alliance is the hope conveyed by the therapist to the patient. Hope is an inherent component of the therapeutic process (Cooper, 2000). The therapist's willingness to listen and understand the patient's experience implies that improvement can occur. As Cooper has noted, any interpretive effort conveys not just an understanding of what is, but the implicit message that the current situation can be changed. So, in that sense, hope is implied in the analytic process. But, it is especially important with psychotic individuals that this hope is conveyed in the very earliest sessions by the therapist's interest in the patient's experience. By contrast, if the clinician is only interested in symptoms and prescribes medication as the only remedy, the implication is that there is no hope that the patient can alter his life experience by any human process. The communication to the patient that understanding and relating can shift the experience of the world is effected by the therapist's interest and willingness to engage the patient's experience, and when the patient receives this message, then hope is conveyed. And this hope, now held by both patient and therapist, strengthens the therapeutic alliance.

Hope, then, may be considered an attitude that the therapist provides to the patient. Many patients attribute a large portion of their growth to providers who held out hope through some very difficult years. While we recognize the suffering of the patient and how difficult it is to have a debilitating problem, we hold out hope that their suffering will abate at some point down the line. In other words, we express hope but not in a way that denies the gravity of the patient's situation (Karon and VandenBos, 1981); because to do so is dishonest, or at least naïve, and potentially only a denial of feelings of hopelessness. We promote what Searles (1979) called "mature hope." The provision of hope, while recognizing the gravity of the patient's situation, fosters and maintains a therapeutic alliance because it demonstrates to the patient that we are confident that the work agreement will lead to positive consequences and simultaneously shows him that we recognize his pain.

Excessive provisions can seal over negative states. This result is frequently seen on hospital wards when a patient is immediately provided with something (usually something oral like medication or cigarettes) in response to distressing affect. A clinician may provide this type of gratification because she herself cannot tolerate the patient's negative affect. The "improvement" in the patient's affective state is then based on the patient's positive feelings toward the clinician and the satisfaction of less mature urges rather than to interpretive and integrative work. Such an improvement disappears when the patient is out of the clinician's range. In this situation, the clinician persistently satisfies the patient's wishes as they are expressed without facilitating his capacity to manage unsatisfied desires. The alliance must be built by responsiveness, but not total accommodation to the patient's wishes, for that will interfere with the therapeutic goal of helping the patient develop new psychic capacities. In this way, the patient and therapist are acting in accordance with a therapeutic alliance rather than establishing an alliance geared solely toward avoiding pain.

Therapeutic action is contingent upon the establishment and maintenance of the agreement that the patient and therapist are working toward the patient's self-understanding. The agreement is fostered by the gratification that allows the patient to stay in the relationship and the frustration necessary for self-reflection.

Action supporting the alliance and alliance supporting further action

It happens all too often that therapists are not deeply engaged with their patients even if they are meeting with them in intensive psychotherapy or psychoanalysis. In many cases the therapist or analyst's investment in the patient is predominantly intellectual. Feeling little or no affective connection with the patient, the therapist observes her solely as an object of intellectual interest and perhaps curiosity, like a specimen seen through a microscope. The upshot is a gulf between patient and therapist that is counterproductive to the formation of a therapeutic alliance. While a relationship of convenience might develop in such an environment, this type of interaction has no therapeutic benefit. A relationship contains a therapeutic alliance only when it is characterized by the therapist's openness to the patient's whole experience. As described earlier, this requires a certain kind of "taking in" of the patient, which then allows the patient to experience the therapist as receptive to her experience. When the patient has this experience, it makes possible the eventual formation of a new self-image based on the therapist's experience of the patient.

So, the alliance only emerges if the therapist is non-impinging and emotionally receptive toward the patient, and further therapeutic action only occurs if a therapeutic alliance is established and maintained. When there is no trust that the therapist will carefully attend to what is meaningful to the patient, there is no alliance, and when there is no alliance, there is little chance for therapeutic action.

Affective registration between patient and therapist: Amber

Now we will turn to a brief clinical example that illustrates the oscillating process of alliance building and therapeutic action. We will see how the therapist's behavior fosters the emergence of a therapeutic alliance and how the emergence of the alliance supports further therapeutic action, which then further strengthens the alliance.

Amber

At the 2004 meeting of the United States Chapter of the International Society for the Psychological Treatments of the Schizophrenias and Other Psychoses, Jessica Wall, LCSW, reported her work with a patient she has called "Amber" (Wall, 2004). Amber was 10 when she began a 4-year treatment with Jessica. Amber had already been involved with several practitioners, many of whom were prescribers and none of whom were able to help her. Jessica, however, was able to engage Amber in intensive psychotherapy, resulting in improvement in Amber's sense of self and a reduction in symptoms. Prior to Amber's therapy, she had received a multitude of diagnoses that included, among others, schizophrenia, autism, and ADHD. Amber presented with auditory hallucinations, arm flapping, a tendency to relate to objects rather than people, ritualized behaviors, severe emotional disruption, isolation, and depression.

We have heard many cases presented in which symptoms less extreme than Amber's were taken as proof that the patient is untreatable. It is often argued that patients like Amber can only be helped by medication or only need "support" and are not "accessible" to a therapeutic process. Moreover, even when the therapist is willing to employ an interpretive strategy, the patient is often treated like a specimen to be observed or, as Bollas (1989) puts it, a "decoder of symbols." The motivation of such practice is the therapist shielding herself from the patient's experience resulting in a lack of a real therapeutic alliance.

Fortunately, Amber was given a chance by Jessica, despite the fact that Jessica developed a severe headache after meeting with the family for the intake. This leads us to believe that Jessica was quite connected with Amber's psychic pain and that she was willing to enter into a work-alliance with Amber. Jessica notes that Amber's mother's and grandmother's reporting of Amber's presenting problems "had me feeling bombarded and engulfed, so much so I couldn't wait for their departure." She found Amber's father to be ". . .straightforward and gruff, and often lacking the sensitivity that Amber required." So Jessica's emotional openness and willingness to embark on a therapeutic journey with this chaotic and disturbed family and patient is the first therapeutic occurrence that eventually allowed for the development of the alliance. Jessica uses her reverie of feeling "bombarded and engulfed" to inform herself about the nature of the family's and patient's disturbance. Jessica's openness to her experience of Amber and her family allowed her to understand them in a meaningful way.

Jessica described her first meeting with Amber as follows:

> Her physical presentation was awkward; she looked as if she were in the grip of great turmoil. Life and people moved too quickly for her and she was overwhelmed. At other times, she came across as over-whelming with her intense engagement of a person or object. She had a spooked uncomfortable way about her, as she darted around looking, or remained very still and staring off [into space]. Her presence penetrated me without her ever looking at me. Amber's skittishness made her appear odd and unreliable in her actions. She spoke in a removed and unnatural way.

Over the course of the first year of treatment, Amber began to notice Jessica rather than look right through her, often very excitedly and some-times with fright, and Jessica became "exquisitely aware" of her own feeling states. Jessica's affect, as she put it, "became a useful barometer of what Amber was experiencing and how I could be useful to her." Slowly, Amber began to locate her feelings in her body and began telling Jessica where she would hurt during the session. Eventually, Amber began to talk directly about her feelings. This therapeutic action emerged out of an alliance between Amber and Jessica: Amber became able to do the work of engaging in this growth-oriented intertransmission because Jessica provided the space for it through her receptivity and commitment. Once the alliance was established, Jessica's empathy for Amber and communications about Amber's possible feeling states led to a furthering of Amber's affective development. So here we have an example of therapeutic action leading to the establishment of an alliance, which then leads to further therapeutic action.

Jessica's interactions with Amber allowed Amber to know herself with Jessica as a point of reference. From the beginning, Jessica's intent was to offer an affective exchange in which the therapist feels what the patient conveys. Jessica's construction of this side of the alliance allowed Amber to contact the inside of Jessica and Jessica fed back to Amber Jessica's sense of her. This process allowed for therapeutic action, as throughout the course of the 4-year treatment Amber began to formulate a sense of self, grounded in her own affect, as processed by Jessica. Amber began connecting to others in less bizarre and distancing ways. Jessica described the formation of the alliance and the resultant therapeutic action as follows: "By ingesting her early affects and experience, like a mother with her infant, and slowly feeding them back to her in manageable doses, Amber experienced greater regulation and grounding." Amber's experience meant that Jessica took her seriously, which, in turn, gave Amber a new view of the once disorganizing and socially distancing sensations that had constituted her experience up to that point. Amber's responses, especially her excited states, were no longer simply irritations to the body that needed discharge somehow, but experiences that connected her to the world.

So, we can see why this relationship, characterized by a solid therapeutic alliance, had a profound effect on Amber. Her experience mattered to someone, which meant that it existed inside another subjectively. By being able to see her experience reflected in Jessica, Amber was able to experience her formerly vague and disorganizing excitations and agitations as real. Experience that mattered to another *became real*. While many take for granted the reality of their experience, those who live without a formed affective life can make no such assumption. They need the recognition of the other in order to make the voyage into the world of human interchange, that is, interpersonal reality. In order for a true alliance to develop and for subsequent therapeutic action to occur, the therapist must be a *subject* for the patient because only if the patient can make contact with the therapist's subjectivity does the therapist's look of recognition bring the patient's experience to life.

Over the course of this 4-year treatment, Amber approached Jessica first as an object and then "slowly as a person she could relate to and share herself with" (Jessica's words). Amber began developing other similar affect-laden attachments, including friendships. Jessica's way of being with Amber from the very beginning of the therapy facilitated the positive attachment with her or the "unobjectionable component" of the positive transference that permitted a circulation of affects between patient and therapist and the subsequent growth experienced by Amber.

In sum, the therapeutic alliance that Jessica established with Amber was not a matter of Jessica simply reflecting Amber's affects, because one cannot reflect back what does not yet exist. Nor did it involve seeing Amber as an intellectual curiosity. It involved, from the start: Jessica's use and feeding back of her direct experiencing of Amber, which both fostered the alliance and led to Amber's affective growth. When Amber started treatment, her affective life was not yet born. Desperately trying to make sense of what she felt, Amber was not able to use her affects to form ways of connecting to the world because her experience did not yet consist of formed or defined affects. Jessica did not simply recognize Amber's affects, nor did she label them; she helped to *create* them from her own emotional and bodily resonations and reveries. Such a stance was a component of early therapeutic action, which allowed the alliance to emerge and solidify. The alliance then further stimulated growth and integration.

Jessica attended not to affects, but to experiences in which Jessica saw potential for affective connection to the world. In Loewald's (1980) terms, Jessica had a vision of who Amber could become that went beyond the immediacy of the patient's experience. By responding to these incipient excitations, Jessica assisted their elaboration into ways of being and relating, that is, she helped to establish and maintain an alliance with Amber in the service of facilitating and building Amber's affective life and reducing her symptoms.

Conclusion

The therapeutic alliance, which emerges from certain conditions established by the therapist, provides the foundation for therapeutic action. The therapeutic alliance is defined as the part of the clinical relationship that involves an agreement between patient and therapist that the two will be working toward the patient's betterment through their exploration and understanding of him. Such an agreement is based on the patient's trust that the therapist will fully, openly, and non-intrusively attend to what is real and meaningful for him.

The alliance is distinguished from the transference in that the transference is often a less mature, more emotionally chaotic part of the treatment relationship, whereas the alliance, while containing some positive transference, is mature and fosters, rather than interferes with, the patient's psychic development and integration.

Seriously disturbed patients present with particular problems that require close attention when establishing and maintaining the therapeutic alliance. Typically, these patients present with paranoia or a serious lack of trust. As such, great care must be taken with these patients as we try to enter their world and establish a closeness with them. Patients need to know that we are there because we want to help, and that we are not interested in imposing our views or way of living upon them.

The therapeutic frame is the anchor of the alliance and may even be considered a prerequisite for it. The frame allows for some predictability in the midst of what is often chaotic. It binds anxiety for both parties and facilitates the mobilization of the work agreement.

The therapist fosters the development and maintenance of the alliance by allowing the patient sufficient control over the treatment. The direction of the patient's development begins with his or her efforts, that is, it emerges from within the patient and is only *facilitated* by the therapist. When the therapist drives the treatment, as often occurs in psycho-educational-only or medication-only treatments, the alliance is not a therapeutic one because the patient does not get to know himself from the inside out.

There are times when limits do need to be set. We try to balance the importance of allowing a certain degree of the patient's control over the treatment with not allowing total omnipotence. Providing everything for the patient potentially forecloses on his development and creates a non-therapeutic alliance.

The therapeutic alliance supports therapeutic action. It is a certain atmosphere that is encouraging of the patient's expression and growth. The alliance is an attachment that sets the stage for the circulation of affects between patient and therapist, which then allows for the patient's further development of self and understanding and resolution of symptoms.

References

Atwood, G., Orange, D., and Stolorow, R. (2002). Shattered worlds/psychotic states: A post-cartesian view of the experience of personal annihilation. *Psychoanalytic Psychology*, 19: 281–306.

Becker, E. (1973). *The Denial of Death*. New York: Free Press.

Bollas, C. (1989). *Force of Destiny*. London: Free Association Books.

Cooper, S. (2000). *Objects of Hope*. Hillsdale, NJ: Analytic Press.

Demos, V. (1988). Affect and the development of the self: A new frontier. In A. Goldberg (Ed.), *Frontiers in Self Psychology: Progress in Self Psychology* (Vol. 3, pp. 27–53). Hillsdale, NJ: Analytic Press.

Freud, S. (1912). The dynamics of the transference. In E. Jones (Ed.), *Collected Papers* (pp. 312–322). London: Hogarth Press.

Fromm-Reichmann, F. (1950). *Principles of Intensive Psychotherapy*. Chicago: University of Chicago Press.

Karon, B. and VandenBos, G. (1981). *Psychotherapy of Schizophrenia: The Treatment of Choice*. Northvale, NJ: Jason Aronson.

Loewald, H. (1980). On the therapeutic action of psychoanalysis. In *Papers on Psychoanalysis* (pp. 221–256). New Haven, CT: Yale University Press. (Original work published 1960.)

McWilliams, N. (2004). *Psychoanalytic Psychotherapy*. New York: Guilford Press.

Meissner, W. W. (1996). *The Therapeutic Alliance*. New Haven: Yale University Press.

Modell, A. (1990). *Other Times, Other Realities*. Cambridge: Harvard University Press.

Searles, H. (1961). Schizophrenia and the inevitability of death. In H. Searles (Ed.), *Collected Papers on Schizophrenia and Related Subjects* (pp. 487–520). New York: International Universities Press.

Searles, H. (1979). *Countertransference and Related Subjects: Selected Papers*. Madison, CT: International Universities Press.

Sullivan, H. (1970). *The Psychiatric Interview*. New York: W. W. Norton.

Wall, J. (2004). Far talk and tornadoes: Establishing a developmental process with a latency age girl. Frank Summers, PhD (Chair), *Panel Presentation*. Annual Meeting of the International Society for the Psychological Treatments of the Schizophrenias and Other Psychoses – United States Chapter.

Winnicott, D. (1965). The *Maturational Processes and the Facilitating Environment*. Madison, CT: International Universities Press.

Part 2

The elements of change

Chapter 5

Sustaining relationships: cure, care, and recovery

Frank Summers

Editors' Introduction: Frank Summers leads us through a detailed, empathic account of the key therapeutic ingredients involved in the creation of a sense of self in an extremely disturbed, intermittently paranoid patient who floundered between overwhelming affect states of envy and rage and extraordinary loneliness.

Dr. Summers describes the process by which the therapist both stays with and stays "out of the way" of the patient's nascent, developing self. He delineates how this process provides a space or place in the treatment wherein certain conditions, delineated in earlier chapters, are brought into existence so that they can now serve as a platform from which the patient can launch him or herself forward in creating new experience – and a new life.

Summers is the rare clinician and writer who can capture the intimate feel of a difficult and meaningful treatment relationship in evolution. Let us listen in . . .

Introduction

In this chapter, I will describe the type of therapeutic relationship that I have found useful for psychotic and borderline psychotic patients in individual psychotherapy. The emphasis with such patients lies in the type of relationship that evolves between patient and therapist, rather than the insights gained or knowledge provided by the expertise of the therapeutic agent. I will describe the formation of the therapeutic bonds built on responsiveness to the patient's longing for a connection to complete the sense of self. In my view, it is the therapist's responsibility both to adapt to the patient's need and recognize the inherent limitations of the therapeutic connection. It is this delicate balance of responsiveness to the desire for merger and the awareness that the therapeutic environment can never meet the needs as the patient seeks to have them met that defines the unique therapeutic relationship for the characterologically disturbed patient.

I will use the psychotherapeutic process with Martha to illustrate the therapeutic principles to be elucidated. Martha was a pleasant-looking, thin, intense, vivacious, but emotionally labile young woman who talked constantly, as though pouring emotion from her body to relieve herself of an overfilled psyche. A previous bout of therapy had ended in disaster as the therapist became impatient with Martha's constant demands and screamed at her, "You're a borderline! It will take 10 more years for you to get any better!" The therapist then terminated Martha's treatment and recommended she see me. Martha was early for every session, began talking the instant she sat down, and hated the session endings, often feeling she was dismissed abruptly by their cessation. She kept close track of the time and let me know if she felt she had been cheated out of a minute. The sessions were filled with drama. She worked as an inpatient nurse, and every case seemed to involve a crisis requiring her attention. She complained incessantly about her coworkers, whom she felt lacked the necessary commitment and work ethic to do the job properly. When not working, Martha was lonely with little social contact, feeling she did not fit in well with peers. Martha filled the message box on my answering machine with lengthy disquisitions on some work drama that often ended with a melodramatic flair, such as "This is a tough job. Damn. Damn." Her jealousy surfaced early as she made clear her hatred of other patients, especially women. Martha was certain I preferred my easier, more sophisticated patients. She called me frequently to talk between sessions, often concocting what seemed to be a clearly invented problem to justify the phone call.

Her anxiety at seeing other patients escalated to the point of rage reactions at seeing any of them. Most sessions began with outbursts to which I responded by talking to her about the pain of having to share me, and noted that she had never had anyone care who was focused just on her. She felt deeply understood by comments of this type and was often as dramatic in her appreciation and relief as in the rage. The result was momentary calm, but she would invariably explode again in response to another slight. For example, she complained that my fee was prohibiting her from coming more frequently, and that I did not need to have such a "fancy" office with expensive items in it. The fact that she received a reduced fee was of no moment to her. Martha accused me of being so successful I did not care for her and should see fewer patients in order to devote more attention to her. She hated my vacations and proposed that I not go away for periods of 5 or 6 years. Almost every session included caustic criticisms of me for caring more about my wife and family than her and leaving her bereft while I enjoyed other relationships. All of these complaints evolved quickly into vitriolic attacks on me, my values, and my character. Frequently, she began to get up to leave before the session, ending in a fit of rage, but never did so. In her view, I was self-centered, morally corrupt, and devoid of human feeling. Many times she said she was quitting because she "could not take it anymore."

Nonetheless, when her rage abated, Martha openly expressed affection for me, acknowledged that she wanted the life I had, and often used me for guidance. When my comments calmed her, she expressed deep gratitude and a sense of such relief that she felt a momentary beatific peacefulness and love for me. She made efforts to absorb herself into me. She tried wearing the same color clothes I wore. If she detected that I liked a particular type of décor, she grew fond of the same type of interior decorating. If she heard music coming from my office when she was in the waiting room, she felt she should cultivate an interest in that type of music. It was as impossible to draw her attention to her attacks on me when she felt this way as it was to show her the "good side" when she was in a fit of rage. In each case, she dismissed the other side as a fraudulent defense that I should be able to see through.

In the same way, Martha persistently asked my opinion on her conflicts with her coworkers. They complained that her work ethic was too rigid, and that she should not hold others or herself to what they regarded as an impossibly high standard. Martha wanted me to tell her who was right: Were her ethical and work standards too high or were her coworkers lax? In response, I insisted that we explore why she asked and what her view was of her coworkers' attitudes. This response frustrated her, but it was clear that she felt there was nothing wrong with her expectations for a solid day's work and that she asked out of her anxiety that others felt she was "wrong."

Martha could not tolerate being alone, and when not working she was mostly by herself. In fact, the only arena in which she seemed to function was her job. She seemed to organize her life around doing her job as close to perfection as possible. But, even in her work life there were endless problems as she felt her coworkers held themselves to subnormal standards and were casual about malfeasance she considered to be serious. Martha came from a rural environment, and she regarded her coworkers as privileged, more worldly than her, urbane, and possessing normal social lives into which she did not fit. In addition, her work ethic set her apart and, in fact, she felt connected to a piece of the world only in her therapy. Without the structure of job expectations and goals, Martha seemed lost in a sea of confusion, even disorientation, and painful isolation. Her therapy, both with her previous two therapists and me, consumed her life with overwhelming longing and envy-laden rage. When she could not contain the envy and desperation, Martha understood the separations between us as my hatred of her, and she then suspected I was trying to evict her from therapy and talking about her with other patients. Although these paranoid beliefs were intermittent rather than persistent, they were not infrequent.

To afford psychotherapy twice a week, she lived frugally. But, she wanted to come more often and berated my greed that she believed prevented her from doing so. As her connection to me grew, she became

increasingly enraged at the infrequency of the meetings and at my unavail-
ability for immediate response to phone calls. I noted the pain of the
loneliness she felt when without me. Comments of that type caused her to
burst into tears. She felt I understood, but times without me were not easy.
Her anxiety grew until she needed to call me for relief.

The pivotal point occurred when my wife gave birth during the period of
Martha's treatment. She was so enraged that she kept me on the phone
while my wife needed to go to the hospital. Completely unconcerned about
my need to leave, she attacked me viciously for abandoning her. While I
took time from work, she called a colleague of mine to complain, rather
than the person covering my practice. She hated my wife and newborn
child. I talked to her by phone during my few days away from the office,
and during that time she threatened to kill herself. When I returned to my
practice, Martha was in a rage; she berated me for leaving her for my wife
and child, while she suffered, bereft and forgotten by the world. She said
she would not leave the office because it was not 'fair" for her to be thrown
out into the world by herself. I said that she could not tolerate the gap
between us under any circumstances, but this separation was especially
painful because it involved other people. As usual, this comment calmed
her temporarily, but later she went on to say that she could not bear the
separations, and it was clear to both of us that the gaps between sessions
were not tolerable for her. Martha then arranged with her parents to receive
money that would have been her inheritance in order to afford four sessions
a week. This schedule reduced her anxiety between sessions, and she called
less often during the week, but calls continued on weekends. She felt less
abandoned and, as a result, less angry, but she continued to express the
painful feelings that I preferred my family and excluded her from parts of
my life.

What the patient seeks

We will return to the therapeutic process with Martha later in the chapter,
but I believe this brief description of her therapeutic behavior illustrates the
dynamics of people who form psychotic transferences. Such patients feel
painfully helpless and unable to influence others, have only minimal ability
to control their reactions to disappointments and frustrations, and seem to
have great difficulty in handling what for other people are relatively routine
human conflicts and tension. Lacking conviction in their experience renders
the sense of self fragile, and the result is a desperate effort to maintain a
sense of self by a tenacious clinging to others (Summers, 2005, 2007). As we
have seen, when she was alone, Martha was lost, as though she had no
compass for navigating the world. In her isolation, Martha's anxiety often
mounted to the point that she felt she was going to "jump out of her skin."
In an effort to quell her escalating annihilation anxiety, she would call me

either to leave dramatic, lengthy messages, or to have a conversation in which she seemed to want to hold me there to maintain a connection that would not end, as though letting go would return her to a void. Nonetheless, she was continually confronted with the reality of our separateness, and each moment of this realization issued a traumatic reaction that often led her to withdraw and sparked the thought of ending the relationship. This pattern typifies the therapeutic sojourns of patients who oscillate between clinging and the potential loss of self, on the one hand, and painful isolation, on the other.

For that reason, people who possess a fragile self at any given moment will either feel isolated from others or smother them with demands. Many patients tend to gravitate toward one of these poles most of the time, but all have the potential to swing to the alternative side when the predominant mode of interaction becomes too painful. The demanding patient, such as Martha, does not recognize the separate subjectivity of the other, and the withdrawn patient has walled off human contact after failing to erase it. Neither respects the separateness of the other when the effort is made to form a relationship. Therefore, these positions are not opposites, but two sides of the same dynamic. We saw with Martha that she had great trouble forming relationships of any type, but when her longing was evoked by therapeutic understanding she attempted to blur the self–other boundary.

Because there is minimal self-regulating capacity, the patient suffers from a feeling of being broken, as though something is simply not there, and the other is viewed as an opportunity for self-completion. That is why Martha could not tolerate the fact that I had a life apart from her. Others are meaningful or useful only as a potential source of self-completion. So, while the patient's push for an unbounded fusion of psychic states places great strain on the therapist, to fail to respond is to rebuff the only effort the patient can make to form a relationship. Therefore, the patient's insistence on fusion must be welcomed as an opportunity for the development of an affective bond between the pair. However, as mentioned, the same affective contact the patient seeks elicits its opposite, either because her fragile boundaries are threatened or because the awareness of separateness is too painful to bear. Whatever the particular pattern of distancing, the therapeutic process undergoes an oscillation between contact and defense that strains the therapist's emotional resources. Although Martha was demanding of my attention and resources, when her frustration with my failure to meet her needs became unbearable she exploded with a resolve to end our relationship.

Because any relationship without a mingling of boundaries feels empty to such a patient, a special therapeutic sensibility is required. The therapist is called upon to be exceptionally quick, accurate, and penetrating in her responses in order to form an affective synchrony with the patient. It is not only the alacrity of response that helps to form the connection, but also the grasp of the depth of despair and pain. For example, one patient had suffered persistent sexual, physical, and emotional humiliation from her father throughout childhood. Living in continual fear of others, she was easily injured by what she regarded as others' slights and insults. She lived alone physically and emotionally. I commented one day that it seemed as though she lived in a concentration camp, imprisoned by guards watching her every step. She burst into tears and felt for the first time that *she* had become fully aware of how she felt. It was not simply a question of my understanding what she was saying, but that she felt my comment gave words to what she had been feeling all her life but had not been able to articulate. That comment was the first step in the solidification of our relationship.

Unable to understand the value of demarcating a distinction between self and other, such patients put the therapist in the unenviable dilemma of having to either offer himself as a piece of human clay to be molded at will by the patient or face the wrath of a person who has little ability to control his rage reactions to the therapist's separateness. Given the excruciating dilemma in which the therapist finds herself, it is incumbent on her to pay especially close attention to her own reactions to determine the extent to which she is willing to accommodate her behavior to the patient's exigencies. Successful treatment in these situations demands a delicate skill of responsiveness and self-protection. The boundary dilemma is not a peripheral issue here, but the very essence of the therapy (Summers, 1999). Martha sought to become a part of my life beyond the therapeutic relationship, and the fact that I would not allow this to happen elicited venomous rage attacks. Nonetheless, I had to draw the line at the protection of my personal life. The establishment of this boundary drawing only made more imperative my immersion in Martha's emotional life. The art of therapeutic strategy with the patient suffering from a fragile self is to provide an enduring connection without the patient or therapist having to pay the price of losing the sense of self.

As we have seen with Martha, the therapeutic synchrony typically does not end with the close of the session. Not atypically, patients who suffer from psychotic transferences become overwhelmingly anxious between sessions and call the therapist, seeking contact to calm the impending threat to the sense of self. A pattern often develops in which the patient calls in a state of panic, sometimes fearing an imagined conspiracy, and is calmed only upon contact with the therapist. In these situations, the patient seeks continual contact in and out of sessions, sometimes coming four or five times per week and asking for much extra-session communication. Even after we increased the session frequency to four times per week, Martha needed some phone contact to calm the terror of her isolation. Even if the patient feels a deep affective resonance during the hour, that feeling often dissipates as the direct encounter fades into the past. Some patients will lose the connection at the moment of leaving the therapist's office. I have worked with patients who, after considerable opposition and conflict, are able to form a sustaining bond during sessions that they lose almost immediately upon departing my office. For example, one patient felt an emerging despair begin to overtake her the moment she got up to leave, and before she reached the elevator down the hall she had lost the bond with me, and before she exited the building she was consumed with depression. At times she refused to walk out when the time was up. Frequently, she needed to call me in a desperate attempt to regain the feeling of connection before we met again. For a prolonged phase of the therapy she called almost nightly for brief contacts that reassured her that I had her in my mind.

How the therapist responds

Despite the therapist's best efforts to resonate with the patient's experience, the gaps in the relationship force awareness of separateness, as happened with Martha at the end of each session or phone contact. The therapist will not always respond immediately in the way the patient seeks, may have difficulty understanding the patient's meaning, may misunderstand it, or may forget a detail. Or, it may happen that the time taken for the therapist to return the patient's call forces the recognition that the therapist has a separate mind. In a myriad of ways, the therapist unintentionally forces moments of separateness upon the patient. With Martha, the endings of sessions and my life outside of the office were sufficient to elicit the panic of isolation and abandonment. The therapist, of course, will respond to the patient's pain, but the damage is difficult to repair and empathy with the sense of loss may be insufficient to heal the rift. In Martha's case, my recognition of her pain and loneliness usually assuaged her anxiety at the moment, but the sense of threat remained. Sometimes such a patient requires continual reworking of a seemingly minor failure before the relationship is restored. The psychotic patient may interpret the lapse in synchrony in a delusional manner that is little affected by empathy. We saw that Martha made paranoid interpretations of my separate life, although her beliefs were responsive to my understanding of her plight. The intensity of the pain in response to routine gaps in communication taxes the therapist's capacity to manage emotional turmoil and accounts for the volatile nature of the therapeutic relationship.

For her part, the therapist would be operating in an illusory world to believe she could offer the patient the fusion that is sought. In full recognition of this limitation, the therapist can only be sufficiently gratifying for the patient to feel periods of fusion that will be continually dented by the reality of the patient–therapist interaction. The therapist feels the pressure from the patient to be in continual empathic synchrony while bracing for

assaults in response to minor failures. Riding this roller coaster of resonance and disruption is the lot of both parties to the relationship.

The tendency to saturate the relationship with the longing for fusion and
its disappointments means that the patient splits her affective states. When
the patient is in the midst of a strong response, she cannot be reminded of
opposing affects articulated at other times in the same relationship, even if
they appear in the same session. Such opposing emotions will be denied,
and the therapist is mocked for suggesting that they are "real." This principle applies no less to the patient's love than to her hate. While the
therapist should not reject the patient's intense positive feelings, she has a
responsibility not to confuse them with the whole of the relationship any
more than she would mistake the patient's rage for the therapeutic relationship. The patient's injuries can be neither disavowed by the therapist
nor mistaken for the defining feature of the patient–therapist dyad. We saw
this split in emotional life in our discussion of Martha, who avowed only
her feeling of the moment. When she raged at me, she denied ever having
any positive feeling for me, and when she acknowledged her love, the anger
was dismissed as a fake response that I surely should be able to see through.

Because the patient cannot articulate her experience, she does not so
much tell the therapist her most intense feelings as much as *show* them by
inducing them in the therapist. The major Kleinian contribution to the
formation of a relationship with the severely disturbed patient is the insight
that the primary communicative mode for split-off negative parts of the self
is projective identification (e.g., Kernberg, 1975, 1984; Ogden, 1982;
Racker, 1960). The patient induces in the therapist the anger and helplessness with which the patient has been afflicted since childhood. Many
patients use projective identification as a defense and/or mode of communication, but for the patient who forms a psychotic transference the
communication of affects by induction is persistent and the primary means
of affective communication (Kernberg, 1975, 1984; Rosenfeld, 1983; Segal,
1981). Indeed, the rapid oscillation of mood inductions promotes the
confusion between self and other. This tendency to confuse self and other
makes it imperative that the therapist maintains clear boundaries and does
not act on the feelings induced by the patient's affective storms. The
therapist accepts the patient's projections in order to understand the
intensity of the patient's feelings, but it is both an indulgence and a collu-
sion to act as hopeless or rageful as the patient.

The forbearance and willingness to maintain empathic immersion with
someone who is attempting to destroy the self–other boundary requires the
therapist to bear the strain of an emotional roller coaster. The therapist's
ability to sustain this stance across points of connection and the repair of
breaks facilitates a relationship that the patient is able to hold over the
separations. The patient, seeing the therapist survive his attempts to destroy
the developing relationship, begins to register the therapist as a figure with

sustaining interest in him. When the patient can conjure up the image of the therapist as a way to tolerate moments of despair or pain, then the relationship is beginning to form. The therapist's image becomes encoded as a stable presence, and at this point the patient experiences what Winnicott (1965) called an "ego relationship," a connection that endures without physical contact, a step forward from the "id relationship" that had been demanded. This "ego relationship" assuages the pain of isolation.

The development of agency

From these considerations it can be seen that several critical therapeutic benefits accrue to the patient if the therapeutic couple is able to endure this tumultuous relationship. The mixture of gratification and frustration offers the patient a meaningful relationship without the complete fusion that has been demanded through so much of the therapy. The sense of loneliness and abandonment dissipates as the patient is able to maintain the sense of relatedness across separations and frustrations. The patient finds that the therapeutic endeavor has sharply reduced her sense of threat, and it eventually occurs to the patient that this ability to manage affective disturbances has grown without the merger that is sought.

While this achievement is an important step forward, it is not the only clinical payoff. Assuming this burden allows the therapist to nourish an emotional synchrony that gives pride of place to the patient's affective experience, even when the patient is unable to access it. As the patient reacts and the therapist responds, the rhythm of the interaction is directed by the patient's emerging affects, desires, and interests. The patient finds that the therapist will adapt to his experience, even if the patient herself has difficulty articulating it. The fact that the therapist responds consistently to the patient's longings, despite repeated opposition from the defenses, demonstrates to the patient that her affects can achieve a desired response. This awareness is no small realization. Patients whose selves are fragile do not believe that their psychic states matter, that they can have an impact on others. This sense of ineffectiveness impels the longing for fusion. Belief in the ability to penetrate the other's subjectivity constitutes a transformation of the patient's view of her ability to be effective in the interpersonal world and therefore diminishes the desire to appropriate the other.

The patient sees that her subjective states are not only heard but also adapted to, that is, the therapist's behavior is a response to her expressed desires. The therapist's willingness to live through the emotional roller coaster while recognizing the patient's affects and adapting to them demonstrates to the patient that her longings and desires have gained a response in another person. The patient's realization that she has had an impact on the therapist provides the beginnings of a sense of *agency*. As many analytic theorists have argued, the need for effectiveness is a primary human motivation (e.g., Greenberg, 1991; Hendrick, 1942, 1943; White, 1963). The developmental studies of Fonagy et al. (2002) have led these researchers to conclude that the sense of agency originates in the child's recognition that her behavior has elicited an empathic response from the parent. I suggest that an analogous process occurs with psychotic patients who, feeling that they are neither seen nor heard by others, tend to assume they cannot have an impact on people. The violation of this expectation of non-responsiveness by the therapist's empathy gives birth to the patient's belief in her effectiveness, the ability to penetrate the psyche of the other. The growing conviction that "I can do something that gets you to respond to me" is the first sense of agency or, we might say, the birth of the self.

Many years ago I had a patient who literally screamed upon her arrival at the office. I told her that she needed me to know how much distress she was in, and the decibel level of her voice returned to normal. Once the patient knew that I had received and understood her communication that she was in great pain, she had no motive to scream. The value of this experience was not that the patient now "internalized" my soothing, but that she realized she could be *effective*, that is, her message was registered in my psyche. The accumulation of these experiences of efficacy eventually crystallizes in the belief that her affective dispositions, desires, and passions can form the direction of her life. It is this belief in one's potential to be effective by relying on authentic experience that leads to the authorship of one's psyche and one's life.

Once the sense of agency begins to emerge, space is opened for the creation of alternatives to the fusion/withdrawal syndrome. This movement takes place not because the therapist suggests thinking about it, but because the patient finds that she has participated in the establishment of a useful relationship that fell short of its goal to obliterate boundaries. This realization evokes the thought "I can create a relationship that is useful to me even if the other is separate!"

Of equal significance, the engagement between Martha and me around her work ethic involved a new way of using me. Despite the value Martha found in the relationship, it was not lost on her that I had not provided her with the answers she sought, such as whether her work ethic was too stringent, and her frustration with this refusal was evident. What surprised Martha was the value she received from my insistent pursuit of her states. She had never thought that what she felt was a good guide for her conduct. How could it be when she suffered from so much anxiety and depression? Of course my "answers" would be superior. My steadfast attitude that the issue was not to achieve the "right" or "wrong" way but to understand the importance of what she felt, and that her attitude expressed her self most deeply, shifted her view of how I could be helpful to her. It struck Martha that I was being useful as a guide to her buried life and how to use it to live, rather than as a consultant on how to behave. It was no longer necessary that I be absorbed into the same being with her because I could be useful as a separate center of subjectivity. Furthermore, she noted that in learning to rely on herself she was potentially in far greater control of her life than she had been when she sought anxiety relief through fusion. Now Martha recognized that even when she felt such relief it would inevitably fade, only to be reawakened by the next fissure in our relationship. When she was able to have faith in herself, she felt an enduring sense of commitment and control over her destiny.

From agency to selfhood

There were two key therapeutic advances that evolved from this inter-change. First, Martha's attitudinal shift toward others' opinions and emboldened desire to pursue her own path marked a transformation in the way she guided her life. I did not give her the answer she sought, but she came to a realization about herself – that the work ethic she held dearly was critical to who she was. This recognition was the first moment of belief in herself. That session initiated a growing conviction about the way work should be done, and she insisted that her viewpoint was an ethical stance. This change then led to the realization that while her coworkers and she were never going to have an easy relationship, she would hold her stance because she valued her commitment to the highest standards. She put her faith in organizing her life around her ethical beliefs and was willing to pay the price of alienating those who disagreed and thought she was "too rigid." Importantly, now that she was beginning to gain a sense of who she was, Martha found it much easier to reach out to others. Her willingness to embrace her beliefs and values, irrespective of how they were viewed by other people, gave her the feeling that she had a sense of self with which she could encounter others. She knew that most people felt she was too rigid, but such disagreement now had little importance to her. The commitment to her convictions gave her the ability to reach out to others, and for the first time in her adult life Martha began to make friends. She found people who did not consider her "weird" even if they did not share her work ethic. And those who did share her work ethic became close friends, almost kindred spirits.

In this context, Martha began to consider what kind of romantic relationship she wanted. She began to date and eventually found a man who loved her deeply. The couple became devoted to each other, but the most striking feature of the relationship was Martha's insistence that the relationship evolve according to certain principles on which she would not compromise. It was important to her to continue working even after the couple had children. However, Martha was willing to concede many issues to her husband, such as living in a rural environment. After discussing with her husband all the areas of disagreement, she determined the issues on which she was willing to accede to his requests and those on which she felt she could not bend. The negotiation of this relationship was a meeting of the minds. For Martha, this exchange of feelings, values, views, and ideas both affirmed and strengthened her sense of self. She was now in possession of a self. The idea of demanding fusion was now an anathema to her, and she could barely believe she had ever desired such a state. Her self-development obviated and even rendered absurd the notion of obliterating boundaries. Martha held her boundaries proudly in her relationship with both her husband – whom she loved deeply and who was equally devoted to her – and her growing number of friendships.

We can see from the therapeutic process with Martha that the fragile self does not strengthen as a result of direct work on the patient's defects. The relationship that is needed to complete a recovery from psychotic and intermittently psychotic individuals consists of responding to and living through the patient's demands. The therapist has to engage actively the patient's longings and attempt to meet them, while recognizing that they can never be gratified in the way the patient desires. The importance of this forbearance is that it provides, for the patient, the first experience of efficacy. The self is strengthened as the patient's desires gain a response in the other. As the stirrings from the patient's subjectivity become the source of ways of being and relating, the patient is creating a new self that is no longer fragile because it is relied upon to master the routines and challenges of daily life. Ultimately, the process is about the patient's ability to create the self from long-buried affects and desires.

As the patient assumes ownership of her psyche, she gains the awareness that a relationship with imperfections has been useful. The result is a willingness to accept the subjectivity of the other, that is, the patient for the first time realizes that another person, separated by her own experience, can provide a needed relationship. It is this recognition along with the sense of efficacy that obviates the need for clinging and transforms the patient's way of relating to others. Now the patient has the freedom to assess people for their qualities, rather than their ability to gratify the need for fusion. The latter criterion confines the other to either a "good object" who is a source of endless gratification, or a "bad object" who frustrates. But, with a solid sense of self, the patient is free to recognize and assess a wide variety of qualities in other people. Once the self begins to emerge, the ultimate decision about the kind of relationship sought, if any, becomes a free choice. We saw this transformation occur when Martha began to use her deeply held beliefs and values to lead her to or away from people.

Conclusion

Patients are labeled "psychotic" because their minimal sense of self forces delusional expectations of others. The therapeutic goal is not so much to transform the self as for the patient to create a self that had not been brought to fruition, and it is this self that obviates the need for a blurring of self–other boundaries. As we saw with Martha, when the therapeutic relationship eventuates in a strengthened self, the psychotic transference dissipates. The therapeutic relationship heals by finding long-buried affects and desires and facilitating their articulation into ways of being and relating. The belief in spontaneous experience, which should have occurred in the earliest experiences, initiates the ownership of the self. The therapist sees and responds to previously unrealized affective dispositions and nascent interests. This therapeutic "gaze" makes real the patient's subjectivity and originates its becoming a self. The patient then is able to create the self that was always there in *status nascendu*. Once the therapeutic relationship uncovers and brings to fruition the patient's potential for being, the self is an enduring reality that can be relied on for a lifetime.

References

Fonagy, P., Gergely, G., Jurist, E., and Target, M. (2002). *Affect Regulation, Mentalization, and the Development of the Self.* New York: Other Press.

Greenberg, J. (1991). *Oedipus and Beyond.* Cambridge, MA: Harvard University Press.

Hendrick, I. (1942). Instinct and the ego during infancy. *Psychoanalysis Quarterly*, 11: 33–58.

Hendrick, I. (1943). Work and the pleasure principle. *Psychoanalysis Quarterly*, 12: 311–329.

Kernberg, O. (1975). *Borderline Conditions and Pathological Narcissism.* New York: Jason Aronson.

Kernberg, O. (1984). *Severe Personality Disorders.* New Haven, CT: Yale University Press.

Ogden, T. (1982). *Projective Identification and Psychoanalytic Technique.* New York: Jason Aronson.

Racker, H. (1960). *Transference and Countertransference.* New York: International Universities Press.

Rosenfeld, H. (1983). Primitive object relations and mechanisms. *International Journal of Psycho-Analysis*, 64: 261–267.

Segal, H. (1981). *The Work of Hannah Segal.* New York: Jason Aronson.

Summers, F. (1999). Transitional space and psychoanalytic boundaries. *Psychoanalytic Psychology*, 16: 3–20.

Summers, F. (2005). *Self Creation: Psychoanalytic Therapy and the Art of the Possible.* Hillsdale, NJ: Analytic Press.

Summers, F. (2007). When one and one makes one . . . well, almost. *Contemporary Psychoanalysis*, 43: 638–665.

White, R. (1963). Ego and reality in psychoanalytic theory. *Psychological Issues*, Monograph 11, Vol. 3, No. 3. New York: International Universities Press.

Winnicott, D.W. (1965). The capacity to be alone. In *Maturational Processes and the Facilitating Environment* (pp. 29–36). New York: International Universities Press.

Chapter 6

Sustaining relationships in milieu treatment: a corollary to Summers

Julie Kipp

Editors' Introduction: Building on the previous chapters, Julie Kipp broadens the scope of this volume to show how milieu treatment, in contrast with individual work, can help to strengthen patients on their paths to recovery and help them resume their place in society. Kipp reminds us of the high percentage of patients with psychosis who are treated in milieu settings, and offers a specific pragmatic guide for how to structure a psychodynamic therapeutic milieu.

Dr. Kipp then re-addresses Frank Summer's case of Martha in light of how this patient might additionally be helped via milieu treatment. Here she draws on many of Summer's key points and illustrates how milieu experiences offer, in fact, "depth" experiences of the same kind of range and intensity that individual relationships can provide. She asserts that it is because of the variety of potential therapeutic relationships available to any one given patient – from other staff or other patients – that any given psychotic patient may find the kind of engagement that will make meaningful recovery possible.

Introduction

Many people with serious mental illness are not treated in the private practices of gifted psychotherapists like Frank Summers, but are more often found in milieu programs of public or private social service agencies. Workers in such settings may not have been exposed to psychodynamic principles of treatment for serious psychiatric problems, or may assume that such an approach is only applicable in individual work, and perhaps then only if the treatment is several times weekly. However, the majority of clients will never have such in-depth individual work available to them. How can these valuable principles of treatment be applied in the actual settings in which the majority of clients are seen?

Milieu programs are settings where clients live or attend regularly, and which offer a daily structure of activities and/or treatment. It should be noted that in the United States the services available for treating mental illness differ a great deal according to the state in which a person resides, as each state administers its own services, with varying commitment and funding for treatment of its mentally ill citizens. A webpage of SAMHSA (Substance Abuse and Mental Health Service Administration of the United States Department of Health and Human Services) confirms that ". . . State mental health systems vary widely" and that ". . . each State mental health agency has its own unique State laws and regulations regarding who it serves, its priority populations, and . . . other variables that impact the number of mental health consumers" (SAMHSA, 2004). However, outpatient milieu programs are utilized in most state mental health systems, again with great variance. As stated in an article on the website of SAMHSA, referring to services for the mentally ill:

> Ambulatory community support services vary widely across the country, but most public services include some type of daytime program. These programs are among the most difficult to define . . . in part because several different types of activities (and levels of care) are sometimes provided within a single program and in part because the use of labels, such as day hospital or clubhouse, has not been standardized. Other programs include vocational rehabilitation, supported employment and case-management.
>
> (Dickey et al., 1999: Ch. 4, sec. 5)

There is little overall information on the treatment provided in such programs across the country. A recent study by this author (Kipp, 2005) explored several aspects of treatment in milieu programs, but there has not been a great deal of research directed toward cataloging and differentiating these forms of treatment, and much less toward assessing the actual services offered or the outcome success rates.

Although there is a lack of solid information describing these programs, or the approaches and philosophies of treatment that they employ, it is probably true that psychodynamic approaches are not in common use. In this author's (Kipp 2005) study of milieu programs, a psychodynamic approach was not present in many programs interviewed. Historically, however, there is a strong tradition of a psychodynamic approach to milieu treatment. In this corollary to Dr. Summers' inspiring chapter (Chapter 5), I will first offer a brief primer on therapeutic community, which is a modality of psychodynamically informed milieu work, and then evaluate how Summers' ideas can contribute to such settings.

In current usage in the United States, the phrase "therapeutic community" has come to apply only to a model of milieu treatment of substance abuse, the so-called "TC." However, the original therapeutic communities treated people with mental illness. These were developed in military hospitals during World War II, first in Great Britain and then in the United States. In the early stages, many of the soldiers in treatment were men incapable of serving in the war effort due to personality disorder or anxiety. Later in the war, therapeutic community was utilized in the treatment of what we now term post-traumatic stress disorder, especially as experienced by soldiers who had spent years brutalized as prisoners of war. As noted by Harrison (2000) and Manning (1989) in reference to the history of the therapeutic community, psychoanalysis was one of the major influences in its development, through the participation of Tavistock Clinic-trained psychiatrists, such as W. R. Bion, who were recruited into the war effort. Other influences were the social psychology of Kurt Lewin, and the newly developing field of group psychotherapy, especially as represented by S. F. Foulkes. Additionally, Maxwell Jones, one of the original innovators, became the most well known and energetic voice of therapeutic community in the decades after World War II.

What is therapeutic community?

Briefly, there are eight defining features of the therapeutic community, based on this author's review of the literature (Kipp, 2005). The first four have actually become quite common in many milieu settings, but the other four are less frequently in use and indicate how therapeutic community differs from other forms of milieu treatment.

1   *Patients can help one another*. Perhaps the most important principle of the therapeutic community, and the most radical concept when first set forth in the British military hospitals of World War II, is the idea that patients can help one another, and that this can be as important as professional help. As Jones (1959) notes:

> The therapeutic community is *distinctive* among other comparable treatment centers in the way the institution's total resources, both staff and patients, are self-consciously pooled in furthering treatment. This implies above all a change in the usual status of patients. In collaboration with the staff, they now become active participants in the therapy of other patients, and in other aspects of overall hospital work – in contrast to their relatively more passive recipient role in conventional treatment regimes.
>
> (p. 200, Jones' italics)

2   *Flattened hierarchy*. Related to the first concept is the idea of a flattened hierarchy among the staff. The medical doctor is no longer considered the patriarchal authority. Instead, all members of the staff are recognized for making an important contribution, each having a unique perspective on the treatment. Robert Rapoport, who researched Maxwell Jones' Belmont Hospital Social Rehabilitation Unit in the late

1950s, reported that "democratization" was one of four themes that defined therapeutic community (Rapoport, 1960).

These first two features of therapeutic community were nothing less than revolutionary when introduced in the hierarchical medical and military settings in the 1940s. However, in contemporary settings it is now common to see patient support groups and team approaches in all kinds of medical settings, and these ideas are no longer so radical, nor so specific, to the therapeutic community. Following are two more original features of the therapeutic community that have become common in milieu programs.

3   *The community meeting.* The early therapeutic communities discovered the use of large groups as a cornerstone of the treatment (Jones, 1953; Bion, 1946/1996). Contemporary milieu programs often include some sort of regular meeting of all clients and staff (Kipp, 2005), although such a meeting is often only used as a sort of bulletin board of announcements and scheduling. In the tradition of the large therapy group, staff in some programs take the meeting further and deeper by considering the community meeting as a place for members to process their feelings and responses to events in the community.

4   *The provision of learning experiences (Clark, 1964) or the living-learning situation (Jones, 1968).* A last aspect of therapeutic community practice that remains in general use is the provision of learning experiences. Although this ideal can be seen as a significant advancement on a completely medical model of treating mental illness, it has currently become quite commonplace. Contemporary milieu programs usually provide a schedule of opportunities for varying kinds of learning, such as "coping skills" groups, medication education groups, as well as current events or music groups or trips. Even lighter activities, like a Bingo group, provide a learning opportunity for severely under-socialized clients to begin to take part in limited, structured interaction with others.

These first four aspects of the original and innovative therapeutic community[1] have become integral to good milieu practice, but workers can certainly expand upon them. In the case of the ideal of patients helping each other, it is easy to find evidence of this in any program, and it can be underscored by expressions of formal appreciation, like a regular time to give verbal "gold stars" for kind deeds. Clients themselves can also lead regular activity and educational groups, with the support of a weekly group leaders' workshop, in which they get training in group skills from staff. This practice may need defending to governing bodies who question paying for client-run activities, but group participants clearly benefit from having access to more groups than could be led by staff only, from seeing their peers in positions of prestige, and from learning leadership skills through running groups themselves. As for the community meeting, if the tradition has become ossified into just a bulletin board – perhaps with the addition of a few oft-repeated complaints that draw groans from the rest of the members – the therapeutic potential of the meeting can be enhanced. Staff can take a group-dynamic approach by, for example, asking about clients' feelings about a recent event in the milieu, such as the departure of a staff member, or an argument between clients that was witnessed by others. In addition, when clients seem to be only expressing predictable and compliant views in the meeting, the leader of the meeting can reach for unpopular feelings. Clients with borderline pathology are especially welcome when trying to heighten the emotional honesty of community meetings, since their dramatic, extreme statements often enliven the discussion, which may tend to be bogged down by the more compliant, regressed clients.

There are four other aspects of milieu work that define the therapeutic community and may be less common in milieu settings today.

5   *Openness of communication or freeing of communications (Clark, 1964).*
    The importance of openness of communication is frequently expressed in milieu programs, and clients are usually encouraged to say what is on their minds, as an obvious step forward in taking more responsibility for their lives. However, the professional mandate for maintaining clients' confidentiality is often considered to be in conflict with this value in the milieu setting (Kipp, 2005). This has become a serious obstacle to the therapeutic potential of milieu programs, in this author's opinion. Certainly, an individual client's wishes should be respected when it comes to revealing information to the community, but there should be a middle ground that recognizes the reality that all members, both staff and clients, give up some privacy by coming into the community. It is unavoidable that numerous personal facts are well known just by being together on a daily basis. In the therapeutic community, the supreme confidentiality of the individual client is as misplaced as the outdated ideal of the blank slate therapist.
    For example, the staff of some programs feel that they cannot report to the community when a client is in the hospital or has left the program, although the client's absence is obvious and worrisome to peers. Remaining clients may feel that "people just disappear around here," making the milieu less of a safe place. A more sophisticated approach allows for staff to share some information, without revealing too much. For example, it is quite possible to report in community meeting on which clients are hospitalized, and whether psychiatrically or medically. It would usually be inappropriate to share what psychiatric problems led the client to be hospitalized, but staff can say, "he's almost ready to come back to program," or "she is still struggling

to get better." On the other hand, if a client had decompensated floridly in the middle of the milieu, it would be crucial to discuss the event with the community, hopefully including the client himself when he returned from the hospital.

6   *Analysis of all events (Clark, 1964), or the culture of enquiry (Haigh, 1996)*. Another of the less common features of contemporary milieu work is the idea of analysis of all events, which represents the most obviously psychoanalytic of the therapeutic community principles. Just as in an individual psychotherapeutic treatment, where all thoughts, feelings, and happenings are "grist for the mill," a milieu program becomes a real opportunity for psychodynamic work when staff and clients learn to look at everything as an opportunity for understanding. In a daily program of 50–100 clients there is obviously a lot of grist available for grinding, and there may not be an opportunity to talk about everything. Still, many things can be processed, and an attitude of considering all events and interactions to be worthy of therapeutic understanding contributes greatly to a deepening of the work. A "culture of enquiry" is established, to use the terminology of Tom Main, one of the original British World War II era innovators.

David Clark (1964) has noted that the French psychiatrist Paul Sivadon once remarked:

> . . . that it was good that there was always something wrong in a hospital, since this could be used as the starting-point for joint problem-solving. Even if the community began to reach an efficient and effective state, the new entrants – the new patients with their distressing problems, the new staff with their adjustment difficulties – would provide a constant flow of problems.
>
> (p. 72)

A therapeutic community approach does not value an institutionalized, compliant milieu, but relishes the difficult issues that arise, considering them as the opportunity to "do the work."

7   *The staff support group*. Upholding all the other aspects of therapeutic community is the staff support group (Clark, 1964; Kennard, 1983; Main, 1977), a regular meeting that gives staff an opportunity to explore their own reactions to the work and their conflicts with each other. It is unfortunate that this element of good milieu practice is not more widely used, because programs treating psychiatric illness are often noxious environments for staff. Optimal treatment for clients requires that staff have the opportunity to detoxify and transform the difficult work they do. Staff need to sort out their own reactions to the work on two levels. First there is the level of the staff members' individual personalities, and the naturally occurring conflicts that come

up in any group of people. If conflicts between staff are left unprocessed, they may negatively affect staff working together to treat the clients. On a more serious level, no matter how collegial the relationships between staff, they will be the recipients of multiple and complex projections from clients, which need to be understood or which may result in increasing polarizations and conflicts. When staff have regular time to process their own feelings and their conflicts with each other, their understanding is passed to their work with clients in a healing way. Thus, the work that the staff do on themselves in the staff support group is a crucial part of the treatment of the clients. It is increasingly difficult to find time for this important aspect of therapeutic community in an era where staff are more accountable for providing billable hours of service at all costs.

8   *Change at one level affects the whole.* Underlying all these therapeutic community principles is the social psychology concept that there cannot be change at one level of an organization that does not affect every other level of the organization. An awareness of this fact gives the worker a deeper understanding of daily happenings, and a way to predict potential issues of concern. A change in cleaning service personnel can have as big an impact on the community as a change of director. Tom Main (1977) reported on his discovery of this principle when, as a result of instituting change on his hospital ward, he was having "almost daily rows" with his commanding officer and beginning "to think about Bion's fate" (which had been to be fired under similar circumstances). Then Main ". . . realized (that) the *whole* community, all staff as well as all patients, needed to be viewed as a troubled larger system which needed treatment" (pp. 11–12, his italics). With this holistic view in mind he was able to address concerns from above, which was crucial to the survival of his innovative new form of treatment.

With these concepts in mind we can begin to see that a milieu conducted as a therapeutic community has the potential to be as psychodynamic and healing to people with serious mental illness as the individual work described in Frank Summers' inspiring chapter (Chapter 5), and in other chapters of this volume.

Application of Frank Summers' principles to milieu treatment

I will turn now to Dr. Summers' chapter, which considers the therapeutic potential of the relationship with seriously disturbed patients. His client Martha was working full-time and was not likely to show up at a day treatment program. However, her pathology is severe and not so different from that of many clients who, perhaps with less education and opportunities, have become unable to support themselves and thus are more likely to undergo the repeated hospitalizations that result in referral to milieu programs. Dr. Summers notes that Martha's flamboyant symptomology is one side of a coin of failure of relationship. On the other side is the withdrawn, isolated client. As Summers notes, "The demanding patient, such as Martha, does not recognize the separate subjectivity of the other, and the withdrawn patient has walled off human contact after failing to erase it. Neither respects the separateness of the other." These two poles represent the range of clients in the contemporary milieu program. Although DSM-IV may indicate discrete diagnoses, it may be more useful clinically to consider clients on this scale, with the common denominator being that all have difficulty in forming mutually enhancing relationships.

An increased capacity to relate to others is the true goal of milieu treatment, and the psychodynamic milieu provides an ideal place for the development of a new experience of relationship for clients on both poles of this spectrum. For some clients the therapeutic community may be a more optimal treatment than an individual psychotherapy. The milieu includes more potential relationships, including those with peers as well as with staff, which can help to challenge the isolation of a withdrawn client, or to spread out the demands of a client like Martha. In his treatment of her, Dr. Summers walks an important and fine line between setting boundaries and tolerating quite a lot of intrusion into his personal life. Certainly this is a familiar story to many of us who treat seriously ill individuals in the private practice setting: the necessity of frequent between-session contacts, repeated filling up of the answering machine when even extra contacts are not enough, and the almost psychotic demands for the therapist to be available without consideration for the therapist's other clients or commitments. Dr. Summers' experience of trying to get off the phone with Martha in order to take his wife to the hospital to have their baby is dramatic, but not so far-fetched to those of us doing this work.

In the milieu, intense therapist–client dyads also develop, but there are more resources available to mitigate the difficulties of the relationship and to capitalize on the opportunities of such relationships. A useful debate often takes place between staff in the milieu regarding the "overinvolvement" of a particular staff member with a client, which not only provides reality testing for the therapeutic couple but also allows the time for overinvolvement to evolve into a more helpful relationship.

For example, a young staff member in a milieu program participated in a complicated ritual involving the pseudo-seizures of a client who will be called Nancy. Periodically, Nancy would begin shaking dramatically and become unresponsive, and would need to be laid down on a sofa in a quiet room, at which point the worker and selected peers would hold her hand and ask her name repeatedly to "bring her back." Senior staff were quick to recognize the attention-getting aspects of Nancy's drama, and the inappropriate "treatment" of the condition by the social worker, if it was indeed a medical condition at all. However, the enactment was repeated several times over the course of a couple of months, until Nancy seemed to develop enough trust to let go of the drama and the worker was able to integrate the team's assessment of the situation. If the senior staff had intervened sooner, Nancy might not have developed the trust in her worker that came from the worker's unquestioning acceptance of her drama and her "protocol" for how she needed to be treated to be "brought back." And if the worker had been on her own in the situation, without the support of the team, she might have continued much longer in an unproductive, unreflected-upon re-enactment with Nancy. The therapeutic community principle of flattened hierarchy is implicit in this example, as senior staff did not dictate how the worker should handle the situation, but supported her efforts, while reflecting together with her. Staff support groups, another of the defining characteristics of therapeutic community, provide crucial processing in situations such as this.

This example also illustrates Dr. Summers' point that a disturbed client may not be able to "articulate her experience, she does not so much tell the therapist her most intense feelings as much as *show* them by inducing them in the therapist" (his italics). As time went on, Nancy's continued dramas came to seem like "lies" to the worker, who had to struggle with losing an idealized view of a "good," victimized Nancy. The worker came to see Nancy as dishonest, manipulative, and "bad." Currently, the worker is struggling to bring together the dissociated good and bad views of Nancy. Successful resolution of this struggle will put the worker in a position to help Nancy bring these dissociated self states into consciousness.

The withdrawn client in the milieu

On the other side of the coin, as described by Dr. Summers, is the withdrawn client, who may remain unconnected for long periods of time despite the efforts of motivated workers. For example, Audrey came to a milieu program after a serious suicide attempt, and spent a couple of years of daily sitting on the couch, isolated, with tears periodically running down her cheeks. When asked why she was crying, Audrey would cry out: "I'm never going to heaven!" Evidently she believed this was her punishment for having tried to kill herself. No amount of individual work seemed to get her much further in her understanding of her situation. However, eventually Audrey was encouraged to assist in the kitchen preparing lunch, which she initially did in an overly compliant and passive way. As several years went by she became more active in the kitchen, as well as in groups in program, and left behind her conviction that she was not going to heaven. After several more years, when a staff member left the program, Audrey took on the responsible task of ordering all the food for the program, and dealt with outside vendors in a professional manner, with humor and maturity. She also took her skills out into the larger community and began volunteering at a soup kitchen, with the promise of eventual paid employment.

In this case, the milieu itself provided a titrated opportunity for Audrey to involve herself slowly in a relationship, and the relationship was initially to a task rather than to any individual. For this client, individual psycho-therapy, which was part of her treatment, would not have provided a sufficient opportunity alone for her to move from her psychotic and with-drawn depression. Her involvement and success in the task eventually led her to relationships with others, and Audrey is now in a good position to leave the program and return to a life outside the psychiatric system. A psychodynamic understanding of her situation contributed to staff having patience with her process, although it was years before this understanding could be conveyed to her. The milieu itself, rather than the relationship with a worker, was there as a transitional object to be used as she needed, at a rate and intensity of involvement that she chose.

Thus, the milieu setting conducted as a therapeutic community provides for the development of agency. Dr. Summers notes that "the need for effectiveness is a primary human motivation, without a belief in one's ability to have an impact on the environment, there is no sense of owner-ship over one's life." In the milieu Nancy plays out an old drama, or Audrey tentatively inserts herself into a milieu task, but at her own speed, and each finds that staff and the program as a whole can tolerate her unique way of reaching out for contact. The relationship with an individual staff member, or with the setting, or with peers, or a combination of all, provides an initial experience of a relationship that is under the client's control yet subject to all the reality testing that living with people on a daily basis can provide.

Perhaps the most important concept presented by Dr. Summers is his emphasis on the "therapist's responsibility both to adapt to the patient's need and recognize the inherent limitations of the therapeutic connection." There must be a balance, at least eventually, between meeting clients' needs, and even neediness, on the one hand, and, on the other, inevitably dis-appointing the client. In milieu programs, many clients have experienced the depersonalization of institutional settings, and may either have given up on themselves as individuals with hopes and dreams, or have become stuck in unproductive anger at family, the mental health system, or the world, as their only way of maintaining individuality. In the therapeutic community, staff regard both kinds of clients as special, unique, and entitled to much more. As a mentor of this writer used to say: "All the clients are princes and princesses!" The statement holds a consciously implied dual meaning. There is a recognition that some clients are demanding, full of their own needs, "entitled," believing that others should do everything for them. But also in this statement there is a recognition that the solution is to cultivate a milieu in which clients *are* seen as special, each in his or her own way, and are encouraged to ask for special treatment. The milieu will of course fail to meet every expectation, but the revealing of expectations and the inevitable "coming up against reality" create the opportunity for the real work of therapeutic community.

For example, Nikolai began working more and more seriously as an artist after coming to a milieu program. He came to be regarded with respect by clients and staff for his abilities, and many of his paintings were hung around the building. In individual therapy with a worker in the program, he became more flexible, less prickly, and more able to empathize with peers. He regarded his painting as an important part of his recovery. However, as time went on, Nikolai's paintings, supplies, and easels took up more and more space in the milieu room. He was given a large closet in which to store artwork and supplies, although many other clients did not even have access to one of the few small lockers. Soon, however, the closet filled up and Nikolai's corner of the milieu room began spreading again. The program coordinator confronted Nikolai, and he quickly returned to his prickly self. He questioned the coordinator's authority, accused the coordinator of trying to take his therapy away from him, and stated that since art helped him he deserved the space. In truth, this situation remains in flux at the time of this writing. The reality of not owning the space he uses in the program may ideally propel Nikolai into a potential next step in recovery: taking himself more seriously as an artist and finding studio space for himself. In any case, Nikolai has realized, and has brought to his individual sessions, how his lifelong difficulties with authority spilled over in his hostile response to the coordinator's request that he clean up his space. He has been able to benefit both from his status as "special" and also from reality's inevitable blows to his specialness.

Conclusion

In conclusion, I believe that the work of experienced therapists/writers on individual treatment of serious psychiatric illness has not always been translated to the real world settings in which people with mental illness are seen. In this chapter I have tried to show how sophisticated concepts of individual treatment, as seen in the previous chapter by Frank Summers, can be applied to the commonplace milieu settings that treat large numbers of the seriously mentally ill in the United States.

Psychodynamic treatment, whether delivered individually or in a milieu setting, has much to offer clients with serious mental illness. It should be noted that none of us have complete control of the treatment that is available to a specific client. We may accept into our private practices those clients whom we believe would be better served by the multiple opportunities for relationship in a milieu program, but the client refuses to consider going "into the mental health system," or there are no programs available. On the other hand, we may encounter clients in a milieu setting who could benefit from an intensive individual psychotherapy, perhaps especially clients who have other supportive relationships in their lives. But there may be no available psychotherapists willing or able to treat serious mental illness, or no psychotherapists able to accept the very, very reduced rate that the client may be able to afford.

In practice we may not have the ideal treatment available. However, a psychodynamic approach and understanding can be applied to milieu work, especially as outlined in the therapeutic community, as well as it can in individual work. The goal of creating a relationship where a client can begin, as Summers writes, "to create the self that was always there in *status nascendu,*" is the same.

Note

1 These features are also shared by the clubhouse model initiated by Fountain House in New York City in 1948, which is somewhat later than the first therapeutic communities in Great Britain. In contrast to the therapeutic community, the clubhouse model does not consider its mission as providing treatment, and takes the anti-hierarchical and self-help values much further. The clubhouse model has been very influential in American milieu programs.

References

Bion, W. (1946/1996). The leaderless group project. *Therapeutic Communities: The International Journal for Therapeutic and Supportive Organizations*, 17: 87–91.

Clark, D. (1964). *Administrative Therapy: The Role of the Doctor in the Therapeutic Community*. London: Tavistock Publications.

Dickey, B., Beecham, J., Latimer, E., and Leff, H. (1999). Community support – the Evaluation Center @ hsri (Human Services Research Institute) toolkit: Estimating per unit treatment costs for mental health and substance abuse programs. Retrieved March 20, 2004, from http://www.mentalhealth.samhsa.gov/cmhs/CommunitySupport/research/toolkits/pn37toc.asp

Haigh, R. (1996). The matrix in the milieu: The ghost in the machine. *ATC Windsor Conference*. Retrieved February 1, 2003, from http://www.winterbourne.demon.co.uk/wtc/papers/ghost.htm

Harrison, T. (2000). *Bion, Rickman, Foulkes and the Northfield Experiments: Advancing on a Different Front* (Vol. 5). Philadelphia: Jessica Kingsley.

Jones, M. (1953). *The Therapeutic Community: A New Treatment Method in Psychiatry*. New York: Basic Books.

Jones, M. (1959). Toward a clarification of the therapeutic community concept. *British Journal of Medical Psychology*, 32: 200–205.

Jones, M. (1968). *Beyond the Therapeutic Community: Social Learning and Social Psychiatry*. New Haven, CT: Yale University Press.

Kennard, D. (1983). *An Introduction to Therapeutic Communities* (Vol. 1). Philadelphia: Jessica Kingsley.

Kipp, J. (2005). *An Exploration of the Prevalence of Therapeutic Community as a Contemporary Treatment Modality for People with Psychiatric Illness in the United States*. New York: New York University.

Main, T. (1977). The concept of the therapeutic community: Variations and vicissitudes. *Group Analysis*, 10: S2–S16.

Manning, N. (1989). *The Therapeutic Community Movement: Charisma and Routinization*. New York: Routledge.

Rapoport, R. (1960). *Community as Doctor: New Perspectives on a Therapeutic Community*. Springfield, IL: Charles C. Thomas.

SAMHSA (2004). *Uniform Reporting System (URS) Data Output Tables*. Retrieved June 13, 2007, from http://mentalhealth.samhsa.gov/cmhs/MentalHealthStatistics/about_urs2002.asp

The process of therapeutic change: trauma, dissociation, and therapeutic symbiosis

Brian Koehler

Editors' Introduction: In an extraordinary and detailed recount of a moment-to-moment psychoanalytic treatment with a thought-disordered, paranoid, schizoid man with overwhelming, yet blocked, needs and murderous feelings, Brian Koehler takes us into the chaotic world of what makes for change in the most disturbed of patients. In navigating the storms of psychosis, Koehler shows us the details of how one regains one's balance when psychotic storms flood the main deck and knock the patient and therapist off their feet.

Here the terror of annihilation takes center stage. Koehler asserts that it is only when the patient undergoes a kind of melding with the therapist, a "therapeutic symbiosis," that a stronger, more individuated self can emerge for the patient. Yet, some patients will fight to the death to avoid this merged connection they so desperately need, want, and fear because it feels to them that the symbiosis will rob them of what little sense of self they still possess.

Drawing on the theoretical and technical advice of Harold Searles and Gaetano Benedetii, Koehler takes on the most difficult of difficult patients, the most terrifying of clinical situations. He lets us know that one cannot hope to help patients tolerate unbearable affects unless one is prepared to experience and tolerate them in oneself.

Introduction: why a relational psychotherapy of psychosis?

This chapter describes the mechanism of therapeutic change in the psychoanalytic psychotherapy of a patient with a chronic mental illness characterized by prominent positive and negative symptomatology. The central core of this chapter is the overriding importance of the relationship, and primarily its establishment and vicissitudes, in the change process. Psychotic disorders are reflective of disturbances in the capacity to establish duality and autonomy, and this results in associated terrifying fears of self-loss.

Why engage with the struggle to formulate a psychotherapeutic-psychoanalytic approach that might be mutative in the schizophrenias if psychopharmacology is considered the "gold standard" and first line treatment approach? Goldstein (2003) noted: "One of the most striking features of modern medicines is how often they fail to work. Even when they do work, they are often associated with serious adverse reactions" (p. 553). Sullivan et al. (2006) noted that although many persons diagnosed with schizophrenia benefit from long-term pharmacotherapy:

> ... the benefits of antipsychotic treatment are inconsistent, incomplete, and often countered by significant side effects, relatively rare life-threatening conditions (e.g., agranulocytosis, sudden cardiac death), side effects associated with long-term morbidity (e.g., tardive dyskinesia, increased body mass, impaired glucose metabolism), and subjectively unpleasant states associated with nonadherence (e.g., akathisia). Although most individuals respond to treatment, poor or partial response is common, and many patients require trials of multiple medications.
>
> (p. 50)

There is also the question of tardive or "withdrawal" psychosis, which may emerge after the person discontinues his or her antipsychotic medications (Jones, 1995). Thus, it behooves us to develop effective psychosocially based interventions to augment or, in some cases, substitute for antipsychotic agents. Thankfully, we are seeing the emergence of effective psychosocial therapies in the field of schizophrenia research (Swartz, Lauriello, and Drake, 2006).

In psychodynamic therapy the therapeutic partners are on more level playing fields and very close attention is given to the relational and emotional processes occurring between and within the therapeutic partners. This viewpoint is partly based on a theory of etiopathogenesis, which privileges developmental psychobiological, sociocultural, and relational processes as significant to the development of psychotic symptoms, particularly the personal and relational processes involved in identity formation, self-esteem, and affect regulation.

The emphasis placed on unconscious mental processes, including internalized relational configurations imbued with strong affects, and transference–countertransference processes is what often distinguishes psychodynamic from other forms of psychosocial therapies. New York University neuroscientist Joseph LeDoux (see Margulis and Punset, 2007) notes that when it comes to processes of self-defense, the unconscious plays a far greater role than conscious processes, despite what many university psychology programs teach their students.

The case of Joseph

Joseph has been diagnosed with severe paranoid schizophrenia for over 30 years. Despite saturation of his dopamine, serotonin, and other receptors with numerous first- and second-generation antipsychotic agents, which has left him with tardive dyskinesia, and despite years of intensive psychotherapy, he has continued to experience ongoing persecutory and grandiose delusions, auditory, visual, and tactile hallucinations, and excessive self-referential thinking involving social rejection and persecution. He experiences his body as being colonized, mutilated, taken over, and controlled by numerous persecutors. He feels that the latter have literally taken up residence within his psyche and body. It is as if his very brain and psyche have turned against him. It is my feeling that, for him, this has relational and transferential roots in his developmental and social experiences.

After spending countless hours in individual psychotherapy with Joseph, I believe that at some level he "needs" these experiences, that is, that they provide him with some form of resonance that *he exists*. They give him reason to be angry and to blame others for his intolerable sense of himself as a "failed" and worthless human being.

Of note, there was a period in his therapy in which his delusions all but disappeared. This occurred at a time when he was given a large sum of money and no longer felt socially marginalized or inferior to others. As soon as his money was spent, however, he reverted back to his delusions and hallucinations. In this experience, one could see the close connection between self-esteem and paranoia. Joseph has strong feelings of envy of others who have more than he does, economically and socially. Moreover, social indifference seems murderous to him. Joseph is enraged that others, whom he believes are envious of him, rob his strength and body parts, as well as shamefully transform his body into that of a woman or transvestite. During these experiences he feels himself to be developing breasts and hips like a woman.

Interestingly, a practical approach to this delusion, such as encouraging Joseph to tape measure his chest before and after the experience, only leads him to become enraged at the implied disbelief in his experiences. He believes that he is continuously being raped by these persecutors. If I do not acknowledge the actual, literal quality of these experiences, Joseph becomes furious at me for implying that he is quite mad.

After about 8 years of intensive psychotherapy, which has, in fairness, resulted in some positive changes in his life, including abstinence from crack abuse and being able to avert homelessness, as well as being able to tolerate a greater degree of emotional closeness, Joseph had entered a stage of strong psychotic transference.

Psychotic transference is sometimes necessary

Joseph has often accused me of various negative things, such as humiliating him, trying to murder him because of my supposed envy, murdering his beloved teacher from 30 years ago, and murdering his father (of which he also believes he is guilty). The day before his father died, Joseph threatened him with violence, which presumably connects with his guilt feelings.

Joseph recently told me that he was planning to kill me and detailed how he would carry this out, such as by stabbing me in the back through the heart after I left the office at night. I think that in his mind this would prove that he is a "man's man" like his father and not the weak, helpless, powerless, dependent child that he often feels. Also, Joseph states that if he cannot bring himself to kill me, he will hire someone else to do it for him. It is noteworthy that Joseph feels metaphorically "stabbed in the back" by me, as he did by his father, partly because I have indicated to him that his delusional and hallucinatory experiences are reflective of past traumas that are held in memory and still continue to persecute, haunt, and humiliate him. In this vein, Joseph cannot accept symbolic interpretations of his concrete experiences. Also, because I am a separate person from him, this feels to him, at times, like an aggressive act on my part.

Joseph experiences human contact, at a very deep level, as murderous to his sense of self. Rosenfeld (see DeMasi, 2001) spoke of a patient who was so lacking a sense of separateness that he felt almost physically penetrated by his analyst; therefore separations felt to him like lacerating bodily occurrences. The emotional atmosphere of the sessions with Joseph continues to be a "kill or be killed" one. He sometimes experiences my empathy of his plight as disingenuous and fake. Meanwhile, I am ashamed to say that this might indeed sometimes be true, as my countertransference fear and hostility can crowd out any of my libidinal, warm feelings. At some point, I think this might be important to convey to Joseph, though at present, at a deeper level, I believe that tenderness induces in him feelings of weakness and vulnerability.

The importance of engaging the patient's symptoms

As Benedetti (1992) points out, it is in the symptoms placed before the therapist that the person's nascent self resides, whereas behind them may reside a persecutory, haunting absence of "self," a state of "negative narcissism." Without this external, hallucinatory substitute, the patient could not perceive himself as existing – hence his resistance to abandoning it. As Benedetti writes:

> So our task is to look for the lost self in the sensorial images which it sets before us, not by interpreting these images for him, but by enriching them with our presence to the point where we give them the consistency of new, positive symbols.

> (p. 7)

In this passage, Benedetti is referring to the need to establish duality with the patient, for it is his belief that intersubjectivity is the root of the self and is, in effect, "antipsychotic."

In Joseph's case, he has created a wall between himself and others that, ironically, is easily breached by the hallucinatory and actual presence of other persons. Paradoxically, I imagine him as being simultaneously overly "thin and thick skinned" – thus, the emotional "kill or be killed" atmosphere. Recently, he has become more able to tolerate emotional closeness, as he wishes us to wear the same kind of medal around our necks as a reminder of our close and enduring connection. This can be viewed as a concrete manifestation of what will be posited as the central therapeutic mechanism of change in the psychotherapy of psychosis – therapeutic symbiosis.

This kind of developmental "achievement" might not be counted as evidence of improvement in quantitative studies of "evidence-based" treatments for the schizophrenias. However, I believe it to be a landmark in Joseph's emotional growth as a person among other persons. One must be careful not to stand in the way of the patient's developing capacity for relatedness or of their individuation. It is in therapeutic symbiosis and then subsequent individuation that the change process occurs.

Individuation

Recently, Joseph stopped coming to his sessions. He would schedule appointments and then repeatedly not show up. I found myself feeling rejected and angry by this. Meanwhile, I encouraged him to continue his sessions. After a month, though, I began to feel defensively relieved that he was dropping out of therapy. However, we have since resumed our twice-weekly sessions and he seems better, despite his ongoing paranoid delusions.

In hindsight, I think the "respite" was good for both of us. I have come to believe that he needed to be able to separate from me without being "thrown out" of treatment. Searles (personal communication) became very interested in the ways analysts keep their patients ill. I think Searles was referring to the situation of the analyst's resistance toward both the patient's eventual separation and individuation as well as the analyst's refusal to allow for the negative transference and the developing therapeutic symbiosis.

In fact, Searles (1979) believed that one of the reasons why psychoanalytic work takes so long was that both analyst and patient defend against the growing emotional closeness between them. My countertransference experience of Joseph has, in the past, evolved into deep feelings of hatred and fear. I felt terrorized by him. We both had mutual feelings of wishing to murder the other. I believe he was treating me the same way that his persecutors treat him – perhaps a case of misery loves company. The wholesale exportation of this murderous internal situation is partly an attempt to deal with his very painful feelings of loneliness.

Rosenfeld (1987) pointed out that a primary reason for the patient's excessive projective identification, often experienced by the psychoanalyst as a violent attack on his mind and person, is that the patient experienced early trauma alone and therefore needs to communicate this to containing and understanding others. Theoretically, I believe that if I can stand up to his onslaught he should be able, through identification, to stand up to his internal persecutors. However, his extreme envy and permeable sense of self with its correlative fears of colonization often prevent him from taking in anything from me.

Nevertheless, I am containing his rage and terror (with the resulting concordant countertransference feelings of counter-hate and terror). We are gradually working toward helping him to see that his persecutory feelings and experiences directly reflect his experience of other persons in his past, as well as in the here and now of the present: that he feels colonized, con-trolled, and annihilated in his contact with others and with me. I think it is crucial to add to this that despite my countertransference hate I do find myself caring about him a great deal, which is a testament to his capacity for inducing positive feelings in others.

More recently, Joseph has become able to accept "gifts" from me, such as an umbrella on a rainy day when he does not have one, or books that he might find interesting, without feeling persecuted or overtly envious. I believe that what has helped Joseph "achieve" this state of mind is my ability to identify with him and to place myself, in vital ways, within the pain of his delusional world – in essence, to meet him on the same "playing field" of his symptoms.

Loneliness and persecutors

Because of his incessant paranoid accusations and externalization of blame, Joseph has managed to cut himself off from almost all relationships. Invariably, friends from his past have stopped returning his phone calls. He has been loosely associated with a psychosocial club in the past, through which he secured temporary employment, but these too resulted in failure. His part-time employment position ended abruptly when he threatened a work colleague for looking down upon him and being hostile toward him. More recently, his psychiatrist and I have tried unsuccessfully to engage him in day treatment.

Meanwhile, at Joseph's request I have conducted infrequent sessions with him outside of the office, and have seen at first hand how his "projections" operate. One day we were sitting in a local cafe, drinking coffee, when Joseph suddenly turned to me and complained bitterly that the two men next to us were giving him contemptuous looks. I glanced at them but as far as I could tell they did not even notice us. Joseph proceeded to tell me that they did not want him in the cafe. I shared my observations, which were different from his, but this did not lead to any abatement of his persecutory anxieties.

The same sequence of events occurred several minutes later as we sat outside. He accused two women walking past us of doing the same thing to him. It seemed to be a projection of Joseph's low self-esteem, self-hatred, and rejection of self. Perhaps this was his anxious attempt to defend against the threat of emerging closeness between us, that is, the terror that closeness will lead to rejection and abandonment, so one had better not trust that such closeness can be trusted.

Social neuroscience research (Lieberman and Eisenberger, 2006) has demonstrated that the same area of the brain, the dorsal anterior cingulate cortex (dACC), which is involved in the mediation of physical pain, also mediates psychic pain, such as the pain of social exclusion and social rejection. Lieberman and Eisenberger noted: "We suggest that because of the role of social attachment in mammals, the social pain system may have piggybacked onto the physical pain system during our evolution" (p. 181).

Joseph's social pain, which hurts as much or more than actual physical pain, seems quite deep. Between his social pain and persecutory delusions, as well as his tardive dyskinesia, Joseph can present a very bizarre appearance that further serves to alienate him from the social-interpersonal world, and therefore from himself as well.

Envy

Many patients who are in poverty and dependent on the meager, dehumanizing, and humiliating financial support from social security disability form a deep hatred for the therapist's social and financial position. Prior to our therapy together, Joseph had been homeless. He would spend his rent money and sell many of his prized belongings to subsidize his crack cocaine use. Eventually, the social system placed him in a single room occupancy (SRO) and appointed a payee to handle his funds. After our therapy together resulted in a protracted period of abstinence from substance abuse, we managed to get back control of his money, placing it squarely in his hands. This worked well for a significant period of time. He later relapsed, however, and engaged in a long spell of periodic crack binges in which he lost a great deal of money and valued possessions.

Over time I began to notice that his crack relapses dovetailed with positive developments in my life, such as my getting married. In addition to relapsing on crack, Joseph was affected by my marriage in other ways. I began wearing a wedding ring at this time, and Joseph, upon noticing this, verbalized his past hope that we would have grown old together as bachelors. This poignant expression of affection for me as well as his expression of deeper feelings of annihilatory loneliness – a key factor in his psychotic symptoms and self-referential paranoia – balance out my countertransference hate towards him, which can at times border on a murderous intensity. At times like these I feel deep empathy for his plight, for his painful feelings of alienation and loneliness.

Bion (1992) suggested that envy plays a strong role in a psychotic person's projections:

> Envy contributes to the belief that external objects are the patient's thought. Since he cannot admit dependence on an external object, he claims (in order ultimately to escape feeling envy) that he is, like the breast that feeds itself, the producer as well as the consumer of that on which he depends for this life.
>
> (p. 120)

Bion (2005, p. 52) also speculated the following: "There is one fundamental experience which I can put in this way: the patient is aware of two very unpleasant experiences – being dependent on something not himself and being all alone, both at the same time."

Early family trauma

Although Joseph's father is deceased, his mother is still alive and he remains quite dependent on her for emotional and financial support. Meanwhile, she "yells" at him that he is not being attacked by others and that he is really doing it to himself. He tells me that his mother thinks I am a "quack" and often asks when he is going to stop seeing me. This situation has also recently changed because Joseph was hospitalized by his psychiatrist. He had experienced increased paranoid delusional thinking, due to moving to a better apartment in a non-SRO building, although this resulted in him losing his connection to a valued female case worker from the SRO placement. With Joseph's permission, I spoke with his mother by phone at this time. As a result of these contacts, his mother became more trusting that I had Joseph's well-being at heart.

His father used to call him a "bum" and that he was "walking up fool's hill." I now feel that in our sessions we do this together. Joseph often describes his father as having been very paranoid and cruel. For example, there was a time in high school when his father forced him to paint the house, causing him to miss a particularly important basketball practice, which resulted in Joseph being dropped from the team. He would never have thought he could have asked his father for an explanatory letter requesting that he be reinstated to his beloved team. Meanwhile, when Joseph suffered various traumas, such as being forced to kiss a boy's penis when he was surrounded by a gang of bullies in the boy's bathroom of his elementary school, or being hit with a board from behind when he was leaving basketball practice, he never felt he could tell his parents because of a fear that he would be blamed for it.

He described a particularly traumatic family experience in which his father discovered he was "stealing" the weekly church offering. Joseph claims that he did so because his father gave him such a small allowance that he had no money to purchase things for himself. The father ordered his son to go into the basement, undress, and then proceeded to whip Joseph's body with a belt that was kept in a bucket of salt water under the kitchen sink. His mother blocked him from running away as he was being whipped.

Joseph attributes his "schizophrenia" (Joseph's word) to have started with this experience of abuse. One can easily see where his symptoms of persecution and colonization and murderous rage had their origin. As I am writing this, I am getting in touch with the terrible pain and heartache he must have felt and wondering what was the pain that drove his father to act like a "slave owner." Scars can run deep and wide across many generations, particularly if the traumas were dissociated and found no valued place in cultural and personal discourse (Davoine and Gaudillière, 2004).

Joseph describes his mother as passive, quiet, and inaccessible. He wished she had been a nurse so she could give him "mental" nursing. He describes himself as a 'latchkey' child who was painfully lonely. His father did not allow talk at dinner, as both parents wanted to relax after a day of hard labor. His mother worked in a factory and his father was a cabdriver. He alternates between idealizing his father and mother and getting in touch with his deep hurt and rage over the way he was neglected and treated.

He has an older brother who he describes as being aggressive and distant. Joseph often depicts his brother as one of the many persecutors who tried to rape and humiliate him. Joseph reports a particularly traumatic childhood experience with his brother in which the latter tied him up with rope and dragged his body out onto the street like a bundle of rubbish. Once, his brother attempted to have sex – anal penetration – with Joseph. The experience was interrupted by their father entering the room to check on what was happening between them.

Recently, Joseph revealed a memory in which he was forced into performing oral sex on a man whom he let into his apartment at a young age when his parents were out for the night. This memory surfaced during a phone session, and afterward Joseph closed the door on any discussion of this memory. I find myself thinking that something really terrible did actually happen to him, though at the same time I find myself wondering if this could be part of his delusional system. There is current research on the role of childhood trauma in the later development of a schizophrenic disorder (Read and Ross, 2003). My own research (Koehler, 2007) confirms the overlap in neuroscience findings between severe mental illness and the effects of psychological and relational trauma on central nervous system structure and function.

Removing more blocks to a therapeutic symbiosis

While on a 1-week vacation during a holiday season, I worked out a schedule of two phone sessions with Joseph. In both sessions he expressed a great deal of murderous rage and envy. There was nothing I could say that he found tolerable. I felt like hanging up the phone and leaving him to his misery, and he actually hung up the phone on me several times. Each time I called him back, despite my wish for a more peaceful vacation, as I was not going to tolerate this as a way for him to respond. Overall, the phone sessions did not get very far. We remained stuck in an impasse. It was the holiday and he was all alone with no one calling him or checking on him except me. I became the container for all of the hate he felt for those who were not there for him. I survived but was left feeling a great deal of hate myself – hatred of him and for those imagined and real others who abandoned him.

I found myself wondering, as has Searles (1979), what is the role of deep hatred in psychotic symptomatology, and also wondering about the importance of allowing oneself to experience deep hatred for a patient one is supposed to be attempting to "cure." Days after our frustrating phone sessions, on New Year's Eve, I found myself thinking about him. I soon spontaneously called Joseph, on what I imagined would be a terribly lonely night for him. After the usual litany of paranoid and hostile accusations directed toward others and me, he poignantly noted that he is so "crazy" that he drives away the very people who wish to protect and care about him. He then thanked me for calling him on the holiday and wished me a Happy New Year! Soon after, I received a call from Joseph's psychiatrist noting his significant improvement – and attributing it to the effects of his antipsychotic medications!

More recently, though, Joseph's psychiatrist again had him hospitalized against his will, and Joseph displaced his rage onto me, even as I was visiting him in hospital. He now has a new psychiatrist who has placed him on three antipsychotic agents, including clozapine (Clozaril). I am aware that there is no research base for doing this, and as time passes I observe his growing waistline. He now has a huge stomach and I worry about his developing a metabolic syndrome.

That said, Joseph informed me that "Snoop Dog" was protecting him. Later I playfully thought to myself, "well if Snoop Dog is on the case, he's in good hands and I am 'outta here'." However, I fully realize, if I were to really be "outta here" at this point in the evolution of the therapeutic symbiosis, it would be, as Searles points out (1965, 1979), a significant loss for both of us.

From therapeutic symbiosis to individuation

Lately, Joseph's frequent phone calls between sessions stopped. Ironically I found myself feeling hurt and abandoned. I understood my own experience within the therapeutic symbiosis and the feelings of loss that had become engaged in the stage of individuation. In the most recent session with Joseph, a startling event occurred that has left me pondering the mystery of the psychotherapeutic work with Joseph, as well as the mystery of the human condition. Out of the blue, Joseph spoke of his father "watching over" him from "the other side." At that precise moment, a photo of two homeless men touching their heads together in friendship and affection, which has been sitting securely on a bookcase in my office for years, came crashing to the ground spontaneously. While I walked over to the photo, Joseph seemed totally unfazed, sensing the presence of a protective figure letting us know that he was, after all, in good hands. It is a strange event to have witnessed, but I have begun to feel relieved that Joseph's life and well-being are not just in my hands. It may be that I experienced a more secure and strengthened sense of self as the therapeutic symbiosis moved forward into this stage of healthy individuation.

Was this "protective force" the internalization of functions of the analyst? Garfield and Dorman, in Chapter 1, have suggested that an ideal-izing self-object experience may be mutative for psychotic patients in intensive psychotherapy and, in many ways, my professional identity was strengthened by my having weathered the storms of intolerable affects while at the same time keeping the therapeutic frame and process intact.

Therapeutic symbiosis works by combating dissociation

Bromberg (2006) has made many significant contributions to psycho-analysis that are relevant in my work with severely mentally ill individuals. He notes that psychological self-continuity plays a central role in human life. When this is threatened, the mind can turn the future into a version of past danger. Bromberg suggests that "future self-continuity is proactively guaranteed by the creation of a dissociative mental structure – an early warning system" (p. 5). The dissociative structure takes as its highest priority the preservation of self-continuity. According to Bromberg, "past trauma is not allowed to enter narrative memory as an authentic part of the past; it is transmuted into affective and body memories in the form of experiences that are beyond relational self-regulation . . ." (p. 5). Dissoci-ation protects the stability and continuity of the self through controlling non-symbolized traumatic affect.

This may explain the chronic nature of Joseph's persecutory delusions. The capacity to tolerate internal conflict and to engage in interpersonal relationships is diminished in those areas of the personality characterized by dissociation. Thus, the therapist's use of words to explain what is going on – interpretation – will not work during times of enactment. Furthermore, interpretation runs the risk of escalating the enactment and the use of dissociation, as it can even feel like an attack to the patient. This highlights the importance of my holding hated parts of Joseph without trying to "push" them back into him. The latter is something that many post-Kleinian psychoanalysts caution us not to do, for this may lead to ever-spiraling counterprojective identifications – enactments – and ultimate impasse.

Searles (1965, 1979) has understood schizophrenic experience to be a defense against intense emotions in a person who has a faltering human identity. He believed that over the course of the analysis each of the patient's symptoms can be discerned to be referable to some early traumatic relationship event. He conjectured that these introjects need to be re-projected upon the analyst during the course of the transference evolution, so that they can be resolved into an increasingly healthy ego of the patient. In particular, psychosomatic symptoms take on transference meanings as the analyst begins to personify part-aspects of significant others. Bodily symptoms and complaints, such as headaches and stomach aches, can be unconscious transference reactions in which the patient is not yet able to experience his contempt and rage toward the therapist, and also can reflect a body-image degree of dependent symbiosis with the therapist. In Joseph's case, he sits and lays on the couch complaining of multiple bodily aches and pains, some of which are related to his tardive dyskinesia and others to persecutory delusional experiences in the transference. For example, he reports feeling that I am pulling at his head, twisting and distorting it, or at the very least sitting idly by, like his mother did, when he is in deep suffering.

Searles (1965, 1979) proposed that it was in the phase of psychotherapy that he and others such as Benedetti (1987) termed *therapeutic symbiosis* (or state of close emotional oneness) between therapeutic partners – which is crucial for all patients, diagnosed with schizophrenia or otherwise – that a process of mutual reconfiguration, reindividuation, and rehumanization is fostered. As Schwartz and Summers noted in Chapter 4, this can occur when the relationship has become strong enough for subjectively common human identity ingredients to come into play in the holding environment of the transference. Joseph and I are engaged in a process of relational negotiation of our sense of likeness and separateness. In this regard, Joseph has commented many times on how we look alike, despite our coming from different racial backgrounds.

Therapeutic action and a different kind of interpretation

The role of interpretation in psychosis psychotherapy is different from the role of interpretation in the therapy of neurosis. Interpretations in the former address the structural needs of the person with schizophrenia: to help the patient discriminate self from non-self, to grasp the boundaries of the self, and to achieve an intrapsychic coherence. Resistance to inter-pretations in psychosis psychotherapy reflects the patient's attempt to survive by means of organizing a psychotic identity in the vacuum of non-existence. Classic interpretations, or "making the unconscious conscious," simply cannot fill the terrible vacuum that exists within patients with schizophrenia. Benedetti (1990) defined the turning point in therapy as occurring when:

> . . . the loss has been compensated for, not only by full participation in the patient's situation but also by the introjection of this patient's image, which allows him, conversely, to introject the therapist as a love object . . .
>
> (p. 7)

Finally, Benedetti (1987) speaks of "therapeutic love" (p. 83), which refers to ". . . our readiness to be with the patient . . . in his dreams, fantasies, and terrifying experiences" (p. 83). This certainly has been my challenge with Joseph.

References

Benedetti, G. (1987). *The Psychotherapy of Schizophrenia*. New York: New York University Press.

Benedetti, G. (1990). *Depression, Psychosis, Schizophrenia*. Unpublished manuscript.

Benedetti, G. (1992). *The Psychotherapy of Psychotic and Schizophrenic Patients and Factors Facilitating This*. Unpublished manuscript.

Bion, W. (1992). *Cogitations: New Extended Edition*. London: Karnac Books.

Bion, W. (2005). *The Italian Seminars*. London: Karnac Books.

Bromberg, P. (2006). *Awakening the Dreamer: Clinical Journeys*. Mahwah, NJ: Analytic Press.

Davoine, F. and Gaudillière, J.-M. (2004). *History Beyond Trauma*. New York: Other Press.

DeMasi, F. (2001). *Herbert Rosenfeld at Work: The Italian Seminars*. London: Karnac Books.

Goldstein, D. (2003). Pharmacogenetics in the laboratory and the clinic. *New England Journal of Medicine*, 348: 553–556.

Jones, B. (1995). Tardive psychosis. In C. Shriqui and H. Nasrallah (Eds.), *Contemporary Issues in the Treatment of Schizophrenia* (pp. 633–649). Washington, DC: American Psychiatric Press.

Koehler, B. (2007). *The Schizophrenias: Brain, Mind and Culture*. Paper presented at ISPS Norway, Hamar, Norway, February 8, 2007.

Lieberman, M. and Eisenberger, N. (2006). A pain by any other name (rejection, exclusion, ostracism) still hurts the same: The role of dorsal anterior cingulate cortex in social and physical pain. In J. Cacioppo, P. Visser, and C. Pickett (Eds.), *Social Neuroscience: People Thinking About Thinking People* (pp. 167–187). Cambridge, MA: MIT Press.

Margulis, L. and Punset, E. (2007). *Mind, Life, and Universe: Conversations with Great Scientists of our Time*. White River Junction, VT: Sciencewriters.

Read, J. and Ross, C. (2003). Psychological trauma and psychosis. *Journal of the American Academy of Psychoanalysis and Dynamic Psychiatry*, 31: 247–268.

Rosenfeld, H. (1987). *Impasse and Interpretation: Therapeutic and Anti-Therapeutic Factors in the Psychoanalytic Treatment of Psychotic, Borderline, and Neurotic Patient*. London: Tavistock Publications.

Searles, H. (1965). *Collected Papers on Schizophrenia and Related Subjects*. New York: International Universities Press.

Searles, H. (1979). *Countertransference and Related Subjects: Selected Papers*. New York: International Universities Press.

Sullivan, P., Owen, M., O'Donnovan, M., and Freedman, R. (2006). Genetics. In J. Lieberman, T. Scott, and D. Perkins (Eds.), *Textbook of Schizophrenia* (pp. 39–53). Washington, DC: American Psychiatric Publishing.

Swartz, M., Lauriello, J., and Drake, R. (2006). Psychosocial therapies. In J. Lieberman, T. Scott, and D. Perkins (Eds.), *Textbook of Schizophrenia* (pp. 327–340). Washington, DC: American Psychiatric Publishing.

Chapter 8

Technical challenges in the psychoanalytic treatment of psychotic depression

Patricia L. Gibbs

Editors' Introduction: Working with different kinds of psychosis requires different tools. Dr. Gibbs lays out these tools of cure in her detailed approach to working with psychotically depressed patients. In a global sense, she follows in Koehler's footsteps with her emphasis on the restoration of identity via a symbiotically organized experience in therapy, but takes it in a unique direction.

In her treatment of Anita and Mr. C., Gibbs focuses on the skillful management of technical impasses that frequently confront the psychotherapist of psychosis. These are, most notably, transference and countertransference tangles that seem impossible to resolve. Here she points to the key role of dissociation in the impasse, something that Koehler also felt was elemental to the psychoses, and offers insight on how reintegration and cohesive identity can be facilitated through therapeutic symbiosis.

Expanding both Summers' and Koehler's reach, Gibbs describes how, even in psychosis, working with dreams can be an integrative therapeutic activity. In addition, she underscores the importance of providing language for the unarticulated, disconnected experiences of the patient, the necessity of mourning, and the emergence of the "true" self alluded to in previous chapters.

Introduction

Therapeutically engaging a psychotically depressed patient at an affective level is essential, though challenging, because of the typical unconscious fantasies, defense mechanisms, and attachment patterns associated with the condition. The central organizing role of unconscious murderousness in psychotic depression will be examined as it is displayed in clinical vignettes. Dissociation was observed and organized the transference and countertransference for significant portions of the treatments. Addressing transference and countertransference phenomena becomes crucial to successfully navigating the affective storms that inevitably arise in the treatment process. In this regard, the analyst's use of language is particularly important.

The patients that will be described, and the assumptions made in this chapter, reflect an impaired symbiotically organized sense of identity seen in psychotically depressed patients (Arieti, 1974; Jacobson, 1971; Searles, 1979). Freud suggested that some patients never establish a symbiotic relationship with the internalized maternal representation, and thus are autistically and profoundly narcissistic, although even Freud himself was not certain of his thesis (Freud, 1915). The object relations work of many analysts has challenged the notion of the failure of symbiotic attachment in the schizophrenias and psychoses (Klein, 1946). As Koehler's work in Chapter 7 has also shown, psychoanalytic work with psychotic and schizophrenic patients involves the therapeutic use of a symbiotically organized object relationship between analyst and patient. Far from preventing analytic work, use of the symbiotically organized transference facilitates work with psychotic patients (Gibbs, 2004, 2007a, 2007b; Novick and Novick, 1997; Searles, 1979).

The transference and countertransference associated with a symbiotically organized identity will place an enormous burden on the analyst, as murderous rage and hatred are central to this kind of object relations capacity (Eigen, 1986; Gibbs, 2004, 2007a; Joseph, 1982; Searles, 1979). Analytic work, however, with its use of language, provides one of the most powerful means of eventually detoxifying this unconscious murderousness. Psychotically depressed and schizophrenic patients have some common features found in all psychotic persons, hence techniques will be drawn from the literature of work with both types of patients. The analyst's wording and interpretation of the patient's hallucinations, delusions, dreams, and fantasies will be examined in this chapter, with an attempt to specify the clinical day-to-day details of such work.

Preliminary considerations: the epigenetic multi-causal model

A comprehensive multi-causal, epigenetic model points to successful interventions that may or may not directly derive from the etiology of a condition (Jablonka and Lamb, 2005). Conditions considered to be caused primarily by biological or genetic factors may improve after a treatment that has focused on psychological and social interventions. Thus, anxious and aggressive temperaments may be largely caused by neurophysiological abnormalities, and yet may be best remedied by environmental interventions and socialization (Suomi, 1997). Contemporary research provides a growing body of evidence that the psychoses and schizophrenias – even if genetically and neurologically influenced – can be improved with psychoanalytic interventions (Boyer, 2000; Gibbs, 2007b; Gottdiener and Haslam, 2002; Karon and VandenBos, 1981; Pick, 1985; Silver, 1989; Ver Eecke, 2003; Villemoes, 2002).

Therapeutic engagement

Two clinical vignettes will be used to illustrate the technical challenges involved in different aspects of the psychoanalytic treatment of psychotic depression. First, a hallucinating and delusional patient in the early years of a symbiotically organized transference/countertransference will be summarized. Next, a chronically depressed, non-hallucinating patient will be examined. Although both patients are understood to have "psychotic cores" (Eigen, 1986), they represent different clinical pictures requiring differing techniques.[1]

ANITA

Silence in the therapeutic symbiosis of early treatment: words that can be said, and words that cannot be said

Anita was initially seen by the author for some years in a community health clinic and then moved into the author's private practice. When first seen, she was 19, living with her family, and had dropped out of college due to severe depression that included self-mutilation. She was exceptionally bright. The presentation of the psychotic depression was typical as it was associated with a separation from the family of origin and a failed romance.

During the first 2 years of treatment Anita was frequently silent. The sessions consisted of long periods of silence, punctuated by my attempts to put into words her subjective experience of her inner psychic life. I did not wait for her to speak beyond a certain point, knowing she would first have to hear her feelings and thoughts verbalized in the unique mutative situation of the transference before she would be able to initiate articulation of her self (Edgcumbe, 1984; Kavanaugh, 2003; Krystal, 1988).

In the early years of therapy, Anita appeared paranoid, avoided eye contact, and alternated between months of silence and infrequent bursts of verbal expression. For years, she would ring the bell to notify me of her presence in the lobby but would always wait for me to come and let her in rather than entering when the door was buzzed open. In these early years, I believed she wanted me to come and greet her, which was related to her symbiotically organized identity in the transference with me at that time. Years later, after routinely entering the building herself, Anita remarked that she feared contamination from touching the doorknob.

Voices

Anita slowly revealed that she heard "voices," which she reported were always condemning and hateful, often instructing her to stab herself with pins, get drunk, or kill herself. She regularly called between sessions and left messages that she could not recall what happened during the sessions. Occasionally she would say "they are here," and she would call by phone or express worry in the session that if I was alone with "them" I could get hurt. Such expression of concern for the analyst is, sometimes, the patient's unconscious fear of having murdered the analyst.

As will be seen, Anita hearing my voice, both in the session and over the phone, became a crucial aspect of her treatment. I have found that allowing patients who experience extreme amounts of terror and self-persecutory paranoia to have brief phone contact between sessions, and to leave voicemail messages for me, has aided in the establishment of a therapeutic alliance. Such phone contact – outside the bounds of the usual therapeutic frame – reflects the symbiotically organized transference/countertransference, and its use for therapeutic benefit.

Just as Anita walked out of one of the early sessions, clearly terrified, I said, "I'll wait." She returned shortly to say, "How do you know therapy will help me . . . if you don't know . . ." and her voice trailed off. I said: "What is it that I don't know?" There was much silence, and I felt mildly afraid, though aware that it was important to remain calm and not allow myself to be derailed by fear. She said at one point: "Would you leave?" I said it sounded very important for her to know that I would not leave and perhaps that helped us understand why she left – she needed to know if I would leave or stay. She said she was not thinking about that when she left – just that she had to go. I should note that this exchange between us now sounds more organized and coherent than it was because Anita eventually brought her psychosis, with her hallucinations, fully into the transference. She stated bluntly: "Don't look at me." I said "OK" and turned slightly to the side so as not to be looking at her.

I realized that she had come back to the session entirely on her own initiative. She then said, "At first, I thought you were saying that I couldn't do this – that you didn't want me here." I said that her coming back was a way of telling us she must have had other thoughts about this. She then said "Do you feel safe here?" I said "Yes, I do. And you are telling us a safe place is very important." There was much silence between all remarks, and at times, so much so, that these clinical summaries do not capture the vast emptiness and silent chaos of the sessions. She said she did not know what to believe – she could hear me, but she did not know, and again slipped into silence. I was certain that she was having auditory hallucinations – hearing voices at that moment – and I said "Perhaps you are hearing my voice, and other voices as well, and you are telling us how frightening it is to *not* know . . . to *not* be sure . . ." She turned towards me slightly, and smiled – a smile of being understood. Anita's smile is evidence of the minute, though crucially important, organizing effect that my words had just had upon her affect. We both quickly looked away, and sat for several more minutes in silence until the end of the session.

The silences in these kinds of treatments are often laced with fear. With Anita I tried to be calm, and not allow myself to nervously play with my fingers. I focused on my foot, so as not to look at her. I said "Anything that comes to mind will help us. . ." There would usually be much more silence. During such sessions I remembered the pre-therapy work Garry Prouty (2003) describes with schizophrenics (see Chapter 3). Such work often involves an enormous amount of time sitting in silence in the early stages of treatment with a psychotic patient.

After some time, she said, "Am I going to get into trouble here?" There was a regressed and childish quality to her question, and I had the impression that it was her speaking but from somewhere far away, though she sat right in front of me. I said something like: "That thought helps us to know you are afraid of getting into trouble here, that feeling that you will be caught, or thought of as doing something bad." More silence, and then she said: "Will you tell on me?" I moved my fingers ever so slightly, so she could not see this, and felt afraid that she would somehow see me moving or fidgeting anyway. I noticed how important it was to me to not move, and I now have a greater understanding of the terror that had been projected and to which I was responding, frozen into not talking, not moving. The analyst's active engagement of these kinds of countertransference experiences is vitally important in being able to understand and then articulate the patient's terror of their own unconscious murderous feelings. Finally, she said: "I'm ready to go." I said she seemed to be telling us that she felt she would get into trouble if she stayed, yet she was also telling us, just by the fact that she had come here, that it was very important to stay, and know that I would stay. She said, ominously: "I make people leave." I said, trying to sound calm and undeterred: "Yes, that seems part of what you're wondering here – will you be able to make me leave?" She then said rather immediately, and with more affect than at any earlier time: "*Why? Why should it be important?!* None of them like it, they all don't want me to talk . . . I get into trouble . . ."

Engaging the defense of dissociation

At this point I felt that I had heard her indicating that the *they* were *her* (the voices in her head), which I believe was correct. Unfortunately, I did not fully appreciate the extent to which Anita at that point heard the voices as actual separate people, talking to her. This is dissociation at work. Overestimating her sense of a unified cohesive self, then, I mistakenly said: "You're telling us you make trouble for yourself, perhaps." She said, after looking somewhat pained and misunderstood, quietly: "No, they don't like it." At the end of the session she leaned forward and said "I still don't want you to look at me. It's not safe for me to come here." I said, "I won't look at you. We will have to work to make it safe here."

As Bion (1957) discovered, I have also found that psychotic patients are aware that their hallucinations are different from non-hallucinatory and non-psychotic experience. However small this discrepancy may be in the patient's subjective experience, I have found that technique should be directed, as much as possible, to the patient's awareness of their non-psychotic self (Gutheil and Haven, 1979). The dissociative quality of this patient's presentation was not to the extent that I ever witnessed the emergence of an alter-personality, although I believe my orientation to address Anita as a whole person composed of different aspects of herself, and "voices" within her, certainly influenced how I understood her. Anita would report not remembering something said in the sessions, or how or when she left the sessions. She would report what the voices said, and the visions she saw. There was profound confusion about the reality of her experience, that is: "Did seeing [her husband] come behind her at the window mean someone was going to die – someone did die in the neighborhood!" Even when I had the faint notion that someone other than Anita was speaking, I made it my technical business to address and relate to Anita. Dissociation was seen as a central defense that Anita used in an attempt to protect herself from her psychotic depression and its murderous hatred and rage.

It is important to distinguish the term "dissociation" from other processes such as splitting or repression. I am using this term in part because of the memory lapses seen in the sessions (Putnam, 1989; Waiess, 2006). This kind of mental activity, which results in a discontinuity of psychic processing, functions differently from splitting. Whereas splitting separates the "endangered" from the "endangering" and infuses the analytic relationship with either sadistic or masochistic qualities, dissociation works in the service of maintaining object ties to others, and to the self, in such a way that patients are initially experienced as sympathetic and non-provocative by others. Rage was not verbally expressed for some time with both of the patients described here. This directs the analyst toward considering that dissociation rather than splitting was operative.

My observations agree with Putnam's (1989) assessment that contemporary references to dissociation are on the hysterical continuum and indicate a healthier defensive style than that seen when splitting is the predominate defense. On the other hand, the use of repression indicates a healthier adaptation than the patients described here exhibited. Repression is not usually associated with memory alterations to the extent that the patient's identity and mental functioning are fragmented or temporarily lost in the analytic sessions, nor is it typically associated with dissociated experiences in the countertransference. Conceptualizing dissociation as a major defensive style in both cases came in hindsight, as the work developed with these patients. This conceptualization shaped technique in terms of delaying interpretations of aggression and avoiding a confrontational stance during the early years of working in the symbiotically organized transference. Interpreting aggression and oedipal conflicts will be seen in the later years of Mr. C.'s analysis, as he approached termination.

MR. C.

When love goes wrong: the reality of the oedipal crisis and the "murder" of Mr. C.

Although Mr. C. did not have hallucinations or delusions, and was consistently able to work throughout his four times per week analysis on the couch, he did exhibit thought disorder characterized by thought blocking and derailment. He initially reported having "the ideal childhood," although within a few years of analytic work he began recalling severe physical abuse from his father. Dissociative features were pronounced in Mr. C. He would often recall traumatic memories of abuse while on the couch, only to say minutes later: "I can't remember what I just said . . . did you say something? . . . What were we talking about?" Severe fatigue, escape into sleep, social isolation, and underachievement were all aspects of Mr. C.'s depression. Although extremely bright, Mr. C. had a blue-collar job that paid minimally. Most of his time was spent working as a freelance writer, and occasionally attending workshops or university classes. He did sell some of his writing, but suffered months and sometimes years of crippling writer's block.

He consistently reported a very close relationship with his mother, and was unable to fully establish a long-term relationship with a woman until after his mother's death. His symbiotically organized relationship with both of his parents was reflected in the transference. Three dreams will be used to illuminate the death of the symbiotically organized self/other in Mr. C.'s transference, and the mourning associated with the termination of his treatment. This hard work of mourning involves giving up unconscious omnipotence associated with the denial of reality and separateness (Klein, 1946). Done at an intensely charged affective level, it is the final work to be done in the patient's termination of treatment. Reports of patients feeling they will die, or someone close to them will die, or both, are common during this phase of treatment, and speak to the affective reality of the transference.

Mr. C.: Dream 1

My mother came into the room, but she was dead. I knew she was dead when I saw her, her eyes were closed, though she was walking and talking. It was the living room of their old house – (his mother and father's) *– and she walked* *over and sat down on the couch. She said "Oh, Hi" as she walked past me, before she sat down.*

Once he had remembered the dream, he said he felt more like coming to the session, being glad that he would have something to talk about. The patient's "not-remembering," and saying that he has "nothing – nothing to talk about," his remarks about his difficulty writing, and then his relief associated with remembering occurred throughout the analysis. This type of dissociative process seemed to serve a protective function for Mr. C. It allowed him to gradually work through and mourn the many unconscious and partly conscious affective experiences of murderousness, hate, and destructiveness, and to slowly face his memories of abuse.

Three days after the patient reported the above dream, he said he remembered something else, although he did not think that it was particularly relevant. "The color of the coat my mother was wearing in the dream was beige, the same color of the plate in that other dream I had with my mother in it," he said. The dream below, to which the patient referred, occurred about 4 months prior to the one above. It had been an important dream to the patient, with him returning to it frequently.

The technical challenge of bearing loss and sadness

Mr. C.: Dream 2: the oedipal conflict and reality in psychotic depression

I am making a sandwich. My mother is sitting in front of me, and she is sitting alongside of a Black man, who I didn't know. After a while, the patient added: *My Mom and the Black man seem to be mocking me, and laughing at me.* In the next session, the patient said he remembered something else in the dream: *I noticed that the plate I was using was a real plate, a beige colored china plate.*

When I asked for Mr. C.'s thoughts, he said: "It is uncharacteristic of me – I would usually use a paper plate when making a sandwich." He initially said his mother had said nothing he could remember, nothing about the plate, and then he said ". . . Well, she probably would have given me a hard time about it – said something like: "What are you, too good for a paper plate?" At this point Mr. C. had many associations and memories related to being humiliated by his father, as well as stating that he felt guilty about wanting better things than his mother and father had accomplished for themselves. He then said it was clear to him that his mother and the Black man were trying to humiliate him for wanting to improve himself and be successful. "The Black man?" I asked. "That probably is my father, because my Mom would have been ashamed to be with a Black man, and I think she was really ashamed to be with her own husband."

The patient went on to recall many other instances of his mother subtly trying to "keep me in my place," and mocking him for trying to rise above the family's dismal station in life. He recalled that they never had a working shower in the bathroom the entire time they grew up. "Everyone would have to go down to the basement to shower, with no curtain – just an overhead shower head with no stall, no privacy. It was cold," he said.

At this point the patient wondered "is it as simple as me feeling guilty about succeeding, and wanting to surpass my family?" The patient was in the middle of his analysis, and was still underemployed and having difficulty writing. The oedipal dynamics were plain to see: the patient felt guilty about his favored position with his mother, his hate towards his father for his increasing memories of brutal abuse, and his unconscious guilt and murderousness towards himself for wanting to surpass, and leave, both his parents. What he came to see as his mother's complicity in the abuse severely complicated his mourning of his mother's death.

Mr. C. attempted to deal with his past by writing during his analysis. At one point he wrote a gruesome murder story, and read it with much intensity during his sessions. Several months later Mr. C. asked again if I might not have been worried he was writing about something of which he was capable – or, how did I know? – was it something he had really done? The murders in the story became the metaphor for Mr. C.'s rage in the transference for some time, and took on an affective intensity for me, as well, in the countertransference. At times it was difficult for me to trust Mr. C.'s capacity to feel murderous rage in the transference without acting on these strong feelings self-destructively. Similarly, I questioned my ability to contain murderous feelings in the countertransference without enacting these feelings destructively and hindering Mr. C.'s analytic progression.

Mr. C.: Dream 3: entering the termination phase: mourning

I'm in the middle of the freeway, at a toll booth or gas pump. My Dad, who doesn't look like my Dad, comes up in the middle of traffic and causes a terrible traffic jam. He is dressed in overalls, kind of like a hillbilly, and a flannel shirt. And he is yelling, and then all of a sudden he runs back to the car, and in the sky there is this plane. Blue, shiny blue, with red letters – it says U.S. Air. And I'm looking up and thinking – "Oh my God, it's going to crash! It's going down! And my father is running right towards it! I start running in the opposite direction, and I'm thinking "Will I feel the explosion?" I should keep running until I get over that wall ahead. I wasn't thinking at the time of all the people inside.

As Mr. C.'s transference began to be organized around mourning and breaking the symbiotic object tie, oedipal conflicts became prominent. *The oedipal crisis involves the patient's affective unconscious conviction that someone will die.* It is interesting to note that Mr. C. did not develop a committed relationship with a woman until after his mother's death. He then maintained this exclusive relationship throughout the remainder of the analysis. The last dream, and Mr. C.'s associations to it, reflects Mr. C.'s ability to speak of his death wishes, and his restored ego capacity to save himself in the dream: "I ran in the opposite direction . . . I wasn't thinking of all the people on the plane."

The technical challenges of mourning

Technique here was focused on helping Mr. C. relinquish the self-sacrificial stance that is commonly seen in those with psychosis (Balestriere, 2007; Freud, 1911; Searles, 1959). Murdering oneself would be accomplished by Mr. C. maintaining his depression, and not "running in the opposite direction." The self-sacrificial position is reflected in the primitive attempt to avoid being murdered by the other by sacrificing oneself. This symbiotic tie to the other – the attempt to destroy the other, or drive the other crazy – presents major challenges to the analyst. As Balestriere (2007) recently concluded after being asked a question by a psychotic patient: "Not to answer would be tantamount to inviting the patient to perpetuate the sacrificial mode . . ." (p. 409). With psychotic patients, much of the patient's communication involves projected affect, fragments of hallucinations, or, more dangerous, a partial or complete lack of the patient's libidinal object cathexis in the therapeutic engagement (Benedetti, 1987; Bion, 1959). This is initially experienced by the analyst in the vague, non-verbal manner of a countertransference reaction.

The symbiotically organized identity: avoiding an unproductive maternal transference with psychotically depressed, hallucinating, and delusional patients

The reader will note that, especially with Anita, interventions are a mix of beginning to put into words unconscious conflicts, verbalizing affect, and responding to enquiries in a realistic and straightforward manner, such as: "Do you feel safe here?" "Yes I do." Over the years this approach has been modified with hallucinating and delusional patients in the early years of working in the symbiotically organized transference. This modification has been influenced by a consideration of the technical challenges presented in the psychotic's self-sacrificing position. As Searles (1979), Benedetti (1987), Benedetti interviewed by Koehler (2003), Bion, (1957, 1959), and many others have suggested, it is by working in the transference that we gain our most important therapeutic leverage. It is also important, at the same time, not to encourage an unproductive symbiotic or maternal transference with patients profoundly struggling with reality and boundary issues involved in this initial phase of psychoanalytic work (Gibbs, 2004, 2007a; Karon and VandenBos, 1981).

I have found that the symbiotically organized transference, or the dyadic maternal transference, is both the problem and the basis for the solution to the problem (Searles, 1959; Welles and Wrye, 1991). Initially, hallucinations are allowed and interpreted in a way that strengthens the therapeutic alliance. Such non-judgmental acceptance of the patient's world is itself therapeutic. In the hallucinatory process, unconscious conflict is transformed into perception, with the previous conflictual thought acquiring the lower form of perception. Thus, the hallucination loses the higher order processes of verbalization and containment of affect (Arieti, 1974). In order for the highly anxiety-provoking affects associated with the hallucination to be put into words, and re-introjected affectively, much therapeutic containment is necessary. Before the patient is able to benefit from affectively charged transference interpretations, or interpretation of unconscious conflict, the patient must feel – as so many patients seem to communicate in some way – *safe*. I have come to understand this *safety*, which is so important to hallucinating patients in a symbiotically organized transference, as the analyst's acceptance or containment of the patient's hallucinations, *initially without interpretation*. The answer "Yes I do" to the question "Do you feel safe here?" reflects an emphasis on establishing the therapeutic alliance, or engagement. The work of Schwartz and Summers in Chapter 4 also eloquently demonstrates this initial therapeutic engagement with psychotically depressed patients.

The role of language in work with psychotic patients

I later realized that Anita had taken great care to prepare me for what was to be a brutal onslaught of murderousness expressed in the transference/ countertransference. For several months Anita left pages of handwritten notes, poems, and paintings depicting great all-consuming perfect love in my office. Being both a Nationally Registered Art Therapist (ATR-BC) and a psychoanalyst, I have found that writing, drawing, or creative expression is particularly helpful for psychotic patients. The essential role of the creative process in helping the patient to express the "ineffability of psychosis" has been documented by many practitioners (Appollon, Bergeron, and Canton, 2002; Byers, 1991; Naumberg, 1975). This creative expression of the psychotic experience lacks higher verbal secondary process organization, although this kind of expression is essential to the patient being reconnected to the memory and reality of his/her own ineffable psychotic experience. Reclaiming the psychotic experience as one's own ameliorates the psychotic patient's subjective experience of alienation within a surreal and frightening inner and interpersonal world.

Medication may help some patients to tolerate the intense feelings associated with psychotic depression. Only within the safety of the transference/countertransference, however, does a patient learn to live with the feelings of life, as those feelings are transformed from destructive and murderous ones to increasingly complex, loving, and creative organizations in an affectively meaningful relationship with the analyst/self, and with the self. The conceptual and developmental skills related to the ability to contain feelings by talking, writing, artistic expression, and *not immediately acting* are well documented (Edwards, 1987; Piaget, 1962; Silverman, 1991; Winnicott, 1953, 1971).

Without verbalization, and the interpersonal processes involved in communicating to another, one would indefinitely remain in the internal world of omnipotence, or remain symbiotically organized (Bion, 1956; La Farge, 1989; Tustin, 1986). Silence similar to that observed in Anita's treatment reflects a symbiotic identity, and initially limits the separation-individuation processes associated with ambivalence, reality orientation, and mourning. Thus, technique with a symbiotically organized patient must initially allow the patient's experience of merger with the analyst/other/mother in the transference. During the merger transference, the analyst typically avoids asking the patient questions, as this is commonly associated with the patient experiencing persecutory panic (Balestriere, 2007; Karon and VandenBos, 1981; Villemoes, 2002). The symbiotically organized patient will often unconsciously experience the analyst's questions as a rupture of the symbiosis. This rupture results in the patient being flooded with the intensely negative affects of hate, terror, annihilation, and alienation.

This merger is also experienced by the analyst in the countertransference, and involves the subjective experiences of both invulnerability and murderous rage associated with the annihilation of the separate self (Gibbs, 2004, 2007a). This experience of "losing oneself" in the countertransference is beautifully described by Balestriere (2007):

> He explains his convictions . . . I accept being drawn into this . . . Then right in the middle of one of those discussions, I have a terrifying experience; I have the physical impression that my thoughts are detaching themselves from me . . . I had to close my eyes, hold on to that 'no,' turn it around, and finally re-experience the living connection which, in Bion's words, attaches thought to a thinker, which makes that thinking mine . . .
>
> (p. 410)

For the patient, giving up this symbiotic object relations capacity is painful and slow, as the patient struggles to separate, and still feel attached.

Repeatedly, Anita would rage against herself in terms of self-mutilation, self-hate, and escalating persecutory hallucinations, in an attempt to "keep me from going away." Anita's experience of the self and other being affectively oriented around hate and destruction slowly evolved to include the capacity to experience separation and difference, as well as loving affect.

Summary and conclusions

Psychoanalytic technique with the psychotically depressed patient: reality and abuse

The challenges of technique are primarily those associated with transference and countertransference phenomena. Mr. C. expressing rage at his mother for allowing his father's abuse would initially be followed by the analyst affirming the affective experience of the patient: "It sounds hard for you to believe your mother was really there – she saw it. It must have been terrifying . . ." Only after years of analytic work could Mr. C.'s rage be helpfully interpreted, as he read the murder stories he had written: "You, the writer, are creating a murderer, and bringing these stories here to tell us . . . you know how it could be done . . . you can imagine doing it . . . enormous rage, over and over . . ." At this point, perhaps sensing my fear, Mr. C. said: "Don't get me wrong . . . I'm just telling you, I understand it, when I was looking at him, I really felt it . . ." Now close to termination, Mr. C. knew he, like all of us, had murderous rage within him, and could feel this in the safety of the transference/countertranference without regressing back into psychotic depression.

With a patient like Anita, in the early stages of a symbiotically organized transference, although enormous hate and murderousness are certainly part of unconscious and sometimes conscious life, work would not be possible in the way that it was done with Mr. C. above. The following thoughts reveal that Anita is unable to contain murderous rage without debilitating self-hate, unconscious guilt, and severe depression. Thus, the interpretation focuses on accepting the hallucinations and symbiotic identity, in a way that strengthens the treatment alliance: "Your thoughts about the voices telling you to jump from the car – you make people leave! – you tell us this as the session is ending. You wonder – about leaving, about jumping . . . the leaving is hard – it's associated with you jumping from the car, a way of telling us *how important it is to be here – being here.*"

If suicide or self-mutilation was suspected, specific and direct agreements were made about the conditions she would have to meet to remain in outpatient treatment. Medication was used for the first several years of Anita's treatment. Anita seemed to have the most positive outcomes with medications when she had direct access to a prescribing psychiatrist. In her therapy with me she was always encouraged to engage the psychiatrist directly. To the extent that there was a strong engagement, or alliance, with the psychiatrist, Anita felt less afraid of "losing control," being hospitalized against her will, or having to tolerate unbearable side effects. Consulting a psychiatrist on Anita's behalf was most successful when I consulted the psychiatrist by phone in Anita's presence, during her sessions.

Hallucinations and delusions

Memories are present in both the psychotically depressed and schizophrenic patient, although they are remembered through the patient's hallucinations and delusions. The full force of destructive drives is subjectively experienced in the psychotic patient as affective states of hate, guilt, terror, and envy. In an attempt to compassionately spare the patient – and the entire human community – from the agony of these intense affective states, the reality of them may be invalidated and reduced to craziness, delusion, or biochemical imbalance. The psychotic person, however, pays a very high price for denying the reality of his/her memories, even if some palliative relief is gained. Invalidating the patient's hallucinations and delusions further separates the psychotic person from his/her memories, and thus from the human community. Bion (1959) has described the "bizarreness" of the psychotic's experience of the world, as the destructive drives overwhelm the ego's attempts to organize cognitive, affective, and relational functions. Thus, the importance of interpreting the fantasies, hallucinations, and delusions associated with psychotic depression is seen as the essential mutative process that allows not only symptom relief, but also genuine psychological growth and change (Appollon, Bergeron, and Cantin, 2002; Arieti, 1974).

It is the patient who must do the difficult work of affirming the reality of their own experience by slowly containing the intensity of feelings associated with giving up the symbiotic identity. Anita's sense of unconscious omnipotence, however, involves hallucinations and delusions.

For too long, reports of hallucinations and delusions have unnecessarily caused analysts and therapists to refuse treatment to patients. The existence of hallucinations and delusions reflects the same qualitative psychotic organization always associated with a symbiotically organized identity. A part of the patient's identity is stuck at this earlier level of development. The challenge is to understand the differing techniques and counter-transference demands required for hallucinating and non-hallucinating psychotically depressed patients. Anita's refusal to touch the door knob and enter the building herself was handled by the analyst initially by aiming interventions toward the non-psychotic function of the delusion: namely, to establish interpersonal communication and contact. For this reason, the analyst met the patient at the door and let her into the building. Nothing was said about this for years. Later, when Anita verbally revealed her fear of contamination, the contamination delusions could be slowly interpreted:

"Touching what someone else has touched, being touched, this is associated with getting sick . . ."

The dissociative defenses used by Mr. C. allowed him to face his unconscious identification with murderous objects at an affective level, slowly, in a bearable way. He spent many years remembering, and at first, as he would say, "trying to believe . . ." the deprived and violent manner in which he lived as a child. Mr. C.'s aggressively infused feelings toward himself and others would slowly give way to an increased capacity to individuate and relinquish the sadomasochistic tie to the analyst during the termination phase of his treatment. Ultimately, this early primitive attachment and object relations capacity, sadomasochistically organized in a symbiotic manner, provides the basis for the origins of dependency, attachment, and eventually a healthier ability to love. With Anita, technique was initially focused on these primitive origins of dependency and attachment and on maintaining interpersonal contact and communication.

Note

1 In the interest of confidentiality, identifying patient information and circumstances have been changed, omitted, or compiled.

References

Appollon, W., Bergeron, D., and Cantin, L. (2002). *After Lacan: Clinical Practice and the Subject of the Unconscious.* New York: SUNY Press.

Arieti, S. (1974). *Interpretation of Schizophrenia.* New York: New York University Press.

Balestriere, L. (2007). The work of the psychoanalyst in the field of psychosis. *International Journal of Psycho-Analysis*, 88: 407–421.

Benedetti, G. (1987). *Psychotherapy of Schizophrenia.* New York: New York University Press.

Bion, W. R. (1956). Development of schizophrenic thought. *International Journal of Psycho-Analysis.* Reprinted in *Second Thoughts* (pp. 36–42). London: Karnac (1984).

Bion, W. (1957). Differentiation of the psychotic from the non-psychotic personalities. *International Journal of Psycho-Analysis*, 38: 266–276.

Bion, W. (1959). Attacks on linking. *International Journal of Psycho-Analysis*, 40: 308–315.

Boyer, L. B. (2000). *Countertransference and Regression.* Northvale, NJ: Jason Aronson.

Byers, J. G. (1991). Suicide as an abortive life stage of development. In H. B. Landgarten and D. Lubbers (Eds.), *Adult Art Psychotherapy: Issues and Applications* (pp. 21–48). New York: Brunner/Mazel.

Edgcumbe, R. (1984). Modes of communication: The differentiation of somatic and verbal expression. *Psychoanalytic Study of the Child*, 39: 137–154.

Edwards, M. (1987). Jungian analytic art therapy. In J. A. Rubin (Ed.), *Approaches to Art Therapy: Theory and Technique* (pp. 92–113). New York: Brunner/Mazel.

Eigen, M. (1986). *The Psychotic Core*. Northvale, NJ: Jason Aronson.

Freud, S. (1911). Psycho-analytic notes on an autobiographical account of a case of paranoia (dementia paranoids). *Standard Edition*, 12: 9–82.

Freud, S. (1915). Instincts and their vicissitudes. *Standard Edition*, 2.

Gibbs, P. L. (2004). The struggle to know what is real. *Psychoanalytic Review*, 91: 615–641.

Gibbs, P. L. (2007a). Reality in cyberspace: Analysands' use of the internet and ordinary everyday psychosis. *Psychoanalytic Review*, 94: 11–38.

Gibbs, P. L. (2007b). The primacy of psychoanalytic intervention in recovery from the psychoses and schizophrenias. *Journal of the American Academy of Psychoanalysis and Dynamic Psychiatry*, 35: 287–312.

Gottdiener, W. H. and Haslam, N. (2002). The benefits of individual psychotherapy for people diagnosed with schizophrenia: A meta-analytic review. *Ethical Human Science and Services*, 4: 163–187.

Gutheil, T. G. and Haven, L. L. (1979). The therapeutic alliance: Contemporary meanings and confusions. *International Review of Psycho-Analysis*, 6: 467–481.

Jablonka, E. and Lamb, M. (2005). *Evolution in Four Dimensions: Genetic, Epigenetic, Behavioral, and Symbolic Variation in the History of Life*. Cambridge, MA: MIT Press.

Jacobson, E. (1971). *Depression: Comparison Studies of Normal, Neurotic, and Psychotic Conditions*. Madison, CT: International Universities Press.

Joseph, B. (1982). Addiction to near death. *International Journal of Psycho-Analysis*, 63: 449–456.

Karon, B. and VandenBos, G. R. (1981). *Psychotherapy of Schizophrenia: The Treatment of Choice*. New York: Jason Aronson.

Kavanaugh, P. (2003). The dead poets society ventures into a radioactive analytic space. *Psychoanalytic Review*, 90: 341–361.

Klein, M. (1946). Notes on some schizoid mechanisms. *International Journal of Psycho-Analysis*, 27: 99–110.

Koehler, B. (2003). Interview with Gaetano Benedetti, M.D. *Journal of the American Academy of Psychoanalysis and Dynamic Psychiatry*, 31: 75–87.

Krystal, H. (1988). *Integration and Self-healing: Affect, Trauma, Alexithymia*. Hillsdale, NJ: Analytic Press.

La Farge, L. (1989). Emptiness as defense in severe regressive states. *Journal of the American Psychoanalytic Association*, 37: 965–995.

Naumberg, M. (1975). Spontaneous art in education and psychotherapy. In E. Ulman and P. Dachlinger (Eds.), *Art Therapy in Theory and Practice* (pp. 221–239). New York: Schocken Books.

Novick, K. K. and Novick, J. (1997). An application of the concept of the therapeutic alliance to sadomasochistic pathology. *Journal of the American Psychoanalytic Association*, 46: 813–846.

Piaget, J. (1954). *The Construction of Reality in the Child*. New York: Basic Books.

Piaget, J. (1962). *Play, Dreams, and Imitation in Childhood*. New York: Norton.

Pick, I. (1985). Working through in the countertransference. *International Journal of Psycho-Analysis*, 66: 157–166.

Prouty, G. (2003). Pre-Therapy: A newer development in the psychotherapy of schizophrenia. *Journal of the American Academy of Psychoanalysis and Dynamic Psychiatry*, 31: 59–74.

Putnam, F. W. (1989). *Diagnosis and Treatment of Multiple Personality Disorder*. New York: Guilford Press.

Searles, H. F. (1959). The effort to drive the other person crazy – an element in the aetiology and psychotherapy of schizophrenia. In *Collected Papers on Schizophrenia and Related Subjects* (pp. 254–283). New York: International Universities Press.

Searles, H. F. (1979). *Countertransference and Related Subjects*. New York: International Universities Press.

Silver, A.-L. (1989). *Psychoanalysis and Psychosis*. Madison, CT: International Universities Press.

Silverman, D. (1991). Art psychotherapy: An approach to borderline adults. In H. B. Landgarten and D. Lubbers (Eds.), *Adult Art Psychotherapy: Issues and Applications* (pp. 83–110). New York: Brunner/Mazel.

Suomi, S. (1997). Aggression, serotonin, and gene–environment interactions in rhesus monkeys. In J. T. Cacioppo and G. G. Bernston (Eds.), *Essays in Neuroscience*. Cambridge, MA: MIT Press.

Tustin, F. (1986). *Autistic Barriers in Neurotic Patients*. London: Karnac Books.

Ver Eecke, W. (2003). The role of psychoanalytic theory and practice in understanding and treating schizophrenia: A rejoinder to the PORT report's condemnation of psychoanalysis. *Journal of the American Academy of Psychoanalysis and Dynamic Psychiatry*, 31: 11–29.

Villemoes, P. (2002). Ego-structuring psychotherapy. *Journal of the American Academy of Psychoanalysis*, 30: 645–656.

Waiess, E. A. (2006). Treatment of dissociative identity disorder: "Tortured child syndrome." *Psychoanalytic Review*, 93: 477–500.

Welles, J. and Wrye, H. (1991). Maternal erotic countertransference. *International Journal of Psychoanalysis*, 72: 93–106.

Winnicott, D. W. (1953). Transitional objects and transitional phenomena. *International Journal of Psychoanalysis*, 34: 89–97.

Winnicott, D. W. (1971). *Playing and Reality*. London: Tavistock Publications.

Chapter 9

Practicing the "impossible profession" in impossible places

Daniel Mackler

Editors' Introduction: While the previous chapters explored the one-on-one change process and the value of quality milieu therapy in assisting patients in recovering from psychosis, Daniel Mackler illustrates the difficulties that clinicians face in doing therapeutic work with psychotic clients in environments that do not view such work as a legitimate option. Prisons, military settings, religious communities, and a variety of non-Western countries create milieus that are, at times, hostile to therapy.

This chapter focuses on working in an outpatient, inner-city setting where psychotic patients are regularly deemed impossible to work with unless they are first medicated with neuroleptics. In such overburdened, underfunded environments almost all aspects of a patient's clinical situation go unattended. Gross overreliance on getting the patient into a "DSM-IV" box and medicated with the corresponding pharmacologic agent become the justification for a kind of outpatient "warehousing."

Mackler explores various ways in which therapists can successfully connect with such clients and maintain a broader theoretical point of view – beyond medication – in spite of externally imposed limitations. This chapter ultimately seeks to uncover how to make even a hostile environment work in favor of the treatment.

Introduction

It is difficult to do meaningful psychotherapeutic work with severely emotionally disturbed patients in settings that do not believe in the possibility of such work. Therapy with psychotic patients, in any given society or social subculture, can be either facilitative or inhibitory. This chapter will explore some of the environmental blocks that make such therapy difficult, and will then suggest various ways to work around and through these blocks.

Brief review of the literature

Our modern culture's reliance on psychiatric medication for psychosis has rendered it difficult to engage such patients in transformative psychotherapy

(Karon, 2003; Silver, 2000). Other cultures and social subcultures have similarly been resistant to psychotherapy in general, and especially to psychotherapy for psychosis. This makes the job of the therapist, not to mention that of the patient, significantly more arduous and complex.

Prison environments, for example, with their anti-emotional stance that does not facilitate individual emotional vulnerability as a healing tool, are considered less than optimal for successful psychotherapy (Kupers, 2001). Correia (2001) points out the mistrust that inmates commonly have of institutional employees, including mental health workers, and notes how this is only fueled by the compromised therapeutic confidentiality in prison. The difficulty of psychotherapy in this setting is fueled by the other risks that inmates face if they share their emotional problems with therapists, such as being labeled "crazy" by other inmates. This leaves them vulnerable to both bullies and general social stigma. Also, if an inmate reveals enough emotional distress to a prison therapist and gets diagnosed with a more significant mental illness, he risks having his parole board indefinitely postpone his release "based on the assumption that his mental illness would make him a threat to the community" (p. 192).

Likewise, therapists who work in prison settings face difficult challenges that can easily go unrecognized and unacknowledged by colleagues who work in non-prison environments. Towl (2006) notes that in the United Kingdom the public's increased focus on protecting society often comes at the expense of understanding the plight or needs of the prisoner. This does not translate well for the therapist, whose job duties focus increasingly on assessing an inmate's risk, at the expense of providing nurturing psychological help. Therapists invite marginalization if they overempathize with their clients. But perhaps worse yet, Towl points out that inmates themselves introject society's view of them, which only fuels the antitherapeutic nature of the setting.

A similar antitherapeutic environment often exists for psychological sufferers in military environments – especially for combat veterans who have returned to their peacetime societies (Herman, 1992; Williams, 1987). Soldiers are expected, from their peers, from society in general, and from within, to maintain the ideals of stoicism, to downplay emotions in general, and to repress feelings of vulnerability and grief (Sherman, 2007). This makes emotional processing of internal conflicts extremely difficult, and heightens the therapist's struggle to connect with such patients. Many mental health workers have commented on the therapeutic hostility of military environments, and all the more so when the bureaucracy that both funds and oversees the treatment not only imposes its own treatment goals on the therapy but requires that therapeutic confidentiality be compromised in significant and even hostile ways. Kennedy and Zillmer (2006) note that patients who reveal their emotional dilemmas, or even non-pathological sides of their personalities, such as homosexuality, risk being deemed unfit for duty and thus losing their entire livelihood and social structure. Likewise, therapists who retain their own ideals of therapy, and do not conform to the principle of officer first and therapist second, risk the same.

Meanwhile, much in the literature indicates the degree to which many modern psychiatric hospitals offer little in the way of psychotherapy, and instead rely almost wholly on medication as the primary treatment option (Silver, 1992a; Whitaker, 2002). Therapists who struggle to do more meaningful psychotherapeutic work in these settings often face an uphill struggle, and can risk their jobs, not to mention the bonds they are building with their patients, if they deviate from too many accepted norms. The rigid, top-down hierarchical structure and the reductionism of the modern psychiatric establishment so often prove to be the undoing of the very clinical creativity, dynamism, and idealism that itself is the foil for psychological stagnation.

The same antitherapeutic norms can become widely fixed throughout countries as a result of cultural attitudes. China, for example, has historically taken a more dim view of psychotherapy. This is based largely on a stigmatizing attitude toward mental illness and psychological problems and a reliance on more traditional Chinese medicine, although that has been changing in recent decades (Chang et al., 2005; Li et al., 1994). Therapists who work in these environments face skepticism not just from their less psychologically minded colleagues but also from their patients as well. Of course, this can happen in Westernized countries too, such as in the case of therapists who attempt dream analysis with patients who have been ingrained with decades of belief that dreams are just random figments of the mind and not imbued with vital psychological meaning (Miller, 1981).

This echoes the dilemma, expressed by Akhtar (2004), facing sufferers of schizophrenia in rural Pakistan. They are often considered to be possessed by demons or spirits, and one form of local treatment involves brutal punishment – that is, torture – of the sufferer to drive out the offending demon. One wonders, however, how brutal these Pakistani "treatment providers" would consider America's all too recent use of the ice-pick lobotomy – and ongoing use of electroshock. This makes it all the more noteworthy when Karon (2003, citing Lambo, 1957) points out that "quicker recovery [from schizophrenia] in Africa [versus in 'civilized' Westernized countries] is a result of the favorable social environment." Whitaker (2002) also addresses the phenomenon of higher recovery rates from schizophrenia in poor versus developed countries.

Meanwhile, cultures or subcultures with religious proscriptions against psychotherapeutic work form a backdrop of a difficult therapy environment. As an example, Moran (2007) describes how it is not uncommon that "contemporary Muslim patients are receptive to the use of psychopharmacology, but far less receptive to the notion of psychotherapy" (p. 10). And for those who do engage in psychotherapy, Moran notes that clinical

practice can be negatively influenced by such factors as the religious proscriptions against interaction between unmarried men and women. Psychotherapists can feel disempowered in the face of such beliefs or attitudes.
Certainly a patient's positive transference and belief in the curative power
of the therapist eases the burden of those who work in this "impossible"
profession.

Background of the case vignette

This chapter will focus on the difficulty of doing psychotherapy with
psychotic patients from the perspective of working in a public, outpatient
community mental health center in New York City in the 21st century. Such
urban mental health centers are common initial jobs for new therapists
leaving social work and psychology graduate schools. When I finished social
work graduate school in 2001 I began work at one such public mental health
clinic in Manhattan. The clinic, like many of its kind, paid therapists not a
salary, but on a fee-for-service basis (that is, paid therapists a contracted fee
only if the patient came to session). The clinic provided therapists no
benefits, health insurance, or worker's compensation. Technically therapists
were not employees, but independent contractors.

Given this information, one might logically ask why an aspiring therapist
would choose to work in such a financially negating environment. The
answer is that these community mental health centers provide many therapists a transitional step into private practice, offering both a great degree
of clinical experience and freedom. Having previously interned at three
different institutions (one inpatient) where my actions were monitored and
regulated to the degree of blanching creativity from the therapeutic process,
I questioned if there might not be value in working at an agency with little,
or at least less, supervisory oversight. All previous agencies at which I had
interned also had an overreliance on neuroleptics. This was particularly true
with lower functioning patients, and all the more so when these patients
had psychotic disturbances. The prevailing attitude overlapped with the
conventional wisdom of the evening news: that the "mentally ill" needed to
be mellowed, subdued, tranquilized, and have their symptoms kept under
wraps through the use of one, two, or more heavy medications.

Yet I had met enough so-called "schizophrenics" who recovered from
their "illness," and had read enough case studies, starting with Joanne
Greenberg's semi-fictional *I Never Promised You a Rose Garden*, to know
that there could be more to life for a patient with psychosis than the kind of
devitalized, side-effect-ridden existence provided by medication alone.

Upon realizing that my philosophy did not overlap with the philosophy
of these environments, yet retaining the awareness that my passion for
engaging in meaningful psychotherapy remained intact, I chose the most
freeing route possible: an agency that gave me space to do my work – and

did not interfere with my patients' care as long as I kept accurate chart notes that would pass muster in an audit, took the necessary steps to keep suicidal and violent behavior at bay, and, most importantly from the agency's point of view, kept the patients (or in the case of most patients, their government health insurance) paying. Although my agency and many like it are non-profit organizations and define their mission to be the protection and nurturance of society's most wounded and vulnerable, all too often mental health workers who take this mission to heart find themselves in a precarious position. Public and professional opinion in the United States, as Karon (1992, 2003) and Hornstein (2000) point out, has even gone so far as to suggest that it can be considered malpractice to work psychodynamically with psychotic patients.

Yet it is not impossible for a therapist to flourish in such a setting. In my experience, when the doors to my office were closed I was left alone with my own hypotheses, my own vision, and my own slate of patients – and I could set the tone for the healing environment. Of course, this might come across as a harsh indictment of a mental health system, where a young social worker with technically no professional experience could have such control over his patients' therapeutic lives, and at the very least it is a sad commentary.

A therapist, however, can, on an individual level, take strides to compensate for the flaws in the system. He or she can engage in serious self-searching, read broadly about theory and case history, uphold a high degree of personal and professional ethics, struggle to find high-quality, appropriate, independent supervision, and above all maintain a passionate dedication to the well-being of his or her patients. It must be noted, though, that the lack of oversight does create an environment that is ripe for incompetents to partake in therapeutic abuse and acting out, and I have regularly witnessed this happening. From a broader perspective, though, one could reasonably argue that the whole overmedication aspect of the American mental health system is itself a wide-angle lens through which therapists can act out, project, and ablate their fears of their own split-off and unresolved emotional histories.

Managing a difficult supervisor

In my work at the clinic I had an official supervisor. Although I was performing between 30 and 40 therapy sessions a week, with a caseload that included many deinstitutionalized patients carrying diagnoses of severe psychopathology, I was granted a single 45-minute "hour" of weekly supervision. Many of my coworkers complained that this paucity of supervision made it impossible for them to resolve their countertransference problems with their patients. I felt the opposite to be true. The agency supervision I received largely blocked my progress with my patients.

My main dilemma was that my supervisor believed neither in my approach nor my goals. When I stated that I believed patients with schizophrenia might someday taper off their medications and ultimately resolve their emotional conflicts, I was met with disbelief – and treated as naïve. My supervisor stated that she *knew* how impossible it was to resolve and recover from significant psychoses, and based her belief on her own experience of having never witnessed it with her own patients. Also, she avoided literature that contradicted her, and instead trusted the mores of the pharmaceutical industry and the middle-of-the-road mental health field. When I attempted to share alternate literature I found myself treated as a dissident or, worse yet, as irrelevant.

It helped me that I had survived similar limited thinking in the past. Before entering the mental health field I had been trained in biology, a field where animals are not considered to have emotions and where people are only marginally considered to be animals. This taught me a healthy skepticism for both science and conventional training.

My supervisor, on the other hand, was in awe of modern "science." She believed the conventional wisdom about chemical imbalances and genetic etiologies of psychopathology, and believed it so confidently that she shared with me that she herself had a chemical imbalance at the root of her depression, and that she took sertraline (Zoloft), having previously and "unsuccessfully" tried paroxetine (Paxil) and fluoxetine (Prozac). She even told me the dosage.

She also told me in an early supervisory session, in listing what she believed to be one of her strengths, that she was self-aware enough to know that she could not work therapeutically with men with narcissistic issues. She stated that they triggered too many of her countertransference issues, so she behaved "ethically" and referred them to other therapists – and in time came to refer several to me. She stated that my job was to learn which patients overly triggered my countertransference and similarly refer them elsewhere. This shocked me. First of all, in my conception of reality, everyone has narcissistic issues, and all the more so highly narcissistically wounded therapy patients (Miller, 1981, 1997). Second, from my perspective I had a supervisor who did not realize that it was *her* job to work toward resolving her own narcissistic wounds rather than disavowing responsibility for male patients who happened to mirror them. I also found myself trapped by this situation, because how could I, a male not yet so enlightened to be free of all narcissism, sort out my own narcissistically based countertransference issues with her?

The unfortunate solution I found for my dilemma was that I curtailed sharing honest emotional material with her. I learned that when I was fully honest in order to set the stage for optimal use of supervision, as so much of the literature I respected bade me to do (Fromm-Reichmann, 1950; Kadushin, 1968; Schulz, 1989; Silver, 1989), she labeled me cavalier, arrogant, a risk to my patients, even scientifically unfounded. Analyses such as Gottdiener and Haslam's (2003) critique of the flawed Patient Outcome Research Team study (which suggests, among other things, that psychodynamic psychotherapy of schizophrenia is harmful and thus should be avoided) have since provided me some solace, not just for my point of view but for the realities of solid scientific research in the psychological field.

That said, my supervisor was right in one sense: I was entering risky territory with my patients, especially those with psychotic issues. As upheld by many of the pioneers who worked meaningfully with psychotic patients (see Hornstein, 2000), there is risk – both for patient and clinician – in mirroring the horrors of a psychotic person's present existence, in asking them to explore their feelings, and in exploring why they might be having such tortured feelings in the first place – not to mention in tracing these feelings into traumatic roots of childhood and into their split-off and unresolved and projected anger and fury at those who thwarted their healthy development (Dorman, 2003; Miller, 1984, 1997). Time has shown me that it is often safer, both emotionally and legally (considering the mores of the field and the ever-present risk of litigation: see Hornstein, 2000; Karon, 2003; Torrey, 2001), to use one's power as a therapist to "guide" a patient onto heavy medications, to ignore what damage this might be doing to his brain, body, and psyche (Breggin, 1991; Jackson, 2005; Whitaker, 2002), and to use societally sanctioned "socialization techniques," however Machiavellian they might be, to help him "adjust to the realities of his life" – that is, to refuse to be therapeutically supportive until he first complies with society's preconceived ideas of how he should be living.

No doubt anyone would be taking a risk by avoiding my supervisor's template and delving into the pressured unknown, and I understood why my exploring attitude, even if I consider it a strength, caused her anxiety. Aside from the possibility that a patient might experience a worsening of symptoms if he connected too closely with his stifled feelings and history, such exploring caused me anxiety as well. Entering a patient's inner realms of psychosis and severe trauma is inherently stressful to the therapist (Searles, 1962) and, like others who do this work, I experienced chronic vicarious traumatization (Herman, 1992; Howell, 2002), including nightmares, nervousness, and an increased sense of isolation. But these feelings were not unfamiliar to me, and I, along with others (Miller, 1990, 1997), have long accepted them as temporary correlates of the therapist's own psychological growth process.

To this end, I reasoned with myself that what worked for me in my own healing process would also apply to the lives of my patients, especially if they had a committed external ally in me. I took seriously the words of the pioneering therapist Harry Stack Sullivan, who admitted to being a recovered "schizophrenic" himself (M. Green, personal communication, 8/5/2006; Perry, 1982), when he stated that *"everyone is much more simply human than otherwise"* (Sullivan, 1953: 32, his italics).

Finding good supervision outside the unhealthy setting

Like many who have come before me (see Karon and VandenBos, 1981; Koehler, 2003), I found therapeutic work with extremely troubled patients to be too difficult without adequate supervision. I needed more guidance and mirroring than that which could be provided by a supervisor who tacitly required that I narcissistically gratify her in order to maintain not just the emotional stability of the supervisory hour but my very employment.

Of course, one might ask why someone displeased with a supervisor would not request a change. The answer in my case is twofold. First, I explored other options in the clinic and learned that my supervisor was no worse, and actually more benevolent, than most. Second, and perhaps more importantly, clinic culture considered it impolitic to discharge a supervisor – much in the same way that clinic patients were unofficially discouraged from changing therapists if they felt unsatisfied. Patients who insisted on changes tended to garner "bad reputations," which were often bolstered in their charts diagnostically, as Strean (1993) has described elsewhere, with stigmatizing personality disorders as "proof."

Unwilling to risk being pathologized, I employed outside supervision. I knew several experienced therapists in private practice – and I was acquainted with several people who were not therapists but were wiser than most of the therapists I knew – and I began consulting with them regularly, both formally and informally, for hours each week. The intensity of the work demanded it, and the benefits, as Karon and VandenBos (1981) elucidate, were immense.

I also found supervision through books. I read voraciously – from psychological theory, to case studies, to novels, to anthropology, to religion, to Twelve Step literature. I discovered a wealth of helpful information at a relatively low cost, which was a necessity in my case because my pay covered little more than the cost of living, and not even health insurance. This added an ironic twist to my work, considering that almost all of my patients were insured, whereas I, their therapist and guide – like so many therapists I knew – was not. At times, this created some resentment in me, above and beyond the normal frustrations that Hedges (2000), Karon (2003), and Searles (1962) describe as common and even expectable in work with disturbed patients.

Overall, the supervision I found, be it through interpersonal or eclectic channels, enhanced my work with my clients and allowed me to continue and to thrive in the work I was doing. Had I simply remained with agency supervision I could not have functioned effectively. As it was, the work was nearly impossible enough.

Living a healthy lifestyle to avoid burnout

The stress inherent in therapy with emotionally disturbed patients high-lights another key factor in doing successful work in a seemingly impossible setting: keeping one's inner peace. Over the years I witnessed many therapists burn out, in a variety of ways long acknowledged in the literature (Buechler, 2000; Chessick, 2001; Cooper, 1986). Some fell into patterns of substance abuse, others fell into attitudes of cynicism toward patients, others lost hope over healing, and many acted out with patients through other lenses. I struggled to avoid these pitfalls – at least the ones to which I was most susceptible – by striving toward an optimally healing-oriented lifestyle. This, along with the supervision I sought, bolstered my work with my patients and helped me to keep my emotional balance, my focus, and above all my hope. As Kanwal (1997) has emphasized, this hope translates directly into one's work with patients. The more emotionally centered and hopeful the therapist is, the more easily one can guide them in an appro-priate, respectful, and patient manner.

My focus on a healthy lifestyle became a personal dedication, and helped me step above the myopia of a clinic for which the main – and at times it seemed only – focus was staying in business. All too often it seemed that the clinic had no intention of ever having its therapists end the therapy with the disturbed patients, instead preferring to keep them coming forever and, as Karon (2003) notes about the troubled conventions of the field, to neutralize their resistance to taking medications. Many of the more troubled patients at the clinic had been coming weekly or twice-weekly for decades, with no improvement whatsoever. This was the status quo, and the therapists who helped to maintain it became the next generation of clinic supervisors and administrators.

In order to keep my healthy focus, and break some of the environmental pressure to follow the party line, I analyzed my cases in a daily written journal, I analyzed my dreams, and, as trivial as it might sound, I made sure I got a good night's sleep every night. I also exercised prudently and gently, I strove to avoid troubled people and unnecessary conflict in my personal life, and I avoided mood and mind-altering substances. I associ-ated with the most mature people I could and I spent a great deal of time having fun and relaxing. In addition, I ate well and I did my best to enjoy nature – which can be found even in New York City. I kept my days alive and active and I kept my focus on my expanding internal life. And I did a huge amount of personal grieving. In short, I was doing exactly what I asked of my patients – and proving to myself all the while that despite intermittent pain and frustration and hopelessness, a balanced lifestyle ultimately manifests a life of growth, centeredness, self-love, self-esteem, and self-respect.

In time, I became aware that few of my colleagues engaged in similar lifestyles. I attributed this in no small part to the demoralizing tenor of the environment, from top to bottom. The head of our agency was an embittered, elderly psychologist who had become wealthy from the profits he reaped from his "non-profit" clinic. Representative of his attitude toward the therapists was the standard question he would ask when passing in the hallways, with patients just beyond earshot: "How are your numbers?" In common parlance this translated to "How many patients did you see this week and what percentage of your scheduled patients made their appointments?" Time proved that little else in our lives and jobs mattered to him.

For the sake of my job, I was thankful that my "numbers" were good. Mostly it was because I demanded serious therapeutic dedication from my patients – even the troubled ones. Granted, not all could live up to ideal standards and I regularly had to take this into account; I felt it inappropriate to hold it against some of them, but I still felt it important that they make their commitment to therapy, and make it regularly. Of course, because I was being paid only when they came to session, I had my own secondary financial incentive to pressure them to keep their appointments, but since I felt that this motive of mine largely overlapped with what was in their therapeutic interest I did not feel this to be unethical.

In the times, however, when I felt it acceptable for patients to miss sessions, I made it my focus to keep myself centered, resolve my own frustrations on my own, and not to act out on the patients my feelings of (financial) loss – which I came to learn (see Miller, 1981, 1984, 1990) was like most losses, rooted in my historical emotional abandonments of childhood. After all, my financial situation, and the pathology of our clinic, was not their fault. Few of them had any idea – consciously, at least – of the ill state of affairs of their mental health clinic. Perhaps, though, as Milton Erickson noted in his works with couples (Haley and Erickson, 1985), the patients unconsciously sensed everything.

Buffering patients from the toxicity of the therapeutic environment

Another key aspect of working successfully with psychosis is buffering patients from the pathology of the "therapeutic" environment. This can take many forms. The most clear and simple involves the therapist being consistent – be it consistently respectful, consistently interested, or consistently vulnerable and honest, as Karon and VandenBos (1981) suggest, about his or her own human foibles. There is also a value when therapists make all scheduled sessions, and arrive – and finish – on time. This sets a further model of consistency for patients, and does not replicate their all-too-common history of abandonment and object inconstancy. This creates a safe space and steadfast routine so necessary for the nurturance of therapy.

There is also value in setting clear and appropriate boundaries in areas where the setting lacks boundaries. For example, in my clinic I made a point of asking patients not to use the clinic's phone number to reach me, because the overburdened receptionists were unreliable with messages and I learned that the therapy could not risk intrusion by missed communication. Instead, I provided patients with a private, outside phone number through which they could reach me if necessary, although I encouraged the use of such extra-session contact primarily for emergencies and rescheduling.

I also found it invaluable to buffer, and even nurture, my more emotionally disturbed patients' relationships with their psychiatrists, who also worked at the clinic. The primary way I did this was by developing personal alliances with the clinic psychiatrists myself. I interceded for my patients when necessary, I spoke on their behalf, and sometimes I came into their psychiatric appointments with them – or brought the psychiatrist into our therapy sessions. As a result of my personal investment, their psychiatrists spent more time with them, treated them more flexibly, and took more of a personal interest in their therapy and well-being. Consequently, my patients felt, as Ann-Louise Silver describes in hospital work with borderline patients (Silver, 1992b), that they had a caring, parental-like treatment team devoted to them. This was beneficial in and of itself.

But perhaps most importantly, developing a personal bond with my patients' psychiatrists gave me a platform from which I could express my point of view regarding the value of reducing their medications. After all, it was the psychiatrists, not me, who had the power to reduce medication dosages. I shared my point of view with the psychiatrists, and despite their general disagreement I learned that because I had developed positive working relationships, and even friendships, with them, they often considered my ideas.

In this I followed the example of the pharmaceutical companies, who, via their gift-laden drug representatives, discovered the value in bonding with psychiatrists. All too often the clinic – including patients and therapists – treated the overworked psychiatrists as robotic medication dispensers, disconnected from the therapy. Silver (2003) delineates this phenomenon succinctly, and I realized that if I did not find a way to challenge it my patients would suffer.

Interestingly, many of my patients, especially those early in their therapeutic process, were just as pro-neuroleptic as the overall system, in spite of the often debilitating side effects they suffered. Although I shared my point of view and even some literature with most of them, I met with only limited success. On the contrary, I achieved much more success when the therapy itself, despite the neuroleptics, started helping them recover. Here the patients, in a profound, experiential way, came to realize that internal, and not just pharmaceutical, control was possible. Many had never experienced this before, and this, more than any psychoeducation, caused them to question their medications – and question their fears that the television, their past treatment providers, their families, and their own history and introjects whispered and sometimes yelled in their ears about the necessity of medication. At this point they almost all became open to reducing dosages.

I also found that once psychiatrists witnessed a patient's psychotic symptoms abating on their own, they too became more willing to risk lowering a dosage. Many of my patients' psychiatrists, however, shared with me their fears that tapering neuroleptics would result in worsening symptoms. Since I myself sometimes shared this worry I could empathize. I worked through this conflict, however, by being open with both patients and psychiatrists about these fears, and by telling patients that as they went through the process of lowering dosages I felt it appropriate to increase the frequency of their therapy sessions. Given this logic most were amenable, and perhaps not surprisingly the deepening contact generally seemed to help them improve and integrate more rapidly.

And many fully ended their medications: not just antidepressants, but antipsychotics too, with few "relapses." I lack a fuller degree of experience, however, with mood stabilizers for bipolar disorder, because most of the psychiatrists I worked with refused to taper these for fear of a return to mania.

Yet the more the patients did well, the more the psychiatrists were willing to lower their medications further, and this was an exciting process for patients and for myself. Mostly the psychiatrists were not as excited by it, however, not because they lacked caring but simply because they lacked the time or energy to get excited: their massive caseloads, as Silver (1992a) describes, pressured them to view patients more as symptoms rather than ordinary human beings with feelings and hopes. And who were they to be blamed? How can anyone who works with 30 different patients a day, 5 days a week, and sees the same patient only once a month for 15 minutes or less, not sacrifice some degree of human connection with an individual's healing process?

Recovering from the supposedly unrecoverable

My formal supervisor, too, failed to be impressed with the changes in my patients. Mostly, though, she was either uninterested or just considered such changes to be "flukes," a phenomenon reported by Karon (2003) and others. Often the psychiatrists considered my patients' changes as "flukes" as well. When someone stopped hearing voices or stopped being so radically delusional or paranoid or emotionally explosive, or started bathing again and talking to others and asking questions and actually listening – and even making deeper friendships – the psychiatrists and my supervisor largely felt that the change was as a result of an initial misdiagnosis.

Disturbingly, I learned that it was standard operational procedure for clinic therapists, psychiatrists, and supervisors alike to lean largely on a patient's previously prescribed medications to diagnose him at the intake assessment. For instance, if he came to an initial evaluation already taking olanzapine (Zyprexa) or haloperidol (Haldol), conventional (il)logic had it that he must be psychotic, because otherwise his past psychiatrist would never have prescribed him an antipsychotic. Although I fought this thinking, I could understand the underlying motivation to shortcut the deeper information gathering process necessary to complete a more thorough evaluation. When a therapist or psychiatrist has just 45 minutes allotted to complete an intake, when the patient shows up 10 minutes late, when the patient cannot tell his psychiatric history lucidly and bring no supporting paperwork from past treatment, and when he fails to remember the telephone numbers of past treatment providers – and when there is no time to call them anyway, even if he did – there is great incentive to take his aloofness, skepticism, dirty shirt, and pill bottle of antipsychotics as evidence enough to warrant a diagnosis of "295.30": the Diagnostic and Statistical Manual's classification for paranoid schizophrenia.

Not surprisingly, when patients' psychotic symptoms resolved and they tapered off their medications and started behaving more or less "normally," most psychiatrists I worked with tended not to consider that the patient once *had* had schizophrenia and now was recovering from it, but rather that the patient had never had schizophrenia in the first place – and instead must have had obsessive-compulsive disorder or an odd reaction to stress or an underlying "borderline pathology" or just a reaction to having been an alcoholic for too many years or some such other diagnostic revision of history. After all, conventional wisdom states that schizophrenia is a brain disorder that lasts for life, and The National Alliance for the Mentally Ill itself states on its website (www.nami.org) that "there is no cure for schizophrenia . . ."

Early in my work, I felt less alone when I discovered that Joanne Greenberg, who wrote her tale of recovery from schizophrenia in *I Never Promised You a Rose Garden*, faced the same things decades earlier: after she got well, many told her – some to her face – that she had never been schizophrenic in the first place (Greenberg, personal communication, 11/12/2005; also see Chapter 12), despite the fact that her own therapist, Frieda Fromm-Reichmann, was well-recognized as a master diagnostician (Hornstein, 2000).

But if my colleagues in the clinic failed to appreciate what was happening behind the doors of my office, my patients did not. Sometimes they did not understand the precise mechanisms of the transformation, and sometimes I did not either, but what was unmistakable was that recovery was happening. I saw patients who had held the diagnosis of schizophrenia for decades gradually – and sometimes rather abruptly – lose some or all of their psychotic symptoms. Sometimes they were perplexed by this. Sometimes they took this as a loss, which was frightening for them, and sometimes they had reason beyond existential fears to be afraid. Many had never worked, and the loss of their severe diagnosis jeopardized their disability income. Many patients I worked with also did not want to taper entirely off their medications for this reason, because without medications they had no proof, as it were, that they "really were mentally disabled."

Some wanted to fool their psychiatrists and simply pretend to take their medications, but I could not abide that comfortably, although I did tell them that they had a right to do it if they wished but it was just not something I approved of or could hide. But some actually returned to work – or began to work for the first time – and many before they were even fully tapered off their medications. This was incredibly fulfilling to watch, even if I got little collegial acknowledgement.

But even if my colleagues were not aware of what I was doing, they did respect certain aspects of my work. Many referred their difficult cases to me, because they saw that I tended to work well – that is, from their perspective, to have few overt conflicts – with the more difficult patients. A large part of my buffering a pathological system was that I considered hospitalization of troubled patients an option of last resort, or if possible an option of no resort. I made it a point of resolving emotional conflicts within my office with the doors closed, and not seeking the outside help of psychiatrists, police, or ambulance workers. Along with others (Karon and VandenBos, 1981; Silver, 1992a; Wexler, 1971) I felt that psychiatric hospitalization risked crushing the treatment we were accomplishing, and the few times my patients went into the hospital – always on their own volition, with themselves being the ones primarily choosing that route – I found my fears confirmed. They generally returned to treatment not just with more medications of higher dosages on their dossiers, but returned feeling less empowered, more isolated, and less confident in themselves and their capacity to change their lives. And sometimes they returned more psychotic – if they returned at all. Many never did.

Meanwhile, the value I derived from getting so many internal referrals within the clinic – first from therapists transferring their "impossible" patients to me, second from therapists seeking me out for referral after their patients requested a change of therapists, and last from therapists who were leaving the clinic and chose me as their successor – is that I got to hear firsthand, in detail, from both ex-therapist and patient, what had happened in the previous therapy. This was enlightening, to say the least.

For every truly brilliant thing I heard about a past therapist I had the privilege of hearing ten confused and unconscious things they said or acted out, if only in a frustrated reaction to their more disturbed patients' hallu-cinations, delusions, and resistances. Although I could relate to my col-leagues' frustrations, I relate more to Karon (2003) when he points out that therapists who are inexperienced and untrained at working with schizo-phrenia tell us little about the potential efficacy of psychotherapy with schizophrenia. Likewise, would we judge the potential efficacy of a topical antibiotic if a patient took it orally?

That said, I had my share of "failures," "schizophrenic" patients who never changed, who had been diagnosed with schizophrenia and kept on neuroleptics for decades and would probably remain as such for the rest of their lives. I tried to reach a part of them beneath the medications, but saw little movement. And while many of them appreciated my attempts to try something different, some did not – and these I did not pressure, or at least pressured less.

Yet I worked with some patients who stated they felt comfortable being pacified by their medications, and when one considers their tragic histories of highs and far worse lows when they were medication-free, it felt inappropriate to contradict them. But I did see enough patients transform to know that healing could happen, and happen within an environment where it was not considered a real and viable option.

Conclusion

Overall, doing meaningful psychotherapy with psychotic patients is diffi-cult, and all the more so in an environment that works against it. This dramatically increases the burden on the therapist, but for a clinician willing to find appropriate, experienced supervision, to institute enough boundaries to create a healthy therapeutic container, to nurture and buffer patients' relationships with their psychiatrists, and most of all to keep in perspective the potential for recovery in even the most disturbed patients, then practicing the impossible profession in an impossible environment may not really be so impossible.

References

Akhtar, S. (2004). *Schizophrenia in Pakistan.* http://www.isps-us.org/articles/pakistan.htm

Breggin, P. (1991). *Toxic Psychiatry.* New York: St. Martin's Press.

Buechler, S. (2000). Necessary and unnecessary losses: The analyst's mourning. *Contemporary Psychoanalysis*, 36: 77–90.

Chang, D., Tong, H., Shi, Q., and Zeng, Q. (2005). Letting a hundred flowers bloom: Counseling and psychotherapy in the People's Republic of China. *Journal of Mental Health Counseling*, 27: 104–116.

Chessick, R. (2001). The secret life of the psychoanalyst. *Journal of the American Academy of Psychoanalysis*, 29: 403–426.

Cooper, A. (1986). Some limitations on therapeutic effectiveness: The "burnout syndrome." *Psychoanalytic Quarterly*, 55: 576–598.

Correia, K. (2001). *A Handbook for Correctional Psychologists: Guidance for the Prison Practitioner*. Springfield, IL: C. C. Thomas.

Dorman, D. (2003). *Dante's Cure: A Journey out of Madness*. New York: Other Press.

Fromm-Reichmann, F. (1950). *Principles of Intensive Psychotherapy*. Chicago: University of Chicago Press.

Gottdiener, W. and Haslam, N. (2003). A critique of the methods and conclusions in the patient outcome research team (PORT) Report on Psychological Treatments for Schizophrenia. *Journal of the American Academy of Psychoanalysis*, 31: 191–208.

Haley, J. and Erickson, M. (1985). *Conversations with Milton Erickson: Changing Couples*. New York: W. W. Norton.

Hedges, L. (2000). *Terrifying Transferences: Aftershocks of Childhood Trauma*. Northvale, NJ: Jason Aronson.

Herman, J. (1992). *Trauma and Recovery*. New York: Basic Books.

Hornstein, G. (2000). *To Redeem One Person is to Redeem the World: The Life of Frieda Fromm-Reichmann*. New York: Free Press.

Howell, E. (2002). Dual visions, dual voices: Reply to commentary. *Psychoanalytic Dialogues*, 12: 971–986.

Jackson, G. (2005). *Rethinking Psychiatric Drugs: A Guide for Informed Consent*. Bloomington, IN: Authorhouse.

Kadushin, A. (1968). Games people play in supervision. *Social Work*, 13: 23–32.

Kanwal, G. (1997). Hope, respect, and flexibility in the psychotherapy of schizophrenia. *Contemporary Psychoanalysis*, 33: 133–150.

Karon, B. (1992). The fear of understanding schizophrenia. *Psychoanalytic Psychology*, 9: 191–211.

Karon, B. (2003). The tragedy of schizophrenia without psychotherapy. *Journal of the American Academy of Psychoanalysis*, 31: 89–118.

Karon, B. and VandenBos, G. (1981). *Psychotherapy of Schizophrenia: The Treatment of Choice*. New York: Jason Aronson.

Kennedy, C. and Zillmer, E. (2006). *Military Psychology: Clinical and Operational Applications*. New York: Guilford Press.

Koehler, B. (2003). Interview with Gaetano Benedetti, M.D. *Journal of the American Academy of Psychoanalysis*, 31: 75–87.

Kupers, T. (2001). Mental health in men's prisons. In D. Sabo, T. Kupers, and W. London (Eds.), *Prison Masculinities* (pp. 192–197). Philadelphia, PA: Temple University Press.

Lambo, T. (1957). *A Study of Social and Health Problems of Nigerian Students in Britain*. Ibadan, Western Nigeria: Government Publications.

Li, M., Duan, C., Ding, B., Yue, D., and Beitman, B. (1994). Psychotherapy integration in modern China. *Journal of Psychotherapy Practice and Research*, 3: 277–283.

Miller, A. (1981). *Prisoners of Childhood*. New York: Basic Books.

Miller, A. (1984). *Thou Shalt Not be Aware*. New York: Farrar, Straus, and Giroux.

Miller, A. (1990). *Banished Knowledge*. New York: Doubleday.

Miller, A. (1997). *The Drama of the Gifted Child*. New York: Basic Books.

Moran, M. (2007). Their religion may differ, but goals are the same. *Psychiatric News*, 42: 10.

Perry, H. (1982). *Psychiatrist of America: The Life of Harry Stack Sullivan*. Cambridge, MA: Harvard University Press.

Schulz, C. (1989). Recollections of supervision with Frieda Fromm-Reichmann. In A.-L. Silver (Ed.), *Psychoanalysis and Psychosis* (pp. 47–77). Madison, CT: International Universities Press.

Searles, H. (1962). Scorn, disillusionment and adoration in the psychotherapy of schizophrenia. *Psychoanalysis and the Psychoanalytical Review*, 49: 39–60.

Sherman, N. (2007). *Stoic Warriors: The Ancient Philosophy Behind the Military Mind*. Oxford: Oxford University Press.

Silver, A. (1989). *Psychoanalysis and Psychosis*. Madison, CT: International Universities Press.

Silver, A. (1992a). Intensive psychotherapy of psychosis in a decade of change. *The Psychiatric Hospital*, 23: 49–54.

Silver, A. (1992b). Treating the hospitalized borderline patient: Reworking trauma of toddlerhood. *Journal of the American Academy of Psychoanalysis*, 20: 114–129.

Silver, A. (2000). The current relevance of Fromm-Reichmann's work. *Psychiatry*, 63: 308–322.

Strean, H. (1993). *Resolving Counterresistances in Psychotherapy*. New York: Brunner/Mazel.

Sullivan, H. (1953). *The Interpersonal Theory of Psychiatry*. New York: W. W. Norton.

Torrey, E. (2001). *Surviving Schizophrenia: A Manual for Families, Patients, and Providers* (4th ed.). New York: Harper Collins.

Towl, G. (2006). *Psychological Research in Prisons*. Malden, MA: BPS Blackwell.

Wexler, M. (1971). Schizophrenia: Conflict and deficiency. *Psychoanalytic Quarterly*, 40: 83–99.

Whitaker, R. (2002) *Mad in America: Bad Science, Bad Medicine, and the Enduring Mistreatment of the Mentally Ill*. Cambridge, MA: Perseus Press.

Williams, T. (1987). *Post-Traumatic Stress Disorders: A Handbook for Clinicians*. Cincinnati, OH: Disabled American Veterans.

Part 3

Listening to the patient: stories of what really works

Chapter 10

Leaving schizophrenia: the returning home of the awakened mind

Catherine Penney

Editors' Introduction: Now we enter the world of the patient, and hear in their words what has really worked in favor of their recovery.

This chapter is Catherine Penney's personal account of her own recovery from schizophrenia. Ms. Penney has been a fully functioning registered nurse in the mental health system in Southern California for the last two decades. Earlier in her life, however, she spent several years in the throes of schizophrenia, experiencing hallucinations, delusions, and many varieties of disorganized thinking and catatonia. This is the gripping personal story of her therapy with Dr. Daniel Dorman (who co-wrote Chapter 1), and her ascent back to sanity – without the use of psychiatric medications.

Penney notes how she began her journey in the mental health system on medication alone and explores how this functioned as a weak starting point for her treatment. The strength in her treatment came from her therapeutic engagement with her therapist, and the trust he invested in her, and she in him.

The end of a long road

I remember the day my mother drove me the 50 miles from our home outside of Los Angeles to UCLA's Neuropsychiatric Institute. I had stopped functioning, I had become isolated and withdrawn, and I rarely left my bedroom. I had also stopped bathing and ate very little. It had been weeks since I had actually carried on a conversation with anyone. My parents knew something was very wrong, and even though I had gone through two previous hospitalizations without any improvement, they were desperately trying to hold on to the hope that I would receive the help that I needed. It was agonizing for my mother to watch me deteriorate day after day and not be sure if I would ever return to being the daughter she had once known.

Earlier that morning I had struggled to put on a pair of nylons and one of my favorite dresses. It was a dress that no longer fitted my 89-pound frame, it just hung on me. My nylons followed suit and pooled at my ankles. I, however, paid little attention, because it was all I could do to muster up enough energy to dress myself. The voices that had harassed me all through the night were getting louder, so it was of the utmost importance for me to upgrade my survival mode to a more critical level. This meant shutting myself down even more. I visualized food items in my mind and created voices of my own that named those particular food items. I then traveled down with the food voices – down to the bottom of the pit. This kept the other voices out. Sometimes electrical impulses interrupted my descent, razor sharp, darting up and down my head. When this happened I had no choice but to allow the murderous influx of uninvited voices to come flooding in.

Such was my state of mind on that bright fall day as I prepared myself for the long drive to UCLA. Earlier that morning my mother had seemed very busy attending to her household duties and making sure my two youngest sisters and my brother had brushed their teeth and made their beds. I was the oldest of five children. My sister Cindy was 1 year younger than me and had married at 18. Although she and her husband lived only 5 miles away she had escaped. My stepfather was staying home to watch the kids and liked to inspect their bedrooms to see if everything was in tiptop shape. It was the Marine in him, Mother told me. He had done 24 years of military service, spanning World War II, Korea, and Vietnam.

The hour-long drive to UCLA seemed to take forever. My mother was quiet, but there was a sense of urgency that this time her daughter would get some help – would get well. Love, spoken not in words but by way of that ineffable connection that happens between a mother and daughter, presented itself in its stillness. A small part of my soul, still intact, felt love amid all the disorganized clutter that was swirling around in my head. A pain and longing emerged, only to be quickly cut off. I could not tell my mother I loved her, that I needed her. It was too dangerous and, as with all dangerous emotion that attempted to breathe its way to the surface, it was quite effectively snuffed out and replaced by voices.

UCLA's Neuropsychiatric Institute loomed larger than life over the many other structures and businesses in Westwood. Westwood was a fairly hip college town in West Los Angeles. I walked mainly with my head down. I literally could not hold my head up. I did, however, manage to hold it up long enough to steal a glimpse of the Neuropsychiatric Institute, which I would come to call NPI. Once inside the busy screening room I sat with my mother and waited. I really had no expectations, just a touch of curiosity and perhaps an ember of hope, buried beneath the wall I had created to keep the outside world out so that I could continue managing the invasion taking place within.

My first hospitalization

My past experiences with psychiatrists and "the system" had been downright bleak. A year earlier, in March of 1968, when I was 18, I had been hospitalized in St. Joseph's Hospital for 14 days. There I first saw Dr. B., a neurologist. During the first three days, which I spent on the medical floor, Dr. B. gave me a battery of tests, including a thorough neurological exam, to see if I had a brain tumor. After my last test, a pneumoencephalogram, which left me with the whopper of all headaches, he met with my parents and me to discuss the results. Looking directly at them, and ignoring me, he stated, "The tests have all come back negative. There is no brain tumor, no cancer. It is my professional opinion that your daughter is suffering from a mental illness." He then went on. "I've arranged for Dr. G., one of our finest psychiatrists, to visit with Catherine before she is discharged from the medical floor. I think it would be best if you both met with Dr. G. first."

My parents did not speak. There was dead silence. Was the silence from relief or dread? I did not know, nor did I care. All I knew was that I wanted to get out of the hospital and go back home. Home was familiar, home was where I could go to my room, shut the door, draw the drapes, and focus on going "down under." Going "down under" was my way of shutting down and creating an alternate space to get away from the murderous voices. It was also my way of concentrating my imagination on certain foods that in the past, when I had embarked on my diet, had given me pleasure. That this ritual of imagining these foods was no longer giving me pleasure was not important. It was all I had and was my only source of control.

I felt annoyed when Dr. G. came to see me the next morning. I was still in my hospital gown and desperately trying to make sure that the blanket from my bed totally covered my thin body. It did, but I still felt naked and exposed. Finally, after about 5 minutes of silence Dr. G. spoke: "Do you hear voices?" "Yes," I replied. Dr. G. said nothing. Instead he slowly backed his chair away from me, and after readjusting his bifocals stood up and walked out of the room. I was transferred from St. Joseph's medical ward to their neuropsychiatric ward the very next day.

I was then in my senior year of high school. It was during my junior year that the voices had started to come, soft whispers at first, accompanied by an overwhelming heaviness and pressure that seemed to pervade all my senses. By my senior year the soft whispers had blown up into full-grown voices telling me to kill myself, to kill my mother, and to kill my youngest sister.

During that first hospitalization Dr. G. saw me for 10 minutes twice a week. He started me on chlorpromazine (Thorazine), trifluoperazine (Stelazine), and benztropine (Cogentin). I do not remember the exact dosages, only that I took them three times a day. I became like a walking zombie. The drugs dulled my senses and put me in a kind of limbo-land where there was no feeling at all. The voices were still there in the background, just not as loud. Each time I saw Dr. G. I told him that the medicine was making me feel sleepy and I asked if they could be decreased. His answer was always the same: "The nurses tell me, Catherine, that you don't attend the ward activities and that you isolate in your room. Sedation is a common side effect of the medication. In time you will adjust." What I did not tell Dr. G., because it was just too hard to think of the words to articulate, was that when I tried going to ward activities I could not focus, I felt too groggy, and I could not hold my head up. So what was the point?

I was discharged and returned home to try to finish my remaining two and a half months of high school. It was agony. I was different, I knew I was different, and in fact I had always had a pervasive feeling of being different. A fleeting desire to embrace normalcy arose within me, fueled by the temporary cessation of the noises in my head, but my motor movements were slow, I could not concentrate, and I could not hold my head up because the feeling of weight was still there. My peers at school noticed this. Although the voices had disappeared into the background, I had the constant feeling of having a monkey on my back. Once again I resorted to hiding out in the library and the girls' rest-rooms during lunch and break times, as I had done during my freshmen and sophomore years.

A prevailing sense of doom followed me everywhere. One day in an act of total desperation I stared up at the crucifix hanging above my bed. I pleaded with the wooden figure of Christ to come down off the cross and save me. I sat for an hour watching the sun disappear behind the scarlet sky. All the rosaries I said every evening while kneeling on hard stone and all the Sunday masses and Holy Days of Obligation that I devoutly attended were all for nothing. As night approached it became apparent to me that no one, not even Jesus, was going to save me. My heart sank. I thought, "I am dead." Death of the body and mind is one thing, but soul death is quite another. There are no words to describe the death of a soul. It was then that thoughts of suicide, once a fearful and uninvited intruder, became the most important weapon in my arsenal of defenses – and my one ultimate means of escape.

My second hospitalization

My second psychiatric hospitalization at St. Joseph's came 7 months later. I had graduated from high school, which was a miracle in and of itself considering how poorly I had functioned, but the limbo-land I was in had only got worse. I felt like I was in a state of suspended animation. One day I was stopped by cops as I drove my car downtown to the local grocery store. The police escorted me home and my mother had the embarrassing task of informing them that I was not on street drugs – but taking medication. "It's for nervous problems," she told them.

By the time of this incident I had started classes at Saddleback Junior College. This lasted about 2 weeks. Paranoia, the feeling that someone was after me, followed me to every class and in between classes. I hid out in my car most of the time. The medications were no longer working. The voices returned and were much louder. There was no point in going to class because I could not understand what the teacher was saying.

It was a 2-week marathon of running, hiding, and dodging – and not just from classes and other students, but from the time bomb waiting to explode inside my head. Making eye contact with anyone became a liability for me. I was sure people could read my mind and I did not want my evil thoughts – which manifested in the form of voices – to be exposed.

I dropped out of college. I had no future, and felt there was no place for me in this world. Despair of unimaginable proportions took up residence inside me – as did a hopelessness that cut to the bone. That led to my second hospitalization, which lasted again for 14 days. My medications were increased. I received no therapy. Not long after returning home I began having dystonic reactions – head and neck stiffness and jerking movements. I also felt an ever-present sense of internal restlessness and agitation that would not go away. My mother and stepfather were more than a little concerned. "It's the schizophrenia," Dr. G. told them.

Finally, one morning after doing internal battle with the voices all night, I walked into the kitchen, took a handful of chlorpromazine (Thorazine), and announced to my mother that I was going to kill myself. The look of sadness, frustration, and pain on her face paralyzed me. I ended up throwing the chlorpromazine on the floor. Better to go "back down under" to that alternate space, absent of all emotion and feeling. Better to pretend that everything was okay.

I meet Dr. Dorman – and therapy begins

I remember the day I met Dr. Dorman. It came in November of 1969 on my first day in UCLA's Neuropsychiatric Institute, where Dr. Dorman was doing his psychiatric residency. Dr. Rubin, the head psychiatrist, saw me first. Quite frankly I was so engrossed in my chaotic inner world that I remember very little of our encounter. What I do recall is a question Dr. Rubin posed to me in a rather abrasive tone of voice: "Why are you punishing yourself?" This was followed by, "Do you hate yourself that much?"

Verbally I did not respond, but internally his questions hit a chord. As was my usual way of dealing with uncomfortable interactions, I relegated it to the nether lands of repression and continued on with the futile management of my underground world. Acknowledging my silence, Dr. Rubin left the room to speak privately with my mother.

Fifteen minutes later, Dr. Daniel Dorman, the admitting doctor that day, walked into the screening room. I do not remember much of this first meeting, only that Dr. Dorman talked *to* me, not *at* me nor *down* to me. I also remember that he did not become impatient when I did not answer all of his questions. This did not make a big impact on me at the time, but on an unconscious level it cleared a space allowing what tiny bit of clarity that existed to later on take seed and grow. Eighty-nine pounds, with head down to my chin and drooling, I must have been a sight! I broke my silence to make one comment: "I need to be in a hospital."

My first session with Dr. Dorman – the entire 50 minutes – was spent in silence. I did not say a word. Other than introducing himself and asking how I was doing, Dr. Dorman said nothing either. I sat in a chair in a fetal position rocking back and forth, quite content with not having to deal with diversions that might take me away from my primary focus of managing my chaotic inner world. At the end of the session I found it odd that Dr. Dorman had stayed the whole 50 minutes without leaving. Equally perplexing was his comment as he walked me out of his office: "See you tomorrow, Catherine, 9:00 am sharp." The one thought that burst its way through the murkiness was "Why?"

The next day our therapy session was pretty much the same. This went on for quite a while, for about 6 months. Dr. Dorman would introduce topics that had to do with hospital life and ward routines, asking my impressions and making comments about how difficult it must be adjusting to a new environment. I *was* having difficulty adjusting to the hospital environment, but I could not articulate these thoughts, and even had I been able to articulate them I did not feel safe enough to expose them. What ran through my mind was that all my thoughts were evil, that I was a bad person, and that it was better just to keep quiet.

Then one morning during our session Dr. Dorman, in reference to my catatonic posturing and rocking, commented, "The world can be a pretty scary place – I bet you feel safe in there." An antenna went up. How did he know? That was the beginning. Although I did not show any outward signs of change or improvement, and would not for two and a half more years, the seed had been planted.

In *Black Elk Speaks* (Neihardt, 2000), Black Elk, the Native American holy man, stated:

> It is from understanding that power comes; and the power in the ceremony was in understanding what it meant; for nothing can live well except in a manner that is suited to the way the sacred Power of the World lives and moves . . . for the growing power is rooted in mystery like the night, and reaches lightward. Seeds sprout in the darkness of the ground before they know the summer and the day. In the night of the womb the spirit quickens into flesh.

> (pp. 160–161)

Little by little I opened up. And as I began to open up I started hearing voices to kill Dr. Dorman. At the staff meetings the nurses would bring up numerous concerns. My weight had plummeted to 85 pounds, I stayed isolated in my room and did not attend activities, I refused to bathe, and I had to be escorted to the tub room by a nurse who literally bathed me. Washing my hair was out of the question. (I felt there was too much electricity centered at the top of my head and that water falling on my head would blow a fuse, causing my head to explode.)

To my dismay, Dr. Dorman kept showing up for therapy 5–6 days a week and staying the full 50 minutes. He brought up abandonment and rejection issues. During our sessions Dr. Dorman never judged. He listened, and then made comments addressing the underlying meaning of what my hallucinations or delusions were trying to communicate. Later, when I was able to engage more, he would validate my interpretations and at the same time add impressions of his own about my interpretations – which helped to lead me into a better understanding of the dynamics of my life's experience that had led me into mental illness.

Dr. Dorman always had a sense of presence. His authenticity and sincerity burned bright, though in the beginning this was too dangerous for me to acknowledge. When I started hearing voices to kill Dr. Dorman, my symptoms started getting worse. My entire psychotic world was being slowly dismantled without my conscious permission. At the same time, tiny pockets of clarity were popping up, causing me to become aware of how hopelessly crazy I was. On one of Dr. Dorman's vacations I attempted to hang myself by using a sash from one of my dresses. I tied it around the bar holding the clothes hangers in my closet. I made a noose, slipped it around my neck, and attempted to step off several overnight bags so my feet would be off the floor. A nurse – tipped off by my roommate – intervened and I was immediately whisked up to 3-South and placed on suicide watch. There the odor of wilted roses permeated the halls, bringing to mind images of cemeteries and dead and dying things. For 3 days I vegetated along with the other patients, most of whom were of college age. A psychiatric technician was my shadow and followed me everywhere, even to the bathroom. Somewhat annoyed by my silence and unresponsiveness, he said, "Most of the kids on this floor went on too many bad trips. They fried their brains using LSD. So what's your excuse?"

As soon as Dr. Dorman returned from his vacation he immediately had me transferred back to the open unit. In an earlier suicide attempt I stole orange shellac from Occupational Therapy and tried to poison myself by pouring it in milk and then drinking it. My stomach was pumped out in the Emergency Room while I was awake. It was an excruciatingly painful experience. I remember thinking, "There must be a better way to get out of Dodge." Dr. Dorman came to see me that evening on his Sunday off to give support and to process the event.

For two and a half years I developed a pattern of evading the ward's daily routines. Instead I established my own, such as going to the patient refrigerator nine or ten times a day and checking on the pie my mother brought me when she visited every Sunday. I ate a piece of pie for dinner 4 days out of the week and gave the remainder of the pie to the nurses. The nursing staff had pretty much given up on their attempts to get me to go to activities. I was like a fixture, never changing, always there, for the most part immobile and non-verbal.

Patients, however, took an interest in me and would come over and try to engage me. Perhaps they sensed a loneliness and alienation in me that they related to and were not yet quite able to conquer in themselves. Later in my recovery when I would look back at this time – when the voices were the loudest and I was about as low as I could get – I recalled people who approached me with kindness and compassion, causing me to feel less ugly and strange.

Onward to a new facility – and to recovery

During the summer of 1972 the buzz around 2-West was that Dr. Dorman would be ending his residency and leaving NPI to go into private practice. *That was it. This was the end.* I prepared my suicide note. UCLA's Neuropsychiatric Institute was not a long-term care facility for the chronically mentally ill and I had already been an inpatient for close to 3 years, longer than anyone else. When Dr. Dorman informed me that he intended to have me transferred over to the Westwood, a private psychiatric facility where he would be on staff, my panic intensified. "I have to die," I told him. "Why?" he replied. There was genuine sadness in his voice. It was the sincerity of his response that lingered far beyond the fear and trauma of the move, which represented to me yet another uprooting, another change to which I would have to adjust my internal world, a world that was already beginning to erode away. I made the transfer.

The Westwood was an old, large estate that had been converted into a private psychiatric hospital. Bougainvillea vines draped over the outside walls and a variety of brightly colored flowers peppered the green, manicured lawns. It was at the Westwood where the seed that had been planted and watered for the past 3 years started to show signs of coming to fruition. In the first week of our therapy sessions I brought up state hospitals. I asked Dr. Dorman why I had not been sent to Camarillo State Hospital. I had a sense that most of the patients at the Westwood were not as sick as I. As was his usual style Dr. Dorman addressed the underlying fear of why it was hard for me to trust that he would not give up on me – like so many others in my life had.

Then one day at a session a strange thing happened. I took a risk and told Dr. Dorman I was glad he did not send me to Camarillo. After that things began to change. I began to get curious. I had to share a room with three other young women who talked incessantly, way into the night – always about guys. I was struggling with trying to stay "down under" so I could control my space. And now it was not working! The voices were getting louder, a reaction to the interruption in my concentration by the human noise around me. My roommates' verbal escapades were competing with the voices for my attention.

We discussed this at our sessions and I demanded to be put in a private room so I could maintain a better hold internally. Dr. Dorman said no, that it was important that I did not isolate myself. I felt like I was being pulled from both sides of a torture rack. Fears of annihilation, of losing an identity, of not having a sense of self – these issues were delicately woven into our therapeutic sessions.

One evening I heard my roommates talking about one of the psych techs. She said, "Have you seen Bruce? What a hunk – he sure would make a good lay!" Although I was 22 years old, I had no idea what the word "lay" meant – in this context. But my interest was sparked. I became more and more curious about my external surroundings. In sessions I began to bring up some of my deepest fantasies, one of which involved saving a whole platoon of Marines from the Vietcong. In reality when I was 10 months old my biological father had been killed in Korea in 1950 after having chosen to spearhead an assault and secure a strategic location rather than send what few men were left in his company. The hill had later been named "Penney's Hill," in his honor. Instead of commenting on how crazy or delusional a fantasy might sound, Dr. Dorman instead pointed out the connections. He created a safe place for me to expose my inner demons – and my inner truth.

I started attending activities. Patients would come up to me and I would not turn away. I began to talk with my roommates a little. My sessions with Dr. Dorman delved more deeply into my family psychodynamics. After my biological father had been killed, my mother, a young widow with a 10-month-old baby and pregnant with my sister Cindy, went through a serious depression and could barely take care of me. Being a small child and not understanding, I felt I was the cause of her sadness. When it became really bad both sets of grandparents took turns babysitting Cindy and me at their homes. During that time abandonment themes dominated my sleep time. I had nightmares frequently. They generally involved my grandparents returning Cindy and me to our home – that had no mother in sight. "Cathy's extremely sensitive" was a phrase used frequently by my mother and grandparents. Also: "She cries at the drop of a hat."

Throughout my early childhood, noises, no matter how small and insignificant – such as water slowly dripping from the bathroom faucet at night – used to cause me to feel extremely nervous and agitated, interrupting my sleep. Whenever my mother used the vacuum cleaner it felt like an explosion was going off in my head – and I literally had to leave the house.

When I was 6 years old my mother married again, to a career Marine and bachelor – my stepfather. They had three more children together. My stepfather turned out to be an alcoholic, but the destructive and insidious disease of alcoholism did not rear its ugly head until 2 years into their marriage. Although some good times with periods of normalcy did exist in my family, most of my recollections are of my parents fighting. From the time my father came home from work, from 4 pm onward, he started on the rum and Coke. By dinner time and sometimes way into the night, there would be name-calling, shouting, and verbal threats. I lived with the ever-present fear that my stepfather would resort to physical violence against my mother. I obsessed about it. What would happen to me, what would happen to Cindy, Bunny, Michael, and Theresa if something happened to our mother?

Because I was the oldest, the responsibility would fall on me – even though I could barely take care of myself. School was not much better. Shy and introverted, I was the odd one – which made me an easy target for ridicule. Since I was also ridiculed at home by my father when he was drunk – which tended to be almost every night – I had nowhere to go with my feelings. It was not okay for me to be sad, it was not okay for me to be angry, in fact it was not okay for me to feel at all.

During our sessions Dr. Dorman and I exposed and gently peeled away more and more layers of trauma and repressed underground "stuff." I began to feel the re-emergence of feelings that had been split off long ago and replaced by voices. I started showing interest in my environment and began going to Group. And with my growing awareness came the dawning of insight. My recovery and letting go of the schizophrenia was done in *little steps*. My improvement externally – the decreasing of my delusions and hallucinations – was just the beginning.

For the first couple of weeks after I initially opened my eyes – as they had been literally closed for two years (except for when I needed to get around, at which point I would crack them open a little) – my visual perceptions were distorted. I experienced objects in my environment as being upside-down and in slow motion. Dr. Dorman was my guide through this maze. In our sessions he told me that what I was experiencing was a normal reaction for someone who, for survival purposes, had totally shut themselves down mentally, emotionally, and physically. He never expressed doubt that my perceptual abilities would return. And of course they did – though slowly. It was an exhilarating experience during this period, for I was beginning to experience myself and life in a whole new way. Excitement and fear coexisted as I ventured out to explore the world and make human contact. When fear got the upper hand the voices returned. But within me, however, motivation had taken the place of apathy and ambivalence. Instead of letting the fear and negativity take over, I read psalms from the Bible while playing rock music on the radio. Instead of listening to the lyrics of the Stones, The Moody Blues, and The Who, I would concentrate on the particular psalm that I was reading, reciting it aloud. This drowned out the voices. The positive words from the psalms together with the loud rhythmic beat of the rock music stimulated positive energy within me. To counteract negative thoughts I recited positive, uplifting affirmations every morning upon getting up and every night before going to bed. As a new sense of "self" was emerging, so too was a profound sense of the sacred and of rebirth.

Recovery after the hospital

The recovery period after leaving the Westwood was the hardest part of my journey – because now I was facing new territory. In places where only voices had ruled my inner terrain there was now nothing but space – deep and expansive space. It was at this time, when I was in my own studio apartment, where I felt the greatest pull to go backwards, to slip back into old patterns. Without that supportive therapeutic alliance with Dr. Dorman I would have most definitely succumbed to the siren's call. I continued to see Dr. Dorman after my discharge at his office for another 4 years. During that time I had relearned to drive a car, and had started back at school again. When I received F grades for Philosophy and Psychology – in my first attempts at taking classes at a community college 4 months after discharge – I was despondent. My mind still could not focus or concentrate. Most disturbing to me was the inability to draw a connection between words such as "cat" or "dog" to an actual cat or dog. Dr. Dorman reassured me that my brain was neither damaged nor broken. He illustrated this through the symbol of an old house, pointing out how an old house that has not been lived in for a while draws dust and cobwebs. When a new family moves in, the house is cleaned, used, and becomes like new again. He told me, "All the faculties you had before you became ill, Cathy, will come back. Give yourself time." I hung on to those words for dear life.

The following semester I retook those classes and received B grades. Recovery, like life, is a journey, not a destination. In *The Soul's Code*, James Hillman (1996) writes: "For even tomato plants and the tallest trees send down roots as they rise towards the light. Yet the metaphors for our lives see mainly the upward part of organic motion" (p. 41).

I found myself spontaneously breaking out into tears with the least notice. I realized I needed to allow myself to grieve for the Cathy I had been before the schizophrenia that was now no more – and to grieve for the schizophrenia itself, which had become my identity for the last 6 years. As my vision of the world expanded, I found myself developing an independent, healthy identity. I began making friends at school and started dating.

Here Dr. Dorman was my reality check. He helped to affirm the reality of my perceptual apparatus. This was crucial to my growth and development and adjustment to a life without psychosis. He acknowledged the vastness of my insecurity, yet at the same time he helped me to explore and discover my own inner strength and resources. For the 8 years I was in therapy with Dr. Dorman I was never treated as a diagnosis, nor as someone with limitations whose symptoms, at best, needed to be managed or subdued. Dr. Dorman did not reduce my inner experience to mere pathology. Most importantly Dr. Dorman believed in my wholeness and capacity to heal even when no one else did. This was conveyed to me throughout the years of therapy at a most profound level.

My life since recovery

It has been 33 years since my hospitalization at UCLA's Neuropsychiatric Institute and 29 years since my last therapy session with Dr. Dorman. No antipsychotic medications were used during the 8 years I was under Dr. Dorman's care. I obtained a Psychiatric Technician license in 1978 and a Registered Nurse license in 1984. I have steadily worked in the mental health field for 28 years. I have not had any recurrence of psychosis, nor do I fear the schizophrenia returning.

Sometimes in the soft silence of an enchanted evening I can recall a sorrowful, tortured creature sitting alone in the sterile room of a hospital, rocking back and forth, and fighting an invisible army of invading terrorist voices trying to take siege of her mind. Amidst all the turmoil an image would appear and then disappear ever so quickly – of a smiling, radiant girl, a Cathy that was finally free. Some might have called it a delusion. I call it a dream. Everyone has a dream no matter what their diagnosis. Thank you Dr. Dorman for believing in my dream.

References

Hillman, J. (1996). *The Soul's Code: In Search of Character and Meaning*. New York: Random House.
Neihardt, J. (2000). *Black Elk Speaks*. Lincoln and London: University of Nebraska Press.

Chapter 11

Life in the mines: a retrospective on my therapy

Joanne Greenberg

Editors' Introduction: Joanne Greenberg, who wrote a bestselling, fiction-alized account of her recovery from schizophrenia in I Never Promised You a Rose Garden, *was, from 1948 to 1952, a patient of Frieda Fromm-Reichmann at Chestnut Lodge (the location of two of the vignettes from Chapter 2). Born in 1932, Greenberg began hearing auditory hallucinations well before her teen years, and also experienced visual hallucinations and significant disorganized thinking. She created her own language, Irian, immortalized in her book, as the language of Yr.*

Although Greenberg recovered fully from schizophrenia before the invention of chlorpromazine (Thorazine), the first neuroleptic medication, her recovery process did involve medications and cold wet sheet packs – and she writes candidly of the positives and negatives of this here in this chapter.

Greenberg is the author of 17 novels and collections of short stories, and has worked for nearly 20 years as a professor of anthropology at the Colorado School of Mines, and prior to that worked as a sixth grade teacher and an emergency medical technician. She has been married for over 50 years, and is the mother of two adult sons.

Introduction

I suppose it is inaccurate to say that I went through hospitalization without the help of drugs. I had a nightly dose of Seconal (a barbiturate) and later switched to chloral hydrate; a shotglass full of that used to astonish the new doctors coming on the ward. We all had industrial strength doses of sleeping drugs, with repeat slugs if we woke up at night and needed them. We all often had screaming nightmares and I liked chloral hydrate because it helped with those. Some time in the third year of our relationship, Frieda remarked that anything that was powerful enough to guarantee me a dreamless night's sleep was powerful enough to cause less desirable things, and I quit cold. A side effect of chloral hydrate was that it helped clear me before I slept, as cold wet sheet packs did, so that I could get a glimpse into what sanity a clear mind felt like. The intimation was extremely valuable to me.

What was helpful in my recovery? First, I think, was my relationship with Frieda. She always, *always* looked on us as partners, and not unequal partners in the process. I have said before that *we were miners in a shaft mine*, following veins of gold-bearing ore, which we dug and sluiced for nuggets of meaning. It was dark in the mine and often dangerous. I had the map; she had the light. She also had – my little joke – the height, by which I meant the height over our situation. It is important that the therapist does not get sucked into the patient's scheme. To mix a metaphor, nobody needs another drowner to help him when he is drowning. Frieda would say, "I've never been mentally ill; I don't know what it's like. This is work for you to tell me, to take me along." And when I would get out of contact, she would say, "Where are you now? Take me along."

Daniel Mackler (2006) has noted Frieda's weaknesses, and some coping mechanisms that might not always have worked well for her. His paper was a poignant reminder to me that the weaknesses of the therapist can and will be enlisted to bring home the necessary – the healing truth that waters the roots of health in the mentally ill colleague. I do not mean that the therapist turns patient. I mean that the therapist gets it wrong, as Frieda often did with her interpretations or suggestions, because the therapist is human and the patient needs to know that.

The best metaphor I can think of for the process we and you go through is the story of the Wizard of Oz. The patient needs to go armed with everything she can bring to the quest: brain, heart, courage, and quintessence (Toto). She seeks the wizard-healer. She finds him through great adversity and much suffering, wrong turns and detours, dust-throwing, and obfuscation. At last there he is, wizard at first, then humbug, then a person, mortal and unsure, who has to admit "I don't know how it works" when he later floats away and leaves the patient not "well" but no longer ill and with a very good fighting chance and some more weapons to use.

A wonderful book has recently been published called *Out of the Woods* by Hauser, Allen, and Golden (2006). The book examines a cross-section of kids in a therapeutic center. Some make it to health, some do not. Why did this girl succeed and that one fail? Why did this boy learn the coping skills he needed and that one not? The difference was not in the therapy but in the peculiar strengths and weaknesses of the kids themselves. What weapons does each bring to the fight? One big impetus to join in the struggle and not stand outside of it is the suffering involved. A doctor once told me that he thought I had a good chance of recovery because I was suffering so much. "People who hurt less are less likely to work hard to overcome their defenses," he said.

I also had some relationships with other people, so Frieda was not my only test of reality. There were two other patients and one or two staff members who were very helpful. I think even the sickest person can have someone with whom he relates in a less sick way. There is a tendency for sick people to relate sickly to others, but it seems to me that there are people who call out the healthier parts of sick people, who seem to be able to show them the potential of an open world. These people do not need to be trained much. They come already equipped. There were a good few, in the years I was at the Lodge, who were working there because the mill had closed or who had come right off the farm. What they had was an accepting open-mindedness about us, a willingness to start at the beginning with us.

I believe that the illness has different phases as treatment continues, and indeed, without treatment, becomes even more sterile and claustral. I went from a minimal socialization when I was unable to differentiate faces, except for my few friends, to a keen need to learn and know people as I recovered. The illness I left behind was not the same one I came in with. Nothing is static and the closer I got to healing, the more labile I seemed and the heavier the defenses got, so it often seemed as though I was sicker. I noticed this with other patients also.

I need to add that recovery itself is a long process and that, for someone who has been non-functioning for years, part of the recovery includes the basics I never learned well to start with: how other people think and feel, and how to establish boundaries and respect the boundaries of others. All this learning is accompanied by anxiety, doubt, and an occasional desire to run back to the familiar world of illness. There is also the "Everest Effect."

Here I was, struggling, throwing all my energy, will, and intelligence into a fight to learn who I was, to stay in contact, to listen carefully, to try to fit in. It is like a climb up Everest, but doing it alone. The climb takes years. Other people were betting on the climber: also doctors and staff, for whom my recovery was a kind of personal validation. Up and up. And then, there is the top. What is up there? Only everyone else, and I am 2 or 3 years later than where they are, and they are all in college, dating, finding life, and I am there, too, but breathless and sobbing with exhaustion, and late. There is an understandable letdown into the dailiness of it all and in how difficult it is to stay sane. We need people to tell us that it gets easier, that it becomes natural and habitual, and that people respond to our sanity. We also need them to let us know that the normal things that we shrank from will soon become all those things that bring us comfort and ease and validation – other people, friends, activity, work, singing, skiing, studying religion. None of these things were available when I was sick; meaning and motive were sick in me. Instead of trying to destroy them as sick, Frieda sought to enlist them as strengths, and so they were ready for me to use as weapons in defense of my health.

Because we really recovered, Catherine and I are often "accused" of never having been sick in the first place. There is no defense against that. The mission of the accusers is a defense of their own vision of illness and its hopelessness. Therapy for them is essentially one-way, a dead-end street, not an interactive process that engages both the therapist and the patient and demands real feeling from both, and real effort from both. The therapist is an artist, not a mechanic.

Is the work worth it? I get this question from the parents of sick people I know, and one yesterday from the parent of a sick student I had. Why not? We spend this kind of time and money on chemotherapy and dialysis and on physical therapy for stroke and paralysis. Mental illness – the social clumsiness some say it is, or creative individualism people in the Sixties say it was – is debilitating and destructive and it should be addressed with every strength that the patient and therapist can bring to its relief.

References

Hauser, S., Allen, J., and Golden, E. (2006). *Out of the Woods: Tales of Resilient Teens*. Cambridge, MA: Harvard University Press.

Mackler, D. (2006) An analysis of the Shadow Side of Frieda Fromm-Reichmann. *ISPS-US Newsletter*, 7(1–3).

Chapter 12

The experience of being medicated in schizophrenia: a subjective inquiry and implications for psychotherapy

Robert Foltz

Editors' Introduction: There is no doubt that thousands of patients have been helped by medications. From antibiotics to antihypertensive drugs, disease after disease has been pushed back by advances in the pharmaceutical industry. Yet it still remains true that there is no substitute for strengthening the patient, as a healthy immune system fights off infection and a healthy lifestyle combats high blood pressure. In this vein, it is only through real therapeutic engagement, as Joanne Greenberg and Catherine Penny pointed out, that psychiatric patients are strengthened in their battle with mental illness. In a fascinating empirical study, Robert Foltz now reminds us also that all medications have their side effects and the mind/brain is a very complex affair.

All too often the experience and words of the patients themselves are ignored. Foltz offers us a chance to listen from the patient's perspective to what it is like to be medicated. Sometimes medication can help, but it is no "rose garden." In many ways this chapter provides a valuable backdrop for the book as a whole, as clinicians who work with the severely emotionally disturbed have learned through hard experience that to really be of assistance in the recovery process one must carefully heed and trust the point of view of the patient.

Introduction

The use of neuroleptic medication is the primary "evidence-based" treatment for schizophrenia. Moreover, treatment providers consistently claim that individuals diagnosed with schizophrenia can only effectively participate in psychotherapy, much less achieve optimal results in it, after being medicated. As Whitaker (2004) notes, "the standard of care for schizophrenia calls for patients to be maintained indefinitely on antipsychotic drugs" (p. 5). Despite these longstanding practices, very little is known about the patient's subjective experience of being medicated. This chapter explores the experience of adults who have been diagnosed with schizophrenia and are being treated with medications as revealed through their participation in a semi-structured interview. In addition, this chapter also examines the notion that medication use is a prerequisite for successful psychotherapy.

Most efforts to study the effects of these medications are based on symptom rating scales, as scored by observers. Hellewell (2002), however, notes that unfortunately "the subjective experience of patients with schizophrenia who are receiving antipsychotic medication has been a neglected research area, as has the satisfaction of patients with their drug treatments" (p. 457). Mizrahi et al. (2005) point out that historically the patient's "perspective is very rarely, if ever, measured or discussed in routine research settings, although it has been suggested that general attitudes toward medication are key factors for adherence and recovery" (p. 860).

Hundreds of studies and decades of research have attempted to demonstrate the efficacy of neuroleptic treatment in schizophrenia. Although it can be argued that antipsychotic medication has allowed for significant acute symptom reduction and has justified the closing of large numbers of psychiatric asylums, Whitaker (2004) notes that "there is a lack of evidence showing that these drugs have improved patients' lives over the long-term" (p. 5). One complicating factor in long-term studies is the marked rate of non-compliance with neuroleptic treatment regimens among patients. To this end, Hellewell (2002) observes that "surveys of patient experience with typical antipsychotics have tended to indicate high levels of dissatisfaction and perceived adverse effects" (p. 458).

Decades of study have revealed significant side effects from neuroleptics. These adverse events are multi-systemic, that is, potentially impacting many different physical functions and systems (Bezchlibnyk-Butler and Jeffries, 2006; Jackson, 2005). Although these side effects vary, depending on the neuroleptics' categorization of "typical" versus "atypical," they often interfere with a patient's willingness to adhere to the recommended regimen of medication, and can negatively impact the process of psychotherapy. Breggin (1997) focuses on the concept of "deactivation," one systemic side effect of neuroleptics. Deactivation refers to "disinterest, indifference, diminished concern, blunting, lack of spontaneity, reduced emotional reactivity, reduced motivation or will, apathy, and in the extreme, a rousable stupor" (Breggin, 1997, p. 14). Clearly, these effects, if experienced by the client, would markedly impair his ability to participate in, and benefit from, psychotherapy. Additionally, and consistent with deactivation, patients have reported that neuroleptics help them feel "detached" from their symptoms but do not eliminate them (Mizrahi et al., 2005).

Neuroleptic dysphoria is also considered to be a relatively common, yet often minimized, side effect of neuroleptic medication. Voruganti and Awad (2004) describe neuroleptic dysphoria as "feeling blah, listless, tired, and lacking interest and ambition" (p. 286). Marder (2005) observes that "both clinical and neuroimaging studies indicate that dopamine blockade is an important determinant of these dysphorias" (p. 45). Moreover, Hellewell (2002) notes that "healthy volunteers have been reported to develop dysphoric states in response to the ingestion of very small doses of typical antipsychotics" (p. 462).

Current medication trends also include the practice of polypharmacy. This practice involves utilizing more than one medication in targeting a symptom or disorder. Consistent with the sample within this study, most subjects were prescribed more than one medication in an attempt to manage their symptoms. Indeed, as noted below, a significant portion of these subjects were also prescribed anticonvulsants as mood stabilizers. As a result, some consideration of the impact of these medications on the experience of psychotherapy is also important, but virtually unexplored.

Anticonvulsants provide wide-ranging benefits and drawbacks. However, these medications can create significant cognitive impairments that can affect a patient's participation in, and benefit from, psychotherapy. For example, Gualtieri and Johnson (2006) point out "high toxicity" resulting from topiramate, valproic acid, and carbamazepine, all of which are popular "mood stabilizers." This toxicity was identified as significantly slowed reaction time, diminished cognitive flexibility, and diminished complex attention (as measured by the Neurocognitive Index [NCI]) (Gualtieri and Johnson, 2006).

It is also important to look closely at the idea of "effectiveness" in the treatment of schizophrenia. Effectiveness may be defined in a variety of ways, ranging from "quality of life" to symptom remission, to symptom elimination, to a reduction of those behaviors requiring a more restrictive treatment setting. All of these measures of effectiveness deserve consideration, although treatment providers "tend to regard symptom control as a more important objective than freedom from adverse effects, whereas patients and relatives are more inclined to value a freedom from adverse effects" (Hellewell, 2002, p. 459). It is clear, however, that even under optimal medication adherence and response, patients often require ongoing assistance in developing skills to avoid decompensation in the future.

Finally, studies that survey the attitudes of patients diagnosed with schizophrenia are commonly criticized for the reliability of their report. In this vein, Awad and Voruganti (2005) note that "As schizophrenic patients frequently experience cognitive deficits, disturbed thinking and communication, their reports about their feelings, values and attitudes are often uncritically dismissed as unreliable" (p. 7). However, Hellewell (2002) makes the important point that "the reliability of subjective self-reports has been demonstrated" (p. 458). In other words, being diagnosed with a psychotic condition does not nullify a person's ability to accurately describe their subjective experiences. For this reason, the design of this study emphasized the subjective experience of how it is to be medicated.

Method of inquiry

In this study, 45 subjects participated in a semi-structured interview specifically designed to explore their experiences of being medicated. The questionnaire, the Experience of Neuroleptic Medication Inquiry (ENMI), was based on the symptom categories of the 18-item Brief Psychiatric Rating Scale. Of this sample, nearly two-thirds (64.4%) were male. The mean age of subjects was 39.6 years and they had an average level of education of 11.86 years. Ethnically, 48.9% were Caucasian while 42.2% were African-American. The subjects were randomly selected following their admission to a state-run psychiatric facility. Their participation in the study was voluntary.

Because of the common argument that "therapeutic effects" of medications may not be obtained for several weeks, all subjects had been medicated for at least 2 weeks prior to their participation in the interview. Sixty-two percent of the respondents were receiving an "atypical" neuroleptic (including quetiapine, risperidone, olanzapine, or clozapine) as their primary medication and 37.8% were receiving a "typical" neuroleptic (including fluphenazine, haloperidol, thiothixene, or decanoate forms) as their primary intervention.

Of the 28 subjects on atypical neuroleptics, 17 were on additional psychotropic medications. Three of these 17 were on mood stabilizers; two were on mood stabilizers and typical neuroleptics; three were on SSRI antidepressants; two were on SSRI antidepressants and mood stabilizers; one was on a mood stabilizer and benztropine (an anticholineric medication to control Parkinsonian side effects); two were on an SSRI antidepressant and benztropine; two were on benztropine; one was on a mood stabilizer and an additional atypical neuroleptic; and one was on an additional atypical neuroleptic.

Of the 17 subjects on typical neuroleptics, 14 were on additional psychotropic medications. These 14 subjects' additional medications are as follows: one was on a mood stabilizer and an atypical neuroleptic; six were on benztropine; four were on a mood stabilizer and benztropine; one was on a mood stabilizer and an anti-anxiety agent; one was on an atypical neuroleptic and an SSRI antidepressant; and one was on an anti-anxiety agent in addition to his typical neuroleptic.

Assessment of positive or negative effects from medication treatment was obtained through the use of a seven-point Likert scale. In this measure, a score of "4" was considered a "no change" response. As a result, positive or negative trends could be determined as ratings moved toward "1" or

"7," respectively. A *t*-test was utilized to determine statistically significant variance away from a score of "4."

Survey results

Hallucinations

Neuroleptics are commonly credited with the ability to quickly and effectively manage the troubling symptom of hallucinations. However, in light of the concept of deactivation, it is worth considering that the medications actually serve to suppress the patient's reaction to the hallucinations rather than to alleviate the symptom itself. Within the ENMI study, 28 subjects admitted to hallucinatory experience. Subjects were asked, "How would you rate the overall impact of medications on the voices or sounds?" Of those acknowledging auditory hallucinations, 42.8% reported them to be less of a problem while 42.9% reported "no change" in the experience of hallucinations being problematic. Fourteen percent reported hallucinations to be more of a problem.

Subjects were also asked, "When taking your medication, are you more or less able to tolerate the voices?" Here, 39.3% reported being more able to tolerate auditory hallucinations, whereas 17.9% reported being less able to tolerate them. Forty-three percent reported "no change" in their ability to tolerate the voices. The near-40% reporting an increased tolerance may provide evidence for the phenomenon of deactivation. Interestingly, only one subject reported that the voices disappeared completely. With 43% reporting "no change" in their ability to tolerate the voices, it is clear that further examination of the treatment of this symptom is warranted.

Additionally, patients were asked, "When taking your medication, are you more or less likely to react to the voices?" Again, consistent with a "deactivation" process, 51.8% of subjects reported being less likely to react to auditory hallucinations while on neuroleptics. Twenty-two percent reported being more likely to react to the voices and 25.9% reported "no change" in their reaction to auditory hallucinations. This dramatic reduction in the patients' reactions to voices supports the idea that the symptom remains and that most patients simply react less to it. This feature also highlights the challenge to the idea of medication effectiveness. Neuroleptics are commonly called "antipsychotic" yet, as reported here, they often only suppress behavioral reaction to the ongoing symptom – and do not alleviate or remove the psychosis itself.

It is also valuable to look at how medication treatment may change the experience of the voices themselves. Within this study, 11% of subjects reported that hallucinations decrease in frequency, but not intensity. An additional 11% reported that hallucinations become quieter, but do not disappear. Several subjects reported decreased frequency of hallucinations, although interestingly several subjects reported that while they were on medications the message of the voices change. For example, one subject discussed how he commonly experienced voices telling him hateful things about himself, yet this experience evolved into an ongoing narrative of his day-to-day events when medicated. Another subject explained how the once-understandable voice became what seemed to be a steady, and over-lapping, flow of whispers. Of note, 20% of subjects reported that the voices do not change while on medications.

Cognitive organization

Neuroleptics have a mixed performance with respect to cognitive func-tioning. Sedation and fatigue appear to be common side effects, with their obvious correlates to sustaining attention, etc. Additionally, neuroleptics can cause confusion, disturbed concentration, and disorientation. Yet there are also reports of improved cognitive performance with respect to reaction time, verbal learning and memory, and executive functioning (Bezchlibnyk-Butler and Jeffries, 2006). As many patients are often placed on multiple medications, including other classes such as anticonvulsants with demon-strated cognitive drawbacks, it is difficult to discern accurately the magni-tude of how medication treatments enhance or interfere with cognitive processes.

In an effort to explore how medications influence a patient's ability to cognitively manage their experience, this study created several prompts. The study asked, "When taking your medication, are your experiences more or less likely to make sense to you?" Significantly, responses indicate that 44.5% of subjects believed that being on medications improved their ability to make sense of their experience. Of this positive response, 35.6% endorsed the prompt "more likely," which is the most positive rating on the seven-point scale. Conversely, 17.8% reported feeling less able to make sense of their experiences.

Subjects were also prompted with the following: "When taking your medication, do you feel more or less able to sort out your thoughts?" Over one-third (37.7%) reported improvements . In contrast, 37.8% reported "no change" in their ability to sort out their thoughts and 24.4% reported being less able to sort out their thoughts when on neuroleptic medications. While this prompt is somewhat similar to the first in this category, the contrasting responses suggest that while a minority of patients found relief in this regard from neuroleptics, most patients' internal world of thoughts may continue to be quite chaotic, even though perceptual experiences occurring to them on a more day-to-day basis may be easier to organize. It is also noteworthy that the subjects were all hospitalized at the time of the study, so all responses must take into account the presence of a more structured schedule and controlled environment.

An additional question asked subjects, "Do you feel smarter when on your prescribed medications?" Forty percent reported feeling smarter on neuroleptics (24.4% feeling "much smarter"). Thirty-one percent reported feeling no change and 28.8% indicated that neuroleptics reduced their ability to feel smart. This range provides useful information into the positive subjective responses that can be obtained from medications. These numbers, however, may not fully express the patients' experiences. In responding to these prompts, subjects added a variety of illuminating comments to this discussion. One subject stated: "Taking the medications – it's chemically induced retardation." Another articulated that the medication "erases thoughts – wipes them away as you're having them." Another subject remarked pointedly, "it [medication] doesn't have an effect on your thoughts, it keeps you from expressing them."

In an attempt to elicit patients' responses of delusional experiences, the study asked a question within the category of conceptual organization. Each subject was asked, "Do you feel your medications can change a specific belief/group of beliefs that you have?" Nearly two-thirds (62.2%) of respondents indicated that they did not believe medications could change a specific belief, whereas 37.8% believed medications could change a belief.

These conceptual organization questions are particularly relevant to the experience of psychotherapy. While subjects seem to be more able to make sense of day-to-day experiences while on medications, they report little change in their ability to sort out their thoughts, as evidenced by nearly a quarter of subjects reporting a worsening in this respect. Moreover, many subjects seem to feel little benefit in terms of improving their ability to "feel smart," and thus have more self-confidence. Finally, in an attempt to explore the possibility that medication may dissipate or correct delusional beliefs, nearly two-thirds of subjects believe that medications cannot change their beliefs. Admittedly, these prompts pull for responses with ill-defined concepts, such as "feeling smart" or changing "beliefs," yet having access to this information could be useful for the process of psychotherapy. Specifically, when working with a client struggling to understand the reality around them, having a "confidence boosting" experience of "feeling smarter" would enhance their comfort in sharing their subjective, day-to-day thoughts and feelings.

Suspiciousness

Subjects were asked, "When taking your medication, do you feel more or less likely to trust people?" Forty-two percent of subjects feel more likely to trust others while over one-third (37.8%) report no change in their ability to trust others. Twenty percent report they are more likely to distrust others. Clearly, a significant proportion of subjects reported an improved ability to trust others. This feature has important implications in many facets of the patients' lives, and is noted to be of significant benefit.

Subjects were also queried, "When taking your medication, do you feel others are more or less likely to be against you?" Here, 24.4% report feeling that others are less likely to be against them while a consistent 22.2% report feeling others are more likely to be against them. Fifty-three percent report no change in their feeling of others being against them.

These questions are particularly relevant to the process of psychotherapy. It is often asserted that the use of medications is actually requisite for effective psychotherapy to occur. Although establishing a trusting relationship is essential for the psychotherapy process, especially when working with patients with psychosis, when we consider patients' perception of trusting and feeling safe with others the neuroleptics demonstrated varying degrees of benefit in this regard. In the interview, if a subject reported "no change" in their feelings that others were against them, it is likely that this represents a fairly negative stance. That is, it is fair to assume that most subjects are more inclined to be skeptical of the intentions of others, so "no change" from this stance remains negative. For example, in one case, a patient initially agreed to participate in the study upon admission. The interviewer's subsequent attempts to get him to complete the questionnaire was met with the patient's silence. He was curled up in a chair and refused to speak. Eventually, the subject tentatively participated in the interview – and a bond formed between them. Upon completion of the interview process, each time the man saw the interviewer in the hospital in the days that followed, he repeatedly requested the interviewer's participation in his treatment planning, as he complained that the treatment team did not understand his feelings.

Emotional withdrawal

Subjects were asked, "How do your medications affect your ability to express your feelings?" Over two-thirds (68.8%) indicated that medications produce "no change" or make them "less able to express their feelings" (42.2% and 26.6% respectively). The remaining 31% reported being "more able to express their feelings."

In an additional prompt, subjects were asked, "When taking your medication, to what extent do you believe your feelings are important?" Overall, subjects reported clear recognition that their feelings were important. Indeed, 80% of respondents indicated that feelings were "very important." Interestingly, given the prospect of deactivation, subjects are less likely to react to their symptoms – presumably they are less upset or agitated – but subjects here noted their awareness that their feelings remain very important.

This study also inquired, "When you are taking your medication, are you more or less likely to talk about your feelings?" When reviewed, 44.4% of subjects reported being "more able to talk about their feelings," whereas

56.6% reported either "no change" (31.1%) or being "less likely" to talk about their feelings (25.5%).

In the final item in this category, the study inquired, "Overall, how would you rate your moods/feelings when on medications?" Thirty-eight percent of respondents noted an improvement in their feelings whereas 40% responded with "no change." Twenty-two percent of respondents indicated a worsening of feelings (with 20% reporting "much worse"). This finding is also noteworthy, as it is occasionally believed that neuroleptics (and the use of anticonvulsants) can offer a mood stabilizing or elevating benefit. However, in examining the medications' mechanisms of action, their mood elevating properties would be inconsistent with other medications promoting the same benefit. For example, antidepressants often increase the availability of serotonin, dopamine, and/or norepinephrine, while antipsychotic medications effectively block the reception of some of these same chemicals in the brain. So any improvement in mood would challenge the prevailing "chemical imbalance" paradigm of depression.

Findings in this category are particularly important, when considering the purported benefits of medications on psychotherapy. As indicated, a significant proportion of subjects did not feel more likely to express their feelings, yet they continue to believe strongly that their feelings are important. It is also noteworthy that subjects did not necessarily feel improvements in their feelings (i.e., less dysphoric) while medicated. Indeed, even though many subjects were on "mood stabilizers" and antidepressants, improved mood did not emerge as a significant outcome for this sample. Moreover, in an additional response to the study's prompts, one subject expressed, "the medications take away my feelings completely." Another remarked, "I've been on them [medications] for 20 years, and they've done nothing for me." This raises Whitaker's point addressed earlier, that long-term quality of subjective life does not necessarily improve on medication.

Disorientation

The study made two general inquiries in an attempt to gauge the person's orientation to their life circumstances. Subjects were asked, "When taking your medication, do you feel more or less like yourself?" A review of these findings reveals that 44.5% of subjects reported "feeling more like yourself" when on medications. The remaining subjects reported "no change" in feeling like themselves (17.8%) or less like themselves (37.8%).

Subjects were also asked, "When taking your medication, to what extent do you feel you have a clear understanding of how good or bad your life is?": 53.3% of subjects reported that they have a clear or "very clear" understanding of their life situation; in contrast, 26.7% reported "no change" in their perception of their life situation and 20% reported having a less clear or "not at all clear" understanding of their life circumstances. Whether this understanding revealed a positive or negative life situation is not determined here.

While difficult to interpret with certainty, these prompts around "disorientation" do provide insight into the value of respecting a person's perspective on their life experience. Clients often feel as though the goals of treatment are incongruent with their own goals, leading them to feel misunderstood. Subjects provided additional comments to these inquiries that shed light on their situations. One subject noted fearfully, "I'm afraid they'll give me more [medication]." In discussing being off his medication as a comparison, another subject noted the following: "Six months without meds – I was a better man." Regarding life circumstances, many subjects raised valid concern, and stated they knew what their lives required in order for them to "get better," including stable housing, financial stability, and being reconnected with family. One subject stated, "I need to understand myself, to slow down a little bit, and deal with deaths."

Blunted affect

In several ways, this study attempted to explore patients' ability to feel their emotions. Subjects were asked, "When taking your medication, do you feel you are able to smile as much as you'd like?" Twenty-two percent of subjects reported smiling as much as they would like to, whereas 26.7% felt less able to smile as much as they would like to when taking medications. One-third (33.3%) of subjects felt no change in their ability to smile when on medications.

An additional item asked, "When taking your medication, do you feel you are more or less able to react to things normally?" Over one-third (42.2%) reported being more able to react to things normally when on medications, whereas 31.1% reported "no change" and 26.6% reported that medications negatively affected their ability to react to things normally.

Finally, subjects were asked, "When taking your medication, do you feel more or less like you are able to cry as much as you need to?" In this item, 22.2% reported that their ability to cry was improved when on medication, while 40% reported no change and 37.7% reported being less able to cry as much as they needed.

As with the emotional withdrawal category, subjects rating questions regarding blunted affect did not report a markedly improved ability to experience emotions. This is, again, very important to the process of psychotherapy, as access to one's emotional experience is critically important in most psychotherapeutic processes. Moreover, the findings in this category are again consistent with deactivation, as over 50% in each blunted affect inquiry reported "no change" or a negative trend in their ability to feel emotion.

Miscellaneous items

Interpersonal relationships

This study utilized additional prompts to explore other categories that are relevant to a person's ability to benefit from psychotherapy. In one prompt, subjects were asked, "When taking your medication, how would you rate your relationships with others?" Forty-two percent of subjects reported that while on their medications their relationships with others were "much better." One subject (2.2%) reported that his relationships were "much worse." Thirty-one percent of subjects reported "no change" in their interpersonal relationships when on medications.

An additional inquiry was made: "When taking your medication, is it easier or harder to be around people?" In response, 44.4% reported that it was "much easier." "No change" was reported by 35.6% of respondents, and 11.1% reported that it was "much harder" to be around others while on their medications.

This finding is noteworthy. It is possible that the use of medication results in significant improvements in the individual's ability to be around others and enjoy relationships. In contrast, this finding may also be an artifact of the setting in which the subjects were evaluated. As noted, all subjects were currently hospitalized in a state-run, psychiatric facility. A standard expectation in this setting was that subjects remain compliant with their prescribed medication. As a result, it is quite likely that subjects were treated more pleasantly if compliant with their medication. Indeed, many privileges were contingent on this compliance and this fact alone could influence their impression of interpersonal comfort. This area is worthy of additional study as hospital staff, as well as family members, coworkers, etc., may put pressure on individuals struggling with psychosis to "fit in," behave themselves, or stop acting in bizarre ways. Several subjects in this study talked about their difficulty making even basic contact with their families after years of feeling ostracized.

Individual psychotherapy

While it was not a specific pursuit of inquiry in this study, subjects were asked the following two questions: (a) if they have ever received individual psychotherapy; and (b) if they did, was individual psychotherapy helpful. A general description of individual psychotherapy was used, such as "being able to meet with someone on a regular basis to talk about your problems." Of the respondents, 64.4% (29 subjects) had received individual psychotherapy at some time in their treatment history. Of those subjects, 86.2% (25 subjects) reported that individual psychotherapy was helpful.

This is one of the most robust findings of the survey. In these brief questions, an overwhelming majority of people felt as though having someone to talk to, on a regular basis, was helpful to them. While this does not specify the theoretical orientation of the clinician, the essential message is clear: talking with someone about their problems was helpful. Additionally, subjects offered several comments related to sharing their thoughts and feelings, even during the ENMI interview process. One subject remarked, "I'm glad you didn't run out of the office," and discussed his thankfulness about someone "interested in asking questions such as these . . . psychiatrists don't pay enough attention." Another subject noted, "I'm better because I was talking to you."

Beliefs concerning etiology

The study asked subjects, "To what extent do you think your symptoms come from a chemical imbalance (or something wrong with your brain)?" Regarding the belief of a chemical imbalance as being the basis for their symptoms, 20% believed this was "completely" the cause, 24.4% believed it was "moderately" the cause, and 48.9% believed it was "not at all the cause." Two subjects refused to answer this question. Several statements illuminate the subjects' perspectives on the chemical imbalance notion. One subject noted that "Lithium zones you, haloperidol distorts bones," while a different subject said the medications are "supposed to treat chemical imbalances." However, another subject remarked that the medications "freeze my blood . . . they made my blood stop circulating."

The long-standing paradigm in psychiatry asserts that neuroleptic medications are "effective" because they correct "chemical imbalances" that have resulted in psychotic symptoms. In contrast, as evidenced here, the psychotic symptoms experienced by those diagnosed with schizophrenia are not ameliorated by the medications. What is more prominent is that their behavioral reactions are reduced, while their symptoms persist, again consistent with deactivation.

Another study question asked subjects, "To what extent do you think your symptoms have developed because of difficult life experiences?" Regarding difficult life experience, 20% believed this was "completely" the cause, 37% believed this to be "moderately" the cause, and 24% believed it was "not at all the cause." As mentioned earlier, a range of subjects raised life events as being important to "getting better," such as improved housing, financial stability, etc. Yet other subjects noted that deaths in their lives had created difficulties for them. These items are important to highlight the variety of beliefs, despite widespread belief in the professional community of a neurochemical cause for schizophrenia. As a clinician adheres to this belief, it is critically important to recognize that their patient may not subscribe to this theory. Undoubtedly, if these beliefs are not explored in psychotherapy, there may not be a shared agreement on the goals of treatment.

Medication effectiveness

This study asked subjects, "To what extent do you feel like your medications effectively treat the symptoms they are supposed to?" In response, 31.1% of subjects believed that medications treated their symptoms with some degree of effectiveness. Meanwhile, 22% believed medications to be only moderately effective, while 46.6% reported more negatively (specifically, 31.1% reported "not at all").

Non-compliance

Twenty-nine subjects (64.4%) reported that they had, within their treatment history, stopped taking their medication. Those who were non-compliant were asked, "To what extent did you feel better or worse after stopping your medication?" Of those who had stopped their medications, 65.5% reported that they felt better when off their medications (48.3% reported feeling "much better"). Approximately 14% reported "no change" in their symptoms after stopping their medications, while only 20.7% reported feeling worse (and, of these, 8.9% indicated "much worse") after discontinuation of neuroleptics. One subject noted after discontinuing his medication, "I was normal . . . I didn't feel like I was dying." In contrast, one subject stated, "my meds are me." These comments, if made in the context of psychotherapy, are critically important. Non-compliance is not just about a patient being oppositional. Often, a clinician may contact the psychiatrist if a patient becomes non-compliant with medication – without even asking the client what their experience of being medicated is.

Discussion

There is limited understanding regarding the subjective experience of being medicated in schizophrenia. This report utilized a semi-structured questionnaire, the Experience of Neuroleptic Medication Inventory, to explore this subjective experience through a variety of symptom categories. Additionally, this review attempted to examine the impact, benefit, or drawback of psychotropic medications, as the use of these medications affects the process of psychotherapy. Of concern, it would appear that many symptom categories respond to medications in a way that is consistent with the concept of deactivation.

Within the study, there was considerable variation in the individual's response to medication treatments. Some subjects reported significant benefit to specific symptom areas, whereas other subjects reported negative outcomes. These differences are particularly important as efforts should be toward individualizing treatment strategies, while acknowledging that medications are not going to obtain optimal outcomes in all patients. Indeed, very positive benefits have been achieved in using alternative methods such as individual therapy or even a change in therapeutic context or living arrangements.

It would appear, based on these findings, that there is substantial reason to continue scrutinizing the subjective effectiveness of medication treatments in schizophrenia. Admittedly, there is an abundance of literature to support their efficacy. However, there was only a modest demonstration of effectiveness when examining the subjective report of those on a polypharmacy regimen. Additionally, it appears that deactivation is a valid construct in viewing one impact of the polypharmacy of schizophrenia. There was also information within the subjects' review to support the construct of neuroleptic dysphoria. These concepts are relevant for treatment providers, as the emergence of these conditions may prove to be a formidable hurdle to successful treatment. Moreover, the experience of deactivation or neuroleptic dysphoria may prove detrimental to the psychotherapy process, if left unexplored.

Importantly, subjects did report certain improvements attributed to their prescribed medication. If considering schizophrenia to be a "chronic terror condition" (Karon and VandenBos, 1981), a reduction in, or an increased sense of control of, their symptoms is critically important, and this was experienced by some subjects. These positive responses are also important in the psychotherapy process.

There are weaknesses to this study. The study included a relatively small sample. Indeed, discerning the different medication effects of typical or atypical neuroleptics is further complicated because of this issue. In addition, the issue of polypharmacy complicates a precise understanding of the impact of neuroleptics. However, in the study's favor, naturalistic studies on the experience of being medicated in schizophrenia are rare.

An additional criticism of this study could focus on the prompts within the semi-structured interview. It is possible that some subjects had difficulty understanding the questions, although efforts were made in the construction of the survey to use clear, understandable prompts. If a subject had difficulty with a prompt, or asked for clarification, efforts were made to stay "true" to the language of the inquiry, to maintain integrity across the survey.

Finally, it would appear that individuals diagnosed with schizophrenia find psychotherapy to be helpful. It would also appear that utilizing a structured survey, such as the ENMI, could provide valuable information for both the psychotherapist as well as within medication management. Indeed, even after the survey, numerous subjects had requested the interviewer's participation as part of their treatment staff team, expressing that they felt more understood in the interview process or that they wished to have the information they shared made known to their treatment providers. Toward this end, the ENMI could illuminate information that may not otherwise emerge in the therapeutic process.

References

Awad, A. G. and Voruganti, L. (2005). Neuroleptic dysphoria: Revisiting the concept 50 years later. *Acta Psychiatrica Scandinavica*, 111: 6–13.

Bezchlibnyk-Butler, K. and Jeffries, J. (2006). *Clinical Handbook of Psychotropic Drugs* (16th ed.). Ashland, OH: Hogrefe & Huber Publishers.

Breggin, P. (1997). *Brain-Disabling Treatments in Psychiatry: Drugs, Electroshock, and the Role of the FDA*. New York: Springer Publishers.

Gualtieri, C. T. and Johnson, L. (2006). Comparative neurocognitive effects of 5 psychotropic anticonvulsants and lithium. *Medscape General Medicine*, 8(3). Online document posted 8/23/06. Available at: http://www.medscape.com/viewarticle/541762.

Hellewell, J. (2002). Patients' subjective experiences of antipsychotics: Clinical relevance. *CNS Drugs*, 16: 457–471.

Jackson, G. (2005). *Rethinking Psychiatric Drugs: A Guide for Informed Consent*. Bloomington, IN: Authorhouse.

Karon, B. and VandenBos, G. (1981). *Psychotherapy of Schizophrenia: Treatment of Choice*. New York: Jason Aronson.

Marder, S. (2005). Subjective experiences on antipsychotic medications: Synthesis and conclusions. *Acta Psychiatrica Scandinavica*, 111: 43–46.

Mizrahi, R., Bagby, R., Zipursky, R., and Kapur, S. (2005). How antipsychotics work: The patients' perspective. *Progress in Neuro-Psychopharmacology and Biological Psychiatry*, 29: 859–864. Available online at: www.elsevier.com/locate/pnpbp.

Voruganti, L. and Awad, A. G. (2004). Is neuroleptic dysphoria a variant of drug-induced extrapyramidal side effects? *Canadian Journal of Psychiatry*, 49: 285–289.

Whitaker, R. (2004). The case against antipsychotic drugs: A 50-year record of doing more harm than good. *Medical Hypotheses*, 62: 5–13.

Part 4

Concluding chapter

Chapter 13

Sustaining the therapeutic approach: therapists may need help too!

Ira Steinman

Editors' Introduction: Ira Steinman is a talented and experienced therapist and seems to have been able to help patients recover from psychoses that have defeated other experienced and skilled clinicians. However, all therapists have limitations and blind spots, even when they have been able to face some of these in their own therapies and with supervisory and other forms of help and support. Although some readers may be skeptical as to whether, even in near-ideal conditions, most therapy impasses can be overcome, as may seem to be the claim of this chapter, all of the authors in this book are familiar with many patients being helped to move on in their lives as a result of therapists receiving additional help along the lines that Steinman lays out. We hope we have convinced many that medication is certainly not enough and we hope that this final chapter is both inspirational and aspirational to all therapists to persevere when the work gets difficult and we encourage them to search deeply and widely to identify the probable reason.

Steinman reminds us that unbearable affects are necessarily stirred up in the analyst as unbearable affects are discovered in the patient. It is not only the patient who needs strengthening but the analyst needs strengthening as well. Harold Searles (1965) spoke convincingly about the parallel process common to both dyads – patient/therapist and therapist/supervisor. Steinman's illustrative consultations with stymied clinicians bring us to the solar plexus of these taxing dilemmas. In these stories, he reminds us how we need to be aware of how patients use metaphor, how they cling tenaciously to symptoms and just how fragile psychotic patients are not!

As a wise, tough, and compassionate psychiatric psychoanalyst, Steinman is not "anti-medication," but he knows that one must go "beyond medication" in order to find solutions. At the heart of these solutions are deep and meaningful therapeutic engagements.

Introduction

What of the healer? What of the person on the front lines of treatment? Not only can the psychotherapeutic work be glacial in its movement, not only

can pessimism and discouragement sap the energy of even the most committed therapist, but unacknowledged transference–countertransference
binds can subvert our best therapeutic intentions.

Skepticism of dynamic psychotherapy with the deeply disturbed

There are two main reasons why therapists have difficulties with those with
schizophrenia and other severely disturbed patients. First, many therapists
doubt that one can do much more than offer supportive psychotherapeutic
care. They doubt that salutary and curative goals can be achieved in a
psychodynamic psychotherapeutic exploration of psychosis. Second, many
therapists of severely disturbed patients become caught in transference–
countertransference binds with these very difficult patients. Such unanalyzed
predicaments can lead to therapeutic stasis and discouragement on the
therapist's part. At their worst, these transference–countertransference
dilemmas can lead to unintended actions and boundary violations in the
name of helping the patient.

When such stasis occurs in the course of psychotherapy with the severely
disturbed patient, it is very useful to question what is going on. If it does
not become clear to the healer, as evidenced by the free flow of material
during the therapy hours and some improvement in the clinical picture, it is
a very good idea to seek supervision.

Individual and peer supervision

Individual supervision and peer supervision groups often clarify such
difficulties and aid the therapist in continuing the psychodynamic work
required in healing even the most disorganized and chaotic patients. In most
cities there are therapists who do well with the seriously disturbed. It is a
good idea to seek consultation with one of these practitioners or to become
involved in a peer group consultation process, where each of the members
presents cases that are difficult to handle. One might take some additional
courses if there are institutes or other facilities where such courses on the
treatment of the severely disturbed are taught. In addition, the International
Society for the Psychological Treatment of Schizophrenia and Other
Psychoses (ISPS) has meetings at local, national, and international levels
and a thorough, ongoing e-mail listserve intended to enhance the understanding of the psychological treatments of schizophrenia and to allow
practitioners to exchange ideas and provide support to one another.

Hopelessness and therapeutic nihilism may doom the therapeutic dyad
when treating a schizophrenic or otherwise deeply disturbed patient. Part of
that hopelessness may be the result of the expectation on the part of most
practitioners that little can be done with the schizophrenic patient. The

common wisdom is to give them some antipsychotic medication, try to aid them through their isolation, but not really expect to change their thinking. Just keep them on medicine and maybe the whole clinical picture will improve, which it rarely does with medication alone.

I have the opposite view. Rather than believing that psychotic people should have a short visit to a psychiatrist once a month for antipsychotic medicines, I believe it is possible to engage them in an intensive psychotherapeutic exploration, using antipsychotic medication as required, and trying, over the course of the treatment, to titrate down antipsychotics as they work through intense psychological issues, including delusions and hallucinations.

Rather than feel hopelessness at the slowness of change, it is important to realize that there will be quiet periods in the course of the treatment of psychosis. During these seemingly quiescent times a great deal goes on, as psychotic defenses shift and loosen; properly done, the self gradually emerges in the container of an intensive psychotherapy. What we have to do, as therapists, is to recognize the potential for change and engage in a psychodynamic psychotherapy, exploring all aspects of the patient and his or her disturbance.

Letting therapeutic progress work is a path ensnared with pitfalls. All too often, our own transference–countertransference difficulties get in the way and we require support and help to maintain our therapeutic helm.

We must keep in mind that the onion of schizophrenic psychosis can be peeled away even in the most extreme cases, until the terrified person within emerges. Then, recovery, healing, and sometimes cure can be achieved through a psychoanalytically oriented psychotherapy, even in schizophrenic or delusional patients who have been disturbed for decades.

Love is not enough: dynamic therapy is required

In an attempt to diminish suffering and alienation and to help people cope with the world, the therapist's caring attitude and closeness in an otherwise isolated person's life is potentially healing and restorative. I have found over the years, though, that there are a number of patients who remain profoundly psychotic, even after various psychotherapies, medication trials and supportive halfway houses, day care, and hospital services. It was only when they began to engage in an inquiring psychodynamic psychotherapy that we discovered a previously unmentioned, yet tightly held delusional system that had impeded a life in the world outside their misperceptions.

Closeness and support are often not enough in the treatment of schizophrenic and delusional patients. Occasionally, a kindly, supportive presence is enough to help the delusional patient back to reality for a while; generally this is a fragile arrangement, with a great potential for exacerbation of psychosis during stressful times. Such a supportive, reality-based approach attempts to replace a harsh critical persecutory superego with the therapist's more giving and caring attentions. Such an approach alone, to the exclusion of a psychodynamic exploration, often leaves the therapist jumping through hoops trying to keep the patient together, rather than helping the patient see what he or she is actually up to.

More frequently, though, a more thorough exploration is required of both transference–countertransference interactions and the meaning to the patient of delusions and hallucinations, as well as of the life circumstances leading to psychotic thought and schizophrenic orientation, if one wants to achieve lasting gains with schizophrenic patients.

What is required is an analytic orientation, taking cognizance of the fact that hallucinations and delusions have a meaning to the patient, that there will be resistances to therapy, as well as transference and intense countertransference phenomena. Most importantly, the aspiring therapist needs to know that the unwinding of a delusional or schizophrenic orientation can lead to change, healing, and occasionally cure.

Many factors can get in the way of the progress of psychotherapy with a schizophrenic or delusional patient. For example, there is the paranoid who craves and fears closeness and involves us in his delusional system. There is the delusional patient who filters everything through other beings that only he can see. There is the schizophrenic who is buffeted by hallucinations or misperceptions that destroy any ability to live in the world of consensually agreed upon reality.

Here, more is necessary; here, an insight-oriented approach is required to cut through the morass of psychotic distortions and aid the patient in both identifying the distortions and understanding their origins. Such an approach in a sustained psychotherapy over a period of time may lead the schizophrenic patient and his psychological energy away from his internal preoccupations toward the world of actual people and things outside of the confusions within.

Necessity for individual or peer supervision

As a psychodynamically oriented therapist, one must be alert to the ever-present possibility that the slowness and interpersonally painful aspects of treatment may not be just the usual halting pace of therapy with the severely disturbed borderline, schizophrenic, or delusional patient. It is necessary to assess the ever-present danger of hidden delusions or one's own unacknowledged countertransference reactions impeding the progress of psychotherapy.

Our goal with deeply disturbed patients is to alleviate suffering and, if possible, diminish the psychotic thinking that leaves the patient in such distress. To my mind, the best approach is an exploratory, psychodynamic psychotherapy of the patient and his or her disturbed beliefs. Such a psychotherapy is built upon the cornerstone of a belief in the unconscious, the existence of transference and countertransference during the course of treatment, and the presence of resistance to change on the part of the patient. Often, though, we need help in figuring out what is going on in the treatment.

Transference–countertransference difficulties

I was consulted by a therapist who was aware of a rising titer of irritation building up within him during hours with a depressed and helpless-appearing borderline patient with bipolar features. No matter how much he discussed both the psychological issues of presenting herself as a victim and her own unexpressed anger at family and situations and the repetition of those feelings in therapy, she remained in stasis. As we looked at his irritation with the patient, during supervision he was able to see that he was feeling as her parents and other family members had felt with her: angry and resentful in the face of the patient's helplessness, passivity, and outbursts of anger.

As expected, once the transference–countertransference situation had been illuminated and clarified in his mind, the therapist's irritation with the patient diminished and ceased. From that point on in therapy, the therapist could maintain his therapeutic neutrality and the patient became able to see how her actions, verbal explosions, and apparent helplessness in therapy both mimicked her role in the family situation and elicited similar feelings in others. Subsequently, relationships with others improved and the cornerstone of an observational capacity was laid down as the transference–countertransference situation in the therapy was explored.

Here is another example from my own work with a chronic paranoid patient. The patient had an extremely paranoid view to which he had clung for a number of years, through a number of therapists, hospitalizations, and psychiatrists. With me, too, he continued with the same orientation. Numbers meant something special to him; radios and television talked to him; signals were sent to him in all manner of ways. Most of the time, I was able to explore with him the nature of these beliefs and how they developed, but during one particularly prolonged siege of paranoid and delusional beliefs I found myself becoming increasingly frustrated with him.

After several sessions of this frustration, I became aware that my internal reactions were mimicking the paranoid patient's father's anger with his son's delusional beliefs. Here, too, as knowledge of this transference–countertransference dynamic became consolidated in my mind, my irritation ceased. I was then able to work with the patient on his delusions and on the reactions of others to his beliefs, and how he felt in the face of the irritation of others. Some of other people's irritation with him, of course, had been incorporated into delusions.

These are but two examples of transference–countertransference difficulties that impeded work with severely disturbed patients, just as would have happened in the psychodynamic psychotherapy of a less disturbed individual. In the course of such an intensive psychotherapy, one's own countertransference reactions, if unexplored, can get in the way of the process of psychotherapy. Countertransference, however, is but one of the factors to deal with in the course of a mutative exploratory psychodynamic psychotherapy of schizophrenia.

Countertransference as a source of difficulty in limit setting

Dr. J. came in for supervision. She was an extremely capable, intelligent, and compassionate practitioner, treating a very depressed and chaotic man, R., who would bypass and extend any rule she made. She thought R. might be borderline, or bipolar, or profoundly depressed. Various antidepressants and mood stabilizing drugs had been tried, with little success. She had seen R. for years, with R. escalating demands for time and attention. Dr. J.'s husband had begun to get concerned about how much time Dr. J. was spending with R.

It became very difficult for Dr. J. to end sessions on time due to R.'s beseeching her for more time, with threats of suicide. Soon, R., with threats of suicide, began to get Dr. J. to spend long periods of time on the phone during evenings and weekends: 20 minutes would be a short period of time but an hour and a half on the phone would frequently occur. Dr. J. was at her wits' end.

She described several sessions, with a great deal of emphasis on how she just could not adhere to any limits in this therapy. R. was her most severely disturbed patient. With her other patients there was no difficulty adhering to a psychotherapeutic format. Here, for some reason, she was unable to stick with any frame of therapeutic benefit.

How had she got into such a bind? She was walking on tenterhooks with the patient exploding at her if she was not always compassionate, understanding, and giving. She was not sure but she thought it had to do with R. having had critical and difficult parents, as well as tempestuous and sometimes sadistic relationships with his siblings.

Even though Dr. J. thought she was trying to provide a warm, supportive environment for the patient to gradually change, she had not quite put together the fact that she was engaged in a countertransference attempt to make up for the previously harsh critical parental introjects. In addition, she could not quite see that R. was acting to her in a hostile and sadistic way, as he had acted with his siblings.

I asked Dr. J. if she had the idea that a loving, nurturing, constantly giving attitude, without an analysis of the factors involved in the transference, would gradually change a patient's orientation? She immediately said that she did not think that would work at all.

When we talked about how she could not say much to R. or he would yell, scream, carry on, and threaten suicide, she quickly saw the transference aspects. Gradually, Dr. J. realized that she had operated with this very disturbed patient in a different, non-analytic fashion. Somehow, she had the idea that a severely disturbed patient required her to be more solicitous and supportive than she would have been with her better-put-together patients.

As Dr. J. understood that it was possible to weather R.'s outbursts and neediness by talking about the psychological factors involved, she was able to see how her underlying countertransference attitude toward R. had been to fill him up with maternal goodness. Unconsciously, against her conscious intent, she thought that enough of the milk of human empathy and support would work with a severely disturbed patient, when it was not her usual modus operandi with the rest of her patients.

As Dr. J. talked about her difficulties in coping with R.'s outbursts, it became clear that she was ashamed of having a patient act out so loudly and persistently. I asked what this could be about, because it sounded to me as if she had some idealized therapist image, an image in which the therapist was skilled enough that the patient would never act up.

In fact this was the case; she believed that a really good therapist could control R., diminishing his anxiety and defensiveness to the point that he would never act up. Even though she knew that R.'s history included volatile behavior in both the family and relationships, she pilloried herself for not being a good enough therapist to keep him calm at all times.

The result of this belief was that she turned herself into a pretzel in order to not upset R. She did not ask certain obvious questions or make interpretations, and found herself placating R. and spending more and more after-hours time with him, both in the office and on the phone.

I, of course, do not have such scruples about patients making a lot of noise and asked why she was so concerned about her patient being upset and angry. She did not know; she thought she was just trying to keep him stable, in hopes that she would eventually be able to do some interpretive and integrative work.

I asked if there was any similarity in her relationship to R. and her own familial interactions when growing up or currently. Bingo! Dr. J. immediately began to talk about her volatile father and the pattern of her mother trying to placate him. Not only had her mother tried to humor her father's outbursts, but her grandmother had done the same with her grandfather, going out of the way not to upset the volatile figure in the family. Her siblings also acted the same way, deferring to explosive men and doing their very best not to upset them.

When Dr. J. realized her own underlying countertransference attitude, she was able to proceed with R. in a much more effective and therapeutic fashion. Little by little, she was able to get R. to see what he was doing in treatment and in his life. Most importantly, she was able to limit extra contact with the patient to a much more manageable amount, thereby aiding R. in forming new ways of dealing with life. In addition, Dr. J.'s husband was delighted to have her back in the evenings.

Pitfalls for the therapist and supervisor

With the severely disturbed patient so much can get in the way of therapy flowing smoothly. As therapists and as the supervisor of therapists, we need to be aware of the levels of metaphor in which the disturbed patient speaks; we need to learn to speak his or her language, understand the meaning and intent of delusions and hallucinations, and make sense of previously incomprehensible phenomena. Not only will such an approach aid us in making contact with the patient, but our understanding of his metaphor, language, and the meaning of delusions, hallucinations, and symbols will begin to lead the patient out of his confused, schizophrenic state.

We also need to keep open the very strong likelihood that the patient is holding on to delusions that are comforting and hidden away in an internal world that he does not want to share or risk losing. We need to listen with the third ear and see with the third eye, always on the lookout for signs of delusional life that bind the patient in psychosis. Patients do not easily give up their delusions.

We need to observe the psychotic transference reactions that so cunningly appear and reappear. For example, a paranoid patient might be certain that the office is bugged and that others listen to our conversations. Although we think that the office is a safe setting, delusional patients may view it through the filter of their distorted perceptions. For this, we must be ready and alert.

Attunement not only to the patient but also to the likelihood of delusional or hallucinatory presences

Some therapists feel that being attuned to the patient is the sine qua non. Who could argue such a concept? Every therapist, no matter what his or her orientation, would agree that it is necessary to be sensitive to the actual person hiding behind the mask of psychotic behavior and thought. Gradually, if exploratory psychotherapy works as it is supposed to, we get to what Harry Guntrip (1968) called the "lost heart of the self." Here, in the container of a psychodynamic psychotherapy, much work is done as the self emerges, frightened and yearning for contact.

Yet, for some with schizophrenia or chronic delusions who are in apparently very good psychotherapy with well-trained people, things never proceed. There is a quality of being stuck, of never moving from a psychotic world view. How can this be? Our therapeutic attempts are made in good faith and in earnest. Something, however, has gone wrong in much of what passes for therapeutic working with schizophrenic and delusional patients.

What frequently goes wrong in the attempt to help a severely disturbed patient uncover the source of his or her difficulties and work them through is related to a failure of attunement. This failure, however, is related to the failure of being attuned to the fact that the person sitting with us has lived such a painful life that they have gone off into a delusional world. Understanding another's pain does not automatically dissolve the adaptive/ defensive structures that the individual has adopted to deal with life's disappointments.

This lack of attunement on our part extends to the fact that a patient who is delusional will often not talk of their most basic delusions and will have created an inner world so tempting and compelling that much of the aberrant behavior stems from the preoccupation with internal, unmentioned, or unanalyzed delusional figures – imaginary companions who have come to stay and aid the patient with the very real difficulties and torment of their lives.

Here, healing attunement is not only to the person, but to the likelihood of a delusional world that the severely disturbed or schizophrenic patient does not want to talk about. Not only must we empathically work with the patient and the patient's life, we must also be attuned to the possibility of a reactive inner life of psychotic proportions.

Clinical example of the failure of attunement to the psychotic presence

An eminent psychoanalyst who had been trained at one of the world's leading centers for the treatment of psychosis was retiring and wanted to turn over to my care a 50-year-old chronic schizoaffective patient who had had 35 hospitalizations, numerous suicide attempts, four times per week supportive psychotherapy, and every medication known to man over the previous 20 years that he had treated her.

During our first session, I saw that the patient did not make eye contact with me and appeared to be staring over my head; within a few minutes, I asked "What are you looking at?" Of course, she replied, "Nothing." But I kept at it, in my usual persistent enquiring fashion, and within 6 months she told me that she was looking at "Mary."

The previous therapist had once stumbled onto the existence of "Mary" and had asked the patient to show him "Mary" but the patient had hit him. His mistake was twofold. He asked the patient to show him "Mary" and, having once been hit, he never raised the issue of "Mary" again.

A better approach, the one that worked here, was to inquire about "Mary." I asked about how "Mary" developed, what she was like, how she had originated, and what she looked like and said. Little by little over the next 6 months, as I took a history from both the patient and, at times, from "Mary" of the situations and feelings involved in the childhood development of "Mary" – and several other believed-in and terrifying delusional figures – the origin of "Mary" became comprehensible to both me and the patient. Within a few more months, the patient's more than 50-year delusional and psychotic orientation resolved and cleared.

Parenthetically, one of the patient's children told me that, "Mom always looked as if she was talking to someone who wasn't really there." Her staring off had been noticeable to her own child, and I assume to others.

When I discussed the case with the previous very-well-trained psychoanalyst, he said he did not think that her delusions could be unwound and evaporate, and hence had adopted the usual supportive view of our psychotherapeutic field and stayed away from exploring the origin of the delusion he had stumbled into. He was both delighted that the patient had improved to the point of returning to work and relationships after such a previous downhill course, and somewhat chagrined that he had not followed his own analytic understanding into a healing psychotherapeutic treatment of his own severely disturbed patient.

The need for the courage of our psychodynamic principles in the treatment of the severely disturbed

This becomes a crucial point. There are very few practitioners who have the courage of their analytic convictions in the treatment of the severely disturbed patient. Most adopt the view that medications and supportive care are the best that can be done for these very difficult patients.

Primarily, potential healers need the knowledge that it is, in fact, possible to treat schizophrenic patients with an intensive psychodynamic psychotherapy. If successful in this approach, some patients will be able to have their antipsychotic medication titrated down and, perhaps, stopped.

The prescription of medication as the primary mode of treatment leads patients to believe that medicines are requisite to keep their demons under control. With this primarily antipsychotic medication approach, neither doctor nor patient thinks that the patient's clinical picture can improve and, perhaps, be resolved through an in-depth psychoanalytic psychotherapy. Now that it is clear that there are very destructive lipid and glucose metabolism side effects from the atypical antipsychotics, one should use these medications with caution.

Psychiatric rationalization defending multi-antipsychotic use

Yet practitioners can justify the use of these atypical antipsychotic medications, citing chapter and verse and inventing new forms of schizophrenia that defy comprehension.

One young woman was being treated by an extremely articulate and well-informed psychiatrist, who had her on three different antipsychotics simultaneously. Since lipid and glucose disturbances had developed in the course of treatment, the patient was also on medication for diabetes and elevated cholesterol.

When I saw the patient in consultation, she did not look schizophrenic at all to me. She looked young and immature, with some fantasies that needed to be explored. Most importantly, she was gregarious and vivacious. I relayed this information to the treating psychiatrist, telling him that the patient did not look schizophrenic to me, and recommended that he try titrating down the antipsychotics. Needless to say, he had many articulate, rational explanations for the use of all these drugs and continued them all.

When the patient came to see me 2 months after having stopped seeing the previous psychiatrist, she had stopped taking all medicines against the previous psychiatrist's advice. The patient was fine, showing no evidence of schizophrenia; laboratory tests no longer showed glucose or lipid disorders.

Had this patient not impulsively stopped everything, I would have tried titrating down the drugs as I explored her clinical condition. Her clinical improvement demonstrates that the diagnosis of schizophrenia and the premature prescription of antipsychotic drugs, without understanding the true nature of the patient's difficulties, can do both physical and psychological harm to patients.

As practitioners in the field of the severely disturbed, delusional, and schizophrenic patient, we need to heed the adage of "doing no harm." The excessive prescription of antipsychotics may do harm, as this case and its very happy conclusion so clearly demonstrate. We can also see how some healers become very defensive about their excessive prescription of antipsychotics and refuse to look at the underlying causes for both excessive prescription and the harm that can be done by it.

Lessons learned

The most useful ideas I can pass on to supervisors, colleagues, and aspiring therapists of the severely disturbed patient have to do with what works best with schizophrenic and delusional patients. What are some of the lessons to be drawn for the healer?

I have found that a reality-oriented therapy with antipsychotic medication helps some patients but often leaves open the possibility of both drug side effects and the persistence of psychotic thought and recurrence of overt psychosis.

For me, personally, I have found that a more in-depth approach is frequently much more advantageous in the treatment of the severely disturbed patient. With an insight-oriented approach, understanding the origins of delusions and hallucinations within the context of the person's life allows the schizophrenic patient to begin to gain some control over previously inchoate experience.

Primarily, schizophrenics and other severely disturbed patients are people, filled with the same human qualities as the healers they seek. It is incumbent on the treating practitioner to drop the objectifying and alienating attitudes of treating the very sick as *other*, and different from us. It is important not to use medication as a tool for that reification and distancing, but to use medication to try to get a little help while one is engaged in a psychotherapeutic exploration.

If medication alone does the trick with no side effects, and the patient is happy with that, then fine. But if medication causes physical and psychological difficulties (as Robert Foltz has shown in Chapter 12) and is part of a countertransference attitude of objectification of the patient, then we need to look closely at our own beliefs and countertransference attitudes, hopefully acknowledging when we are mistaken.

Support for the healer

1   *Reading the literature.* What happens when we get in our own way? How do we deal with our own frustration, blind spots, or countertransference? Perhaps we pick up Harold Searles'(1965) "Collected Papers" or Harry Guntrip's (1968) "Schizoid Phenomena, Object Relations, and the Self" or turn to Murray Jackson's (2001) "Weathering the Storms" or Rudolph Eckstein and Bob Wallerstein's (1972) "Learning Psychotherapy" or P. N. Pao's (1979) "Schizophrenic Disorders" or some other favorite book and read about how others have dealt with patient difficulties.

2   *Peer, colleague, and individual supervision.* Perhaps we join a group of colleagues, presenting material and discussing both areas of difficulty in dealing with schizophrenic patients and our own reactions to them. The International Society for the Psychological Treatment of Schizophrenia and Other Psychoses (ISPS) is such a group. Perhaps we call a learned colleague or psychologically minded friend to talk about our impasses. Perhaps we have a walking or running friend with whom we discuss cases for years; maybe we talk to a colleague at lunch about problems in the treatment of psychosis.

3   *Self-reflection.* For others of us, self-reflection on the treatment may make clear the countertransference difficulties. This is a potentially hazardous course, however, since blind spots may remain blind unless we can first see and then uncover the underlying sources of our countertransference reactions to schizophrenic patients. For most, if not all, of us the presentation of material and discussion with others is the preferable course.

Any and all of these approaches may help; the important thing is to become aware of any blind spots in our treatment of such complicated and disturbed patients.

Suggestions for supervisor and therapist

For both therapist and supervisor, our most important question is how do we best heal such severely disturbed patients? This is the main issue in dealing with and supporting others as they try to deal with schizophrenic and delusional patients. The comments that follow are meant as a general guideline for supporting the healer.

I hope I have made a strong enough case for an intensive psychodynamic psychotherapy rooted in the knowledge that it is possible to uncover the sources of psychosis through an enquiring psychotherapy of not just the patient's pathology, but also of the origin of the internal psychotic world. We need to aid the patient in the exploration and elaboration of what was going on internally, how it felt, and how the patient coped at the onset of their psychotic experiences.

We need to ask questions in an attempt at a psychodynamic exploration. What did all of this mean to the patient? Were there antecedents in earlier childhood experiences? Often, it is necessary to do psychotherapy of delusional figures – to take a history from the delusional beings, if the patient cannot help, playing along for a while – after one has stumbled onto the presence of a delusional world peopled with comforting and persecutory beings.

Only then, once the inner world has been identified, elaborated, and worked through, can delusional, schizophrenic, schizoaffective, borderline, and multiple personality patients be brought to the possibility of health through a curative intensive psychotherapy.

References

Eckstein, R. and Wallerstein, R. (1972). *Teaching and Learning of Psychotherapy*. New York: International Universities Press.

Guntrip, H. (1968). *Schizoid Phenomena, Object Relations, and the Self*. New York: International Universities Press.

Jackson, M. (2001). *Weathering the Storms: Psychotherapy for Psychosis*. London: Karnac Books.

Pao, P. (1979). *Schizophrenic Disorders: Theory and Treatment from a Psychodynamic Point of View*. New York: International Universities Press.

Searles, H. (1965). *Collected Papers on Schizophrenia and Related Subjects*. New York: International Universities Press.

Index

post-traumatic stress disorder 82
Pre-Expressive Self 34, 35
Pre-Therapy 33–5; effectiveness 45–6;
Evaluation Criterion for the Pre-
Therapy Interview (ECPI) scale 46;
psychological awareness and contact
43–5; techniques 35–43
Pre-Therapy Scale 45, 46
prison environments 125
projective identification 74, 98
provision of learning experiences 83
psychiatric rationalization 186–7
psychic pain 99
psychoanalytic therapy xvi, 82
psychodynamic therapy xii
psychopathology 11
psychotherapy, effectiveness of xv–xvi;
individual xvi, 89, 169–70;
psychoanalytic therapy xvi, 82;
psychodynamic therapy xii;
relational therapy xiii, 93–4;
supportive therapy xv, xvi
psychotic cores 109
psychotic depression 107–23
psychotic transference 95–6
PsychRights 28

quetiapine 162

rage 7, 69, 70, 74, 102, 104, 112, 115,
119; murderous 108
Rapoport, Robert 82
rapport 18
re-contact 36
reality orientation 118
regression 26, 32–47
reiterative reflections 35, 36–7
relational therapy xiii, 93–4
religious attitudes 127
repression 112
respect 12
reverie 53
risperidone (Risperdal) 13, 14, 162

sadism 112
sadness 10, 114–15
sadomasochism 14–15
safety, emotional 54–5
SAMHSA 81
schizophrenia, disorganized 37
Seconal 155
sedation 164

self: absence of 96; authentic 8, 15, 16,
34; developing 4–5; false 8; fragile
71; imaginary 15; Pre-Expressive 34,
35; turning against 7
self-completion 71
self-continuity 103
self-directed dangerous behavior 55
self-disclosure 20
self-esteem 11, 94, 95, 99, 133
self-hatred 7, 99, 119
self-image 58
self-loss 93
self-mutilation 6–7, 8, 109, 119
self-object function 11
self-persecutory paranoia 110
self-protection 72
self psychology xiii
self-reflection 188
self-respect 12, 133
self-sacrificial position 116
selfhood, from agency to 77–8
senility 34
separateness 73
separation–individuation 118
sequelae of psychosis 6–8
sertraline (Zoloft) 129
shame 10
silence 118
situation reflections 35
Sivadon, Paul 85
social pain 99
social psychology 82
socialization 108, 130
Soteria House 29
'space' 9, 54
splitting 112
staff support group 85–6, 88
stigma 126, 131
suicidal behavior 13, 55, 88, 128, 149,
150, 185
suicide xv, 119
Sullivan, Harry Stack xvii, 130
Summers, Frank 86–8
supervision: colleague 188; individual
178–9, 180–1, 188; outside
unhealthy setting 131–2; peer 178–9,
180–1, 188; pitfalls for therapist and
supervisor 184
supervisors, management of 128–31
supportive therapy xv, xvi
suspiciousness 165–6
symbiotic attachment 108